Dismantling Gender Barriers in STEM

Perspectives from the Global South

Edited by
Hannah Whitehead and Matilda Dipieri

**AFRICAN
MINDS**

Published in 2025 by African Minds
4 Eccleston Place, Somerset West, 7130
Cape Town, South Africa
info@africanminds.org.za
www.africanminds.org.za

ISBN (paper): 978-1-0672537-7-6
eBook edition: 978-1-0672537-8-3
ePub edition: 978-1-0672537-9-0

Copies of this book are available for free download at: www.africanminds.org.za

ORDERS:
African Minds
Email: info@africanminds.org.za

To order printed books from outside Africa, please contact:
African Books Collective
PO Box 721, Oxford OX1 9EN, UK
Email: orders@africanbookscollective.com

Contents

Acknowledgements

We would first like to thank Fernando Perini and Katie Bryant, who helped spearhead and support this collection in its early stages of development. We would also like to thank the following past and current program officers at the International Development Research Centre (IDRC) – Alejandra Vargas-Garcia, Matthew Wallace and Ann Weston – for supporting the Breaking Barriers and Gender in STEM projects that contributed to this collection. Finally, we are most grateful to the authors of the collection, without whom these important contributions would not exist.

Foreword

Over the past decades, the global development landscape has undergone a profound transformation. From the rise of digital economies to the growing recognition of inclusive growth as a cornerstone of sustainable development, evidence has shown that equality is not only a human rights mandate but also essential to progress in global development efforts. Still, we must recognise that in Science, Technology, Engineering and Mathematics (STEM), gender equality remains a persistent concern and area for improvement.

Gender equality in STEM is not only a matter of fairness but also a prerequisite for innovation, resilience and inclusive development. Across the world, women continue to face barriers to participation and leadership in STEM fields. These barriers are deeply embedded in cultural norms, institutional structures and policy frameworks, and they manifest in ways that limit access to education, research opportunities, funding and decision-making spaces. Yet, despite these challenges, women scientists, educators and advocates are leading transformative efforts to dismantle these barriers and reshape science systems from the ground up.

This edited collection, *Dismantling gender barriers in STEM: Perspectives from the Global South*, arrives at a pivotal moment. It brings together Southern-led research and lived experiences to illuminate the structural inequities that shape women's trajectories in STEM, as well as the strategies being employed to overcome them. The chapters offer more than analysis; they provide actionable insights, scalable models and a roadmap for change. Importantly, the collection responds to the global call to action embedded in Sustainable Development Goal 5, which aims to achieve gender equality and empower all women and girls.

At the International Development Research Centre (IDRC), we know that research must do more than document disparities; it must challenge the systems that produce them. This is the essence of gender-transformative research: an approach that interrogates the root causes of inequality, promotes shared control over resources and decision-making, and engages diverse communities in co-creating solutions. Gender-transformative research is not just about inclusion; it is about shifting power, challenging norms and building evidence that reflects lived realities and drives systemic change.

This collection exemplifies that approach. It draws on IDRC-supported initiatives, including Breaking Barriers and Gender in STEM, which have invested in building research capacity, fostering collaboration and amplifying the voices of women scientists across Africa, Latin America, Asia and the Caribbean. The work showcased here reflects that commitment – not only to gender equality, but to the broader goal of transforming science systems to be more inclusive, responsive and resilient.

The lessons from this collection echo and expand upon those found in countless publications emerging from IDRC-funded research over the past decades. These contributions have continued to enlighten us about the fact that transformative changes in research institutions require more than policies and checklists; they demand reflective, safe spaces, trust-based relationships and a willingness to confront and disrupt entrenched norms. Change happens when researchers are empowered to define problems in terms that matter to them, when learning is grounded in lived experience and when institutions commit to long-term, iterative processes of transformation.

The chapters in this volume demonstrate that such change is already underway. From participatory methodologies and intersectional analyses to policy reform and institutional innovation, the authors of this collection present a diverse array of strategies that can inform global efforts to close the gender gap in STEM. They show us that gender equity is not a destination, but a dynamic process. It requires courage, collaboration and sustained commitment.

I invite readers – whether policymakers, educators, researchers or advocates – to engage deeply with this collection. Let it serve as both a mirror and a map: reflecting on the challenges we must confront and guiding us toward a more equitable and inclusive future. The journey toward gender equality in STEM is ongoing, and this book provides both evidence and inspiration to continue that path.

Santiago Alba-Corral
Vice-President, Programs and Partnerships, IDRC

Introduction

Hannah Whitehead and Matilda Dipieri

Gender equity in science is more than a moral and social imperative; it is crucial for advancing scientific knowledge and innovation. Yet, women remain underrepresented in Science, Technology, Engineering and Mathematics (STEM) fields worldwide, with only 33% of scientists being women (UNESCO, 2025).

The underrepresentation and overlooking of women in science is not merely a result of individual choices or capabilities. Instead, it stems from deeply rooted systemic and systematic barriers that hinder women's participation and progression in STEM fields. These barriers manifest in various forms, such as gender biases, stereotypes and structural inequalities within educational institutions and workplaces across the globe (OECD, 2015).

Statistical trends reveal a troubling decrease in the enrolment and attainment of women in STEM disciplines. These trends are exacerbated by a lack of supportive policies and initiatives to encourage and retain women in these fields (UNESCO, 2016). The consequences are far-reaching: without the inclusion of diverse perspectives, scientific progress is slowed or stunted, limiting the potential for groundbreaking discoveries and innovations that could address global challenges (National Science Foundation, National Center for Science and Engineering Statistics, 2019). This exclusion risks further entrenching biases and neglecting key research priorities. It is crucial that all voices, especially marginalised communities, shape research agendas and drive innovation.

Despite a recent shift in emphasis on the importance of women's participation in STEM – evidenced by UNESCO's 2024 call to action to close the gender gap in science and findings from the 2023 OECD report on gender, education and skills (Encinas-Martín & Cherian, 2023) – women in the Global South have been particularly underrepresented in these conversations. The majority of discourse surrounding gender equity in STEM comes from the Global North. This edited collection features 12 contributions, most of which are led by women in the Global South, to ensure their voices, perspectives and findings are part of this critical global conversation.

Importantly, this collection comes at a critical moment in global discourse surrounding international development, science systems and gender equity. While there is growing momentum to close the gender gap in STEM, this progress is unfolding against a backdrop of declining development funding and shrinking science budgets in several countries, often accompanied by a troubling retreat from equity-focused policies. That said, amid these challenges, many of the countries featured in this collection are actively advancing inclusive science systems, offering valuable models and insights that warrant attention, support and scaling.

Dismantling gender barriers in STEM: An edited collection

In response to global challenges, *Dismantling gender barriers in STEM: Perspectives from the Global South* addresses the urgent need to close gender gaps in science. It aligns with ongoing international efforts, including UNESCO's call to action, The African Academy of Sciences' initiatives for women in STEM in Africa (The AAS, 2020) and insights from UN Women's (2020) report on women in STEM in Latin America and the Caribbean. This collection offers a unique contribution by providing a Southern-led and contextually grounded exploration of the barriers and solutions related to gender equity in STEM.

The collection draws on research funded by the International Development Research Centre (IDRC), specifically through its Breaking Barriers and Gender in STEM[1] initiatives, which have supported studies across Asia, Africa, Latin America and the Caribbean. Researchers associated with these initiatives have come together to explore synergies, particularly between Latin America and Africa, under the framework of the Breaking Barriers Network. Though all references to the Global South throughout the publication include the aforementioned four regions, this collection primarily focuses on Africa and Latin America, providing just a snapshot of Southern efforts that make up this movement.

Beyond the chapters in this collection, the Network is dedicated to enhancing understanding of the barriers faced by women in STEM, identifying effective

---

1   https://idrc-crdi.ca/en/initiative/gender-stem

strategies to overcome these challenges, improving women's leadership and integrating gender analysis into scientific research.

The editorial team has built this collection, focusing on contributions that not only detail challenges but also suggest evidence-based and practical strategies for change. We included case studies that represent the diversity of institutional, cultural and socio-economic contexts, understanding that gender disparities in STEM vary according to local realities. We also highlight the variety of disciplines within STEM, stressing the unique local settings they address and the key differences in women's experiences across these fields. By emphasising the lived experiences of women scientists, educators, policy-makers and students, the collection provides a nuanced view of the systemic barriers that women in science face and the various ways these barriers are being addressed.

The chapters in this publication also aim to fill a critical gap in the literature. To our knowledge, no existing volume provides a comprehensive, regionally focused analysis of gender barriers in STEM specific to Latin America and Africa. By bringing together evidence from these regions, the book not only enriches the global conversation but also provides a resource for policymakers, educators and advocates seeking context-specific guidance.

Ultimately, this collection is a call to action. It invites readers to rethink how gender equity in STEM is pursued, whose voices are amplified and what kinds of knowledge are valued. It positions researchers from the Global South as key contributors to an international, ever-growing body of literature that seeks to understand and dismantle barriers to women's participation and leadership in STEM. And it underscores the importance of women researchers' insights and leadership in driving progress towards the Sustainable Development Goals, particularly including but certainly not limited to SDG 5, which aims to "achieve gender equality and empower all women and girls" (United Nations, Department of Economic and Social Affairs, n.d.).

Thematic overview

This edited collection is anchored in four interwoven thematic areas that reflect the complex and layered nature of gender disparities in STEM, as well as the multifaceted strategies required to address them. These are: (1) build-ing gender-responsive and equitable STEM institutions; (2) leveraging data to address gender disparities; (3) fostering leadership and mentorship for women in STEM; and (4) ensuring support across academic and career pathways. Each section integrates case studies, critical analyses and policy insights that not only highlight persistent challenges but also showcase innovative responses emerging from the South.

Rather than treating these themes as discrete silos, the collection underscores their deep interconnections. The research questions guiding each chapter reflect the systemic and systematic nature of the barriers to gender equity, barriers that are cultural, structural and institutional in scope. This thematic architecture is designed to move from individual and cultural constraints to broader institutional and policy-level interventions, mirroring the editorial team's conviction that transformative change demands both bottom-up and top-down approaches. However, the chapters themselves do not fit neatly into each of the themes. The insights each chapter brings help build a case for the various components that need to be in place to meaningfully drive change. Additionally, the collection of contributions concludes with a think-piece that, while incorporating ideas from previous sections, also serves to introduce the reader to another way of thinking about gender equity. By organising the chapters in this way, the book offers readers a comprehensive roadmap: from confronting stereotypes and biases to reimagining and reshaping STEM systems. The four interrelated themes are detailed below.

Building gender-responsive and equitable STEM institutions

Researchers have been actively working to institutionalise gender-responsive policies that enhance equity and inclusivity within STEM institutions. While there are several interesting, successful interventions that have been implemented by passionate teachers, researchers and STEM professionals, the systemic nature of the challenges at hand requires fundamental changes to how institutions approach gender mainstreaming and gender, equity and inclusion (GEI) considerations. To ensure that women have access to safe, inclusive environments where they can progress through their educational and professional trajectories and thrive, we must consider and begin to address systemic barriers.

The interrogation of existing policies is one way to consider systemic barriers. A comprehensive evaluation of policies as they relate to gender equality took place at Zimbabwe's Women's University of Africa (WUA) (Chapter 1). Importantly, larger-scale initiatives that investigate policies across multiple institutions, such as reviewing policies at the universities that make up the African Research Universities Alliance (ARUA), can highlight the need for higher-level policies that hold for all member universities (Chapter 3).

Equally beneficial is the inclusion of women's stories to understand how to design policies that best support those underrepresented. Participatory action research, an approach used in Bolivia, has been critical to understanding the barriers to STEM access faced by multiple generations of women (Chapter 11).

Leveraging data to address gender disparities

To address the challenges to women's participation and leadership in STEM, researchers have prioritised data-driven approaches to understand and tackle gender disparities. Comprehensive data collection and digitalisation efforts have been established in countries like South Africa, Uganda, Kenya, Zambia, Bolivia, Brazil and Peru. Beyond mere statistics, initiatives like the ELLAS (Equality in Leadership for Latin America STEM) Network (Chapter 6) are building institutionalised systems for continuous monitoring by universities and research bodies. These gender-disaggregated data form the basis for developing evidence-based policies that directly address gender inequalities.

Integrating gender analysis into STEM research across disciplines uncovers valuable insights into how gender dynamics influence success, leading to more informed and effective policy interventions. In West Africa, participatory research methods like participatory rural appraisal (PRA) have been used to gather insights from women farmers, ensuring their perspectives are included in agricultural data collection and addressing gender disparities in research methodologies (Chapter 4). Additionally, digital platforms are being developed to promote gender equity by showcasing women's contributions in traditionally male-dominated fields, enhancing visibility and recognition of their roles in STEM and contributing to a larger body of evidence needed to advocate for policy changes (Chapter 6).

Fostering leadership and mentorship for women in STEM

Research activities have been designed to create leadership and mentorship pathways for marginalised women, who are often excluded from decision-making and research leadership roles. Through frameworks developed alongside institutional and political actors, such as the African Public Health Research Centre's Gender-Lensed Supervision and Mentorship Framework, emerging female researchers can connect with experienced mentors who guide them through postgraduate training, research careers and professional development (Chapter 7). These programmes not only equip women with the technical skills needed to succeed but also build their confidence and leadership capacities, enabling them to participate in research agenda-setting and policy development.

Additionally, partnerships with advocacy groups and networks provide platforms for women to share best practices, resources and mentorship opportunities. These collaborative networks have scaled efforts and established regional platforms that support female researchers, enhancing their access to leadership opportunities across academic, research and industry settings. Leadership programmes also emphasise intersectionality, ensuring that women from diverse backgrounds, including marginalised and underrepresented communities, are prioritised in leadership and mentorship initiatives. Efforts to support groups of women who are underrepresented, such as the Programa de Apoyo a Mujeres Indígenas en Ciencia, Tecnología, Ingeniería y Matemáticas (PEPMI) initiative, are essential to building inclusive science systems (Chapter 5). This inclusivity ensures that decision-making processes in STEM reflect a wide range of voices and experiences. Further, policies need to be in place to ensure women are provided with equal opportunities to advance into leadership roles. Initiatives that develop or evaluate policies, such as the work of the SISTARS team, which evaluated existing policies within the water sector in Ghana and Kenya, are much needed (Chapter 8).

Ensuring support across education and career pathways

Coordinated, multi-level support systems to help women transition successfully from education into the workforce are an important step in ensuring women's continued participation and success in STEM, acknowledging key moments of potential attrition.

At the educational level, curriculum revisions ensure gender equity is embedded in learning materials and teaching practices, while capacity-building initiatives for lecturers and university staff emphasise gender-sensitivity training and gender-responsive pedagogies. To do so, researchers must develop a clear understanding of the existing state of research on gender-related pedagogies and training. Projects like Inclusive Pedagogies, which systematically reviews gender-responsive pedagogies in Africa's higher education institutions, are critical to these efforts (Chapter 9). Taken together, these efforts create inclusive learning environments where women receive tailored support to address their unique challenges. The gender transformative and organisational learning approach used for training green jobs in Colombia is a great example of this (Chapter 2).

Scholarship programmes, like the Organization for Women in the Developing World's PhD and early career fellowships, go beyond supporting individual women (Chapter 10). They build greater scientific capacity in Global South institutions and ensure the visibility of women who are leaders in science. Beyond individual institutions, support mechanisms are scaled through inter-university networks and regional bodies, providing mentorship frameworks, scholarship programmes and gender awareness programmes that create continuity in support as women move from education into the workforce. Coordinated action between educational institutions, advocacy groups, government agencies and industry builds a seamless pathway for women to enter and thrive in STEM careers.

Conceptual frameworks

To further contextualise the findings and approaches presented in these chapters, we offer key definitions and conceptual frameworks that underpin the collection's analysis. We have been intentional and inclusive in how we define STEM throughout the collection. Our framing encompasses fields such as agricultural sciences (highly prevalent across the Global South) and green growth (a globally developing STEM sector that includes science, technology and engineering approaches) and considers policies across research institutions (although they are not STEM specific). These choices are deliberate, ensuring the collection remains relevant to the regions of focus while challenging narrow definitions that can limit meaningful engagement.

We hope that the strength of this collection is the diversity of perspectives, methodologies and contexts explored throughout its chapters. This intentional variation is designed to provide a more comprehensive understanding of approaches to investigating and dismantling barriers faced by women in STEM in the Global South. Many of the authors of the collection are not feminist scholars or gender researchers, but instead scientists and engineers themselves, who have recently shifted or expanded their focus to investigate gender equity in their fields. Though this means that chapters vary and are sometimes limited in the gender-centric theoretical frameworks that guide their work, they offer instead nuanced field- and region-specific insights.

The authors of these chapters understand first-hand the barriers to participation in their STEM fields in the countries in which they live and work, and they used the insights gained through their lived experiences to shape their work. In doing so, they provide fresh perspectives and approaches to improving gender equity in STEM. Their insights are critical, given that inequities in STEM are pervasive globally. Though these challenges are not specific to the Global South, we highlight how Southern researchers are addressing these challenges in new and innovative ways that have the potential to be adapted across contexts.

Regardless of whether readers are interested in individual chapter contributions or exploring the collection, we suggest that readers consider intersectionality, gender mainstreaming and patriarchal influences as frameworks within which to understand the contributions of the collection.

We define intersectionality as a framework within which we can understand how an individual's intersecting identities may shape their experiences in society (Runyan, 2018). Intersectionality, first introduced by Kimberlé Crenshaw (1989), highlights the role of an individual's identities (e.g. woman and/or indigenous person) in shaping their experiences. In the case of this edited collection, relevant identities may include but are not limited to gender, race, class or national origin, all of which may impact an individual's opportunities in STEM or experiences in STEM. Identities do not act in isolation, but interact, potentially leading to compounding challenges or barriers for those with multiple marginalised identities. For example, multiple chapters highlight the challenges faced by indigenous women (Chapters 2 and 5) as they face barriers related to their indigenous identity as well as their gender identity. We suggest the consideration of intersectionality as a critical component to understanding women's experiences in STEM.

Gender mainstreaming we define as the process of considering the gender implications of legislation, policy and programming to prevent the perpetuation of inequalities (UNESCO, 2017). Gender mainstreaming has been used as an international approach to address gender equity and equality since its adoption by the United Nations at the 1995 Conference on Women in Beijing, meaning it has been defined in many ways and adopted differently by many countries. Within this collection, gender mainstreaming underlies analyses of existing policy (Chapters 3 and 8) and discussions of pedagogical approaches (Chapters 2 and 9). The collection also refers to related terms such as gender-unequal, gender-blind, gender-sensitive, gender-specific and gender-transformative. These terms, which are derived from the World Health Organization's Gender Responsiveness Assessment Scale (Gough & Novikova, 2010), provide a framework to evaluate an organisation, project, or programme's commitment to gender equity (refer to Chapter 3 for a more detailed definition). Together, these terms underscore the importance of gender considerations in all aspects of research and practice.

Finally, we encourage readers to critically reflect on the influence of patriarchy, a recurring theme throughout the collection, in shaping women's experiences in STEM. We define patriarchy as a social structure within which men hold collective power (Beechey, 1979), and the chapters illustrate how its impacts are both enduring and pervasive. Even as policies and practices become more inclusive of women, patriarchal influences remain. In many cases, such influences are evident in domestic spaces and in the perspectives of family and friends; in others, they result from the internalisation of gendered societal expectations and how they inform women's decision-making. These differential patriarchal influences are sometimes referred to dichotomously as public (e.g. policy level) and private (e.g. internalised expectations) patriarchy, respectively. However, as many others have, we caution against rigid dichotomies (Thornton, 1991; Ungs, 2005; Wischermann & Mueller, 2004). The entanglement of these spheres underscores the multifaceted nature of patriarchal influence. Across the chapters, we emphasise this complexity, acknowledging that patriarchy operates simultaneously across professional, domestic and psychological domains, shaping women's trajectories in STEM in profound and often overlooked ways.

In addition to frameworks, we want to recognise the importance of terminology used throughout the collection. The research presented within this edited collection comes from a wide range of countries with differing cultures, perspectives and understandings of gender. We wish to acknowledge the complexity and sensitivity surrounding terms central to this edited collection, such as female, woman and gender. We acknowledge that in many Global North contexts, distinctions are often made between 'female' (typically referring to biological sex assigned at birth), 'woman' (referring to gender identity) and 'gender' (a broader term encompassing diverse identities). However, in various Southern contexts, these terms may be used more fluidly or interchangeably, often reflecting presented identity or local norms around gender expression. As such, while some chapters in this collection differentiate between 'female' and 'woman', others use the terms interchangeably. Rather than imposing a standardised vocabulary, we have chosen to respect the linguistic and cultural choices of contributors, recognising that these variations reflect the complexity and diversity of gendered experiences across regions.

Contribution and impact

By centring research from the Global South, the book challenges dominant narratives and fills a critical gap in the literature, one that has long overlooked the regional specificities, institutional dynamics and lived experiences of women in science across Africa and Latin America.

Critically, the collection does not include randomised control trials or longitudinal studies, which could speak to causal relationships between stereotypes, practice or policies and gender gaps in STEM. Rather, the collection enriches the field of gender and STEM studies by introducing new empirical evidence, theoretical insights and methodological approaches. The chapters engage with existing frameworks, while also proposing context-sensitive models for understanding how gender operates within science systems. The inclusion of diverse case studies, ranging from national policy analyses to institutional interventions, allows for comparative reflection and cross-regional learning. This Southern-led perspective not only diversifies the knowledge base but also repositions researchers from the Global South as central contributors to global scientific discourse.

Practically, the book is not intended to advance theory, but instead serves as a resource for policymakers, researchers, educators, institutional leaders and advocates seeking to implement change. The chapters offer actionable recommendations grounded in evidence, whether through policy reform, educational innovation, or organisational transformation. The thematic structure provides a roadmap for designing comprehensive strategies to promote gender equity in STEM. The publication's emphasis on showcasing successful interventions and scalable models ensures that readers are equipped not only with analysis but also with tools for action.

A call to action

By contributing Southern-led evidence to this international agenda, the book helps to shape future directions for research, policy and practice. The chapters presented here reflect a rich diversity of contexts, strategies and voices from across the Global South, and together they form a compelling narrative of resilience, innovation and transformation.

The concluding chapter of this volume synthesises the key insights from across the thematic sections, drawing connections between cultural, educational and institutional interventions. In it we highlight how Southern-led research challenges dominant paradigms and expands the global evidence base. Importantly, we also build on the research agenda articulated in the IDRC's (2024) *Breaking barriers, building bridges* synthesis report, which calls for a more inclusive and context-sensitive approach to understanding and addressing gender inequities in STEM. This agenda emphasises the need for:

- Intersectional analysis that accounts for how gender interacts with other social identities and structural factors;
- Locally grounded evidence to inform policy and practice in diverse settings;
- Collaborative research models that engage women scientists and practitioners as co-creators of knowledge;

- Monitoring and evaluation frameworks that assess the impact of gender-responsive interventions over time.

By integrating these priorities, the concluding chapter proposes a forward-looking roadmap for future research and action. In our conclusion, we advocate for sustained investment in gender-transformative research, the strengthening of regional research ecosystems and the amplification of women's leadership in science. In doing so, this collection aims to contribute to a global movement that recognises gender equity in STEM not as a peripheral issue, but as a cornerstone of sustainable development and scientific excellence.

This book is an invitation to researchers, educators, policymakers and advocates to engage with the evidence, challenge assumptions and co-create solutions that reflect the realities and aspirations of women in STEM across the Global South. The journey towards equity is ongoing, and this collection offers both a map and a call to continue walking the path together.

About the Editors

Hannah Whitehead is a Program Officer at the International Development Research Centre, Canada.

Matilda Dipieri is a Knowledge Sharing Officer at the International Development Research Centre, Canada.

References

Beechey, V. (1979). On patriarchy. *Feminist Review*, 3(1), 66–82. https://doi.org/10.1057/fr.1979.21

Crenshaw, K. (1989). Demarginalizing the intersection of race and sex: A black feminist critique of antidiscrimination doctrine, feminist theory and antiracist politics. *University of Chicago Legal Forum*, 1989(1), Article 8. https://chicagounbound.uchicago.edu/uclf/vol1989/iss1/8

Encinas-Martín, M., & Cherian, M. (2023). *Gender, education and skills: The persistence of gender gaps in education and skills*. OECD Publishing. https://doi.org/10.1787/34680dd5-en

Gough, B., & Novikova, I. (2010). Table 1: WHO Gender Responsive Assessment Scale: Criteria for assessing programmes and policies. In *Mental health, men and culture: How do sociocultural constructions of masculinities relate to men's mental health help-seeking behaviour in the WHO European Region?* (pp. 8–9). WHO Regional Office for Europe. https://www.ncbi.nlm.nih.gov/books/NBK559709/table/ch2.t1/?report=objectonly

IDRC (International Development Research Centre). (n.d.). *Gender in STEM*. IDRC. https://idrc-crdi.ca/en/initiative/gender-stem

IDRC. (2024). *Breaking barriers, building bridges: A Southern-led research network to advance gender equality in STEM*. IDRC. https://www.breakingbarriersnetwork.com/breaking-barriers-en-mar-2025.pdf

National Science Foundation, National Center for Science and Engineering Statistics. (2019). *Women, minorities and persons with disabilities in science and engineering: 2019.* Special Report NSF 19-304. National Science Foundation. https://www.ncses.nsf.gov/pubs/nsf19304/

OECD (Organisation for Economic Co-operation and Development). (2015). *The ABC of gender equality in education: Aptitude, behaviour, confidence.* OECD Publishing. https://doi.org/10.1787/9789264229945-en

Runyan, A. S. (2018). What is intersectionality and why is it important? *Academe, 104*(6), 10–14. https://www.aaup.org/academe/issues/104-4/what-intersectionality-and-why-it-important

The AAS (The African Academy of Sciences). (2020). Mukhwana, A. M., Abuya, T., Matanda, D., Omumbi, J., & Mabuka, J. *Factors which contribute to or inhibit women in science, technology, engineering, and mathematics in Africa.* The AAS. https://portal.aasciences.app/storage/publications/01112022071736Women%20in%20STEM%20Report_Final.pdf

Thornton, M. (1991). The public/private dichotomy: Gendered and discriminatory. *Journal of Law and Society, 18*(4), 448–463. https://doi.org/10.2307/1410319

UNESCO (United Nations Educational, Scientific and Cultural Organization). (2016). *Closing the gender gap in STEM: Drawing more girls and women into science, technology, engineering and mathematics* [Programme and meeting document]. https://unesdoc.unesco.org/ark:/48223/pf0000245717

UNESCO. (2017). *Measuring gender equality in science and engineering: The SAGA Toolkit.* Working Paper 2. UNESCO. https://uis.unesco.org/sites/default/files/documents/saga-toolkit-wp2-2017-en.pdf

UNESCO. (2024). *Call to action: Closing the gender gap in science* [Programme and meeting document]. UNESCO. https://unesdoc.unesco.org/ark:/48223/pf0000388641

UNESCO. (2025, February 18). *Women in science: Supporting women in science.* UNESCO. https://www.unesco.org/en/articles/women-science

UN Women. (2020). *Women in science, technology, engineering and mathematics (STEM) in the Latin America and the Caribbean region.* UN Women. https://lac.unwomen.org/sites/default/files/Field%20Office%20Americas/Documentos/Publicaciones/2020/09/Women%20in%20STEM%20UN%20Women%20Unesco%20EN32921.pdf

Ungs, G. Y. (2005). Breaking patriarchal bonds: Demythologizing the public/private. In M. H. Marchand & A. S. Runyan (Eds.), *Gender and global restructuring: Sightings, sites and resistances* [eBook edition] (pp. 64–78). Routledge. https://doi.org/10.4324/9780203976111

United Nations, Department of Economic and Social Affairs. (n.d.). *Goal 5: Achieve gender equality and empower all women and girls.* United Nations. https://sdgs.un.org/goals/goal5

Wischermann, U., & Mueller, I. K. (2004). Feminist theories on the separation of the private and the public: Looking back, looking forward. *Women in German yearbook: Feminist studies in German literature and culture, 20*(1), 184–197. https://muse.jhu.edu/article/392669

Educational Pathways for Unlocking the Participation of Women and Girls in Science: Lessons from Zimbabwe's Women's University in Africa

Sunungurai Dominica Chingarande, Tenson Muyambo and Wonder Muchabaiwa

Introduction

Science is identified as one of the vehicles towards the realisation of Zimbabwe's 2030 Vision. The vision also identifies gender equality, a human right and a foundation for peaceful, prosperous and sustainable development, as an enabler and key driver of this vision. To this end, inclusive science initiatives are recognised as fundamental for Zimbabwe's industrialisation agenda. The situation on the ground, however, is that although women have achieved near-parity in several fields of study in the social sciences and humanities, there remain gaps in Science, Technology, Engineering and Mathematics (STEM) disciplines globally (National Science Foundation, 2011). In Zimbabwe, women remain underrepresented among STEM graduates, with 19% of women holding STEM degrees compared to 81% of men (World Economic Forum, 2016). The participation of women in STEM disciplines tends to be hampered by the deeply entrenched patriarchal and cultural norms and practices that can undermine women's agency and perpetuate the perception of women as subservient. Furthermore, the gap is exacerbated by negative stereotypes and the lack of role models, lowering girls' performance, aspirations vis-à-vis science and technology, covert discrimination, implicit biases and career preferences (Gudyanga,

2016). Unfortunately, societal constraints can and do force women to make 'choices' that often lead them away from STEM fields.

In 1995, the Government of Zimbabwe implemented an affirmative action admission policy to facilitate women's entry into public universities. This policy lowered the advanced-level points necessary for females to gain admission to public higher education institutions in the country. At that time, only 25% of enrolled students were women and in 2021, 54% of enrolled students were women. However, only around 20% of enrolled students in STEM disciplines were women (UNESCO-IELSALC, 2021) despite the government providing scholarships for females enrolled in STEM disciplines.

In trying to address persistent barriers to women's participation in higher education and STEM disciplines, women's universities have been established globally, including Hunan Women's University in China, Kiriri Women's University of Science and Technology in Kenya, Philippine Women's University and Ewha Woman's University in Korea, among others. Kiriri Women's University is a women-only university, Philippine Women's University was exclusive to girls until the 1970s when it started to admit boys, Hunan Women's University and Ewha Woman's University admit both girls and boys. In Zimbabwe, the continued gender disparities in higher education and the STEM disciplines saw the founding of Women's University of Africa (WUA) in 2002, with the specific mandate of addressing gender disparities in education.[1]

WUA has policies and practices in place that deliberately promote diversity and inclusion to ensure that barriers to women's access to education in all fields are addressed. However, since its inception, no comprehensive study had been conducted to interrogate WUA's experiences and the effectiveness of its measures to mitigate or eliminate systemic barriers to the greater participation of women and other underrepresented groups. Further, to date, no work has been done to increase diversity of personnel in science fields; hence we conducted this study between 2020 and 2023 to answer the following research questions:

1. To what extent has WUA addressed systemic barriers to the participation of women in STEM?
2. How effective are the gender-mainstreaming strategies implemented by the University?
3. What is the role of multi-stakeholder partnerships in fostering inclusive educational pathways?

---

1 "Addressing gender disparity and fostering equity in university education" (https://www.wua.ac.zw/).

The findings of the study, which inform this chapter, are discussed in detail below.

Methodology

The mixed-methods research project was implemented in two phases over 36 months. Following a qualitative research design with descriptive quantitative elements, the first phase focused on data collection for 12 months from January to December 2020; while the second phase (24 months), from January 2021 to December 2022, used the results to design, implement, monitor and evaluate the results.

Phase 1: Data collection and analysis

The project targeted people knowledgeable in the University's programmes and initiatives who could testify to the measures taken, their effectiveness as well as recommend strategies for inclusive STEM programmes. These included WUA alumni, students, staff and university partners. These participants were notified about the study via email and over the phone.

The project had proposed to design and administer two questionnaires to current and former WUA students as well as to faculty staff that included selected female and male lecturers, staff in the Registry department, key administrators in the University and programme coordinators. The purpose of the student questionnaire was to gather their views and perceptions on their experiences at WUA and its engendering agenda, with a particular focus on STEM. The staff questionnaire was intended to gather data on the extent to which gender mainstreaming and inclusivity have been internalised and enacted by staff, and on the development and delivery of gender-sensitive programmes and services. Overall, the staff questionnaire included information about infrastructure and equipment, mechanisms, practices and attitudes that have made a positive contribution to mainstreaming gender and the promotion of women in STEM at WUA. The questionnaires were also intended to gather staff perspectives on the extent to which policies are gender-sensitive and promote women in STEM, staff gender balance at WUA, the challenges faced and the interventions being implemented to improve the institution's ability to address the barriers to women's participation in STEM, among others.

We also brought together WUA alumni for focus group discussions (FGDs). A total of 19 alumni were interviewed, 9 males and 10 females. The research team resorted to individual virtual discussions with the alumni. This meant that those who lacked access to digital platforms were automatically excluded from the study.

The key stakeholders interviewed virtually included representatives of UN Women, UNESCO, Forum for African Women Educationalists Zimbabwe (FAWEZI), Education Coalition of Zimbabwe (ECOZI) and the Ministry of Primary and Secondary Education (MoPSE).

Key informant interviews with WUA staff were held in person while interviews with the rest of the study's participants were done virtually. At WUA, key informant interviews were conducted with 12 senior administrators. In addition, 14 full-time lecturers in science programmes were also interviewed.

FGDs were conducted with STEM undergraduate and postgraduate students in science programmes at the Harare and Marondera campuses. Undergraduates were separated from postgraduates to allow for unfettered discussions. The groups combined both male and female students. Each group was made up of between eight and nine participants. In total, seven FGDs were conducted with a total of 107 students, 65 females and 42 males.

Thematic analysis was the primary analytical approach for the qualitative data (Caulfield, 2023). This allowed us to identify, organise and categorise themes in the transcripts. This process involved identifying the major themes in the data, based on the study questions and objectives. Thematic coding allowed us to ensure the qualitative analysis remained focused on the study objectives, while also remaining flexible enough to capture emerging themes in the data. Results interpretation considered key themes, who raised certain themes (i.e. students, staff or alumni) and relationships that exist between themes that helped us answer the study questions.

Quantitative data from the staff questionnaire were cleaned and entered into Microsoft Excel for analysis. COVID-19 containment measures resulted in a low questionnaire response rate with only 17 completed questionnaires. Descriptive analysis was therefore conducted to capture perceptions on the commitment to gender equality within the University, staff capacity to mainstream gender, awareness of the existing gender equality policy framework and gender responsiveness of the University infrastructure and facilities, among others. Results are outlined in the following sections.

Phase 2: Implementation, monitoring and evaluation

Using the results from Phase 1, the research team worked with WUA management to design intervention measures for inclusive STEM programmes at the University as well as to devise action plans for implementation. For this second phase of the project, physical monitoring visits to the University were conducted, complemented by regular virtual monitoring calls to members of the Gender Equality Committee. The purpose of the monitoring visits and calls was to measure the progress of implementing the action plan developed by the Gender Equality Committee. Two years were dedicated to implementation, monitoring and evaluation. The research team monitored enrolment intakes (August 2021, February 2022 and August 2022) to establish the enrolment statistics of women in STEM fields and the number of STEM-related programmes available at WUA, as well as changes in policies and practice at WUA. The following section overviews the findings of the study and subsequent intervention measures. The implementation, monitoring and evaluation of intervention measures is discussed.

Findings from Phase 2

Policy transformation

A progressive policy environment for promoting gender equality is critical to reduce the conditions that hinder such equality (Hervías Parejo & Radulović, 2023). According to Hervías Parejo and Radulović (2023), policies may have a major impact on gender equality and attaining equal access to opportunities, resources and rights for women, men and other identities. The Government of Zimbabwe has provided a conducive normative framework for the promotion of gender equality. Section 56 of the Constitution of Zimbabwe guarantees the right to equality and non-discrimination. It highlights that all forms of discrimination on the basis of sex, gender, marital status, custom, culture, pregnancy and disability are not permitted. In addition, Section 80 specifically outlines women's rights. It states unequivocally that all laws, customs, traditions and cultural practices that infringe on the rights of women conferred by the Constitution are void to the extent of the infringement. In addition, in the Government of Zimbabwe's (2020) National Development Strategy (NDS1) 2021–2025, gender equality is a cross-cutting issue. Zimbabwe has also ratified the following continental and regional protocols:

- The African Charter on Human and Peoples' Rights was ratified in 1986. The Protocol to the African Charter on Human and Peoples' Rights on the Rights of Women in Africa (the African Women's Protocol) was signed in 2003 and ratified in 2008.

- The African Union's Agenda 2063, which commits to ending all harmful social practices and removing all barriers to women and girls' access to quality health and education.
- The SADC Protocol on Gender and Development, which calls for gender equality and equity in constitutions and seeks to ensure 50% representation of women in all decision-making positions in the public and private sectors through affirmative action measures.

At the international level, Zimbabwe is party to the following:

- The 2030 Agenda for Sustainable Development, under which Zimbabwe prioritised 10 of the 17 goals, including Goal 5 on achieving gender equality and empowering all women and girls.
- The Convention on the Elimination of All Forms of Discrimination Against Women (CEDAW), ratified by Zimbabwe in 1991. By accepting this convention, Zimbabwe committed to incorporating the principle of equality between men and women into its legal system, abolishing discriminatory laws and adopting appropriate laws that prohibit discrimination against women.
- The Beijing Platform for Action and the Beijing +20 Review, which seek to address women's lack of empowerment and human rights violations through comprehensive laws and policies, as well as transformation of both formal and informal institutions, to achieve gender equality and the full realisation of women's and girls' rights.

Zimbabwe has made significant strides in amending and enacting legislation that promotes gender equality and women's empowerment. Aside from the current Constitution, the country has passed 17 pieces of legislation to advance gender equality and equity objectives. Zimbabwe also made efforts to mainstream gender into its policies. The 2004 Public Sector Gender Policy put in place a system of gender focal points in all ministries and parastatals. In 2015, a Gender Commission was established, and commissioners were appointed in 2016. The country adopted its first National Gender Policy in 2004, followed by the second National Gender Policy in 2017, which aimed to eradicate gender discrimination and inequalities in all spheres of life and development. Furthermore, Zimbabwe has a Domestic Violence Act and a National Gender-Based Violence Strategy that seeks to address GBV through prevention, service provision to survivors of GBV, research, documentation, monitoring and evaluation of the impacts of GBV and coordination of current GBV interventions.

The commitments made by the Government of Zimbabwe all call for women's participation, the transformation of discriminatory practices and upholding women's rights. However, these international and regional conventions and protocols cannot protect women and girls in the manner intended because they are not fully incorporated into law via Acts of Parliament, as stipulated in terms of Section 327(2) of the Constitution.

Ideally, the objectives and approach for higher education institutions should be aligned with the principles and objectives enshrined in Zimbabwe's normative framework to increase the participation of women and girls in Zimbabwe. At WUA, a progressive policy environment plays a pivotal role in defining the University as a safe space for women and girls. At the time of implementing the study, the University did not have policies on gender, disability and human resources, nor an updated anti-sexual harassment policy that enshrined gender-equality provisions. These were developed in response to the recommendations of the study. These policies are important for effective mainstreaming of gender (Morley, 2010). They guide WUA in addressing gender issues in a structured and systematic manner and create more targeted opportunities for female students to take up science programmes. With the University's renewed focus on gender equality as a result of the study recommendations, all University policies were reviewed to ensure their alignment with the gender policy and to make them gender responsive. The revised human resources policy now provides for a compulsory gender module to be completed by all staff within their first two weeks of employment, as well as paternity leave.

That said, having policies in place is not enough to see impactful change in behaviour and practices that promote the participation of women and girls in science. The University also worked to raise student and staff awareness of policy provisions, enabling them to claim and enjoy their rights. In addition, a gender-equality implementation mechanism in the form of the Gender and Diversity Centre was established. This facilitated the reporting of any policy violations, and for the first time, a student reported a case of sexual harassment that led to the dismissal of a staff member and their subsequent prosecution.

In addition to policies, if any meaningful traction is to be realised in the participation of women and girls in science, University plans should be clear on this strategic direction with clear targets, actions, measurable results and a monitoring and evaluation plan. As a result of the study, WUA's Transformational Strategy has gender equality promotion as one of its strategic focus areas, under which the University envisages creating an institutional environment that is gender sensitive and promotes equal opportunities, spearheaded by the Gender and Diversity Centre. The targets are: (1) at least 50% of the decision-making positions occupied by women; (2) at least 85% female student enrolment across all disciplines; and (3) implementation of a wide range of gender-sensitive policies and the creation of at least two functional networks for female scholars. Having such a plan (and a directorate whose performance is measured against a strategic focus area of the plan) has gone a long way to promote a conducive environment and action towards the increased participation of women and girls in science. One such action, aimed at realising 85% female enrolment across all disciplines, has been the establishment of the STEM Centre at the University. The Centre serves to encourage and prepare female high-school students to take up STEM subjects. Policy reform to promote gender equality is therefore imperative for transforming behaviour and practice in university education. Below, we outline three areas within WUA where changes could further improve gender parity in the University's STEM programmes.

Funding

A gender-responsive infrastructure is critical for unlocking opportunities for the increased participation of women and girls in science. A gender-responsive infrastructure calls for funds to support activities and initiatives that address the barriers affecting women and girls' access to university education. Our study revealed barriers that include gender roles and responsibilities, gender stereotyping, limited choice in science programme offerings, entry requirements, lack of female role models and a masculine environment, among others. To address these barriers, WUA has allocated resources for the following initiatives, which were well received by students:

- A mathematics bridging programme to support students without mathematics at Ordinary level who aspire to enrol in disciplines that require mathematics;
- The establishment of a daycare centre and a nursing-mothers lounge to support female students and staff that require such services. The WUA daycare centre was established to provide services to children so that their mothers can concentrate on their studies (Chingarande et al., 2023). This strategy is consistent with those in other countries, such as Nigeria, where a number of higher education institutions have childcare facilities on campuses to cater for the children of students and academics (Gaidzanwa, 2007). However, the daycare centre should be reconfigured to ensure that its calendar is aligned with the University's if it is to be effective in addressing the needs of female students and staff at WUA. The calendar

followed currently is that of the MoPSE, which is not in harmony with tertiary institution calendars. In addition, funding of the centre is critical as fees can be a deterrent for female students and staff who desire to have their children enrolled at the daycare centre. Furthermore, age restrictions at the daycare centre to between 5 and 6 years exclude students and staff whose children are below these ages. Due to these gaps, the number of female students and staff members enrolling their children at the centre is still limited.

- The establishment of a STEM centre, as highlighted in the previous section;
- Capacity-strengthening of staff in gender mainstreaming in general, and in gender-responsive pedagogy in particular.

Despite these important programmes, WUA is yet to have a science laboratory that broadens students' horizons through science-programme variety. Funding is required for the establishment of such a laboratory. Having a science laboratory is a Zimbabwe Council for Higher Education requirement for introducing science programmes. Owing to the financial demands of rolling out science programmes, fees are high compared to other programmes. Therefore, scholarships for female students in science programmes are also necessary.

Additionally, parents and guardians prefer to have their daughters accommodated at the University for their security. The lack of on-campus student accommodation therefore affects their enrolment, especially in science programmes that may require them to be on campus after hours. An investment in on-campus student accommodation is therefore critical for unlocking women and girls' participation in science.

Transformation of the teaching and learning environment

Through our study, we established that a secure learning environment can play a significant role in the recruitment and retention of students across all disciplines, including in STEM. Students need to feel secure in their learning environment – on campus and online. Studies in the Global North have highlighted the pervasiveness of gender violence perpetrated against female students on university campuses (Anitha & Lewis, 2018; Cantor et al., 2015; Wamboldt et al., 2018). Similarly, studies in South Africa have demonstrated that sexual harassment in institutions of higher learning has become rampant; however, victims are unsure where to report these incidents, thereby contributing to underreporting of the phenomenon (Chauke et al., 2015; Mutinta, 2022). Emerging research in South Africa suggests that the subordination and sexual harassment of women, as well as GBV in general are often normalised on campus residences (Anitha & Lewis, 2018; Chauke et al., 2015). Attempts to mitigate sexual violence on campuses globally and at WUA have resulted in the introduction and adoption of anti-sexual harassment policies that attempt to provide support and information to students who experience such incidents (Anitha & Lewis, 2018; Wamboldt et al., 2018). To further ensure women's safety, the University's human resources policy includes a code of conduct for staff and actions to prevent sexual harassment and GBV.

Another way of transforming the teaching and learning environment is to adopt gender-responsive curricula, materials and pedagogical approaches (see Chapter 9 for a detailed discussion on pedagogical approaches to addressing gender equality in sub-Saharan Africa). While the number of women entering different disciplines at WUA has increased, course content in the major academic disciplines has not been revised to give attention to women and gender in the form of language, resources, representation of women, references and teaching styles. Poor pedagogical practices reinforce gender inequalities (Nabbuye, 2018). A study on gender equality in higher education in the Commonwealth (Morley, 2010) revealed discriminatory practices against female students as a result of gender-insensitive pedagogical processes. At WUA, our work has established that some lecturers perceived women and girls through stereotypes – characterising girls as struggling to actively engage in science disciplines. This has resulted in the University introducing a compulsory module on gender for all staff, which new staff must complete within two weeks of employment. The University has also started training academics to apply gender-responsive pedagogies and curricula materials using the INASP Gender Responsive Pedagogy in Higher Education Toolkit (for more information, see Chapin & Warne, 2020). Chapin and Warne (2020, p. 1) elaborate that, in gender-responsive pedagogy, the "learning needs of male and female learners are addressed in teaching and learning processes (inside and outside of the classroom)". Nabbuye (2018) postulates that gender-sensitive pedagogy can make a big difference for women and girls' learning experiences in the classroom. Further, gender-blind teaching practices reinforce classroom gender inequalities, leading to the concept of a 'hidden curriculum', in which male students are permitted to dominate discussions and classroom space (Chapin & Warne, 2020). It is important to note that gender-responsive pedagogy can be enhanced by developing gender-sensitive monitoring and evaluation instruments that capture students' feedback on their learning experiences, needs, challenges and constraints, as well as the opportunities available to female students. Although such a feedback mechanism exists at WUA, the lack of specialists to analyse the data for decision-making purposes has limited their use in the development of trans-formative actions (Anitha & Lewis, 2018; Mutinta, 2022). Therefore, it was difficult to assess the impact of the training on gender-responsive pedagogy. Data from the monitoring and evaluation process provide crucial information for adjusting programmes and activities. To achieve gender-equality goals and understand an institution's progress towards gender equality, gender-sensitive indicators should be developed to measure gender-related change over time.

Transforming the teaching and learning environment may require female role models in science disciplines (see Chapter 12 for a discussion on using role models to address gender disparities in Africa). While female role models help to reduce stereotypes about scientific careers and gendered abilities, they can also make the underrepresentation of women in science more salient (Breda et al., 2020). The underrepresentation of women in these traditionally male-dom-inated fields can also constitute a reinforcing cycle for subsequent generations, as girls have little opportunity to interact with women who could inspire them (Mutinta, 2022). Exposing female students to successful or admirable women scientists could help to break this vicious circle. These role models could poten-tially extend female students' perceptions of the possible, raise their aspirations, alleviate stereotyping and provide relevant information (Anitha & Lewis, 2018). A large body of work has established that female science teachers and professors can serve as role models and that they help improve female students' academic achievement (Eble & Hu, 2017), increase their probability of enroll-ing in STEM disciplines (Lim & Meer, 2017) and influence their occupational choices (Kofoed & McGovney, 2019). At WUA, there is a deliberate attempt to have female role models at all levels. The Board and Council chairpersons are female, the Vice-Chancellor and one of the Pro-Vice-Chancellors are women, three out of four deans are women and the Student Representative Council President is a woman. However, during data collection, a gap still existed in the number of female lecturing staff in science programmes, which, at 40%, is low compared to their male counterparts.

Multi-stakeholder and ecosystems approach

Strengthening institutional partnerships with government, civil society, women's movements and the private sector can enhance social inclusion in higher education. Structural change, especially at the institutional level, requires bold partnerships to review and reform processes that lead to gender-based exclusion (Tizikara, 2019; UNCTAD, 2011). Thus, women's participation in science programmes can be enhanced by a multi-stakeholder approach.

It starts by university administration implementing programmes and policies to support women's participation in science. The government agencies can then chip in with funding initiatives and policies supporting women's participation in science programmes (Tizikara, 2019). Industry partners can also provide scholarship, internship and job opportunities to women in areas requiring sciences. In the same vein, funding agencies like the IDRC, UNESCO and UNICEF, among others, may provide grants and scholarships for women in STEM fields (Tizikara, 2019). More importantly, research institutions may conduct research on gender disparities in STEM disciplines and fields with the aim to provide solutions.

The synergies among these stakeholders can create a supportive ecosystem that addresses systemic barriers and promotes women's participation in science disciplines. To this end, our monitoring visits to WUA established that partnerships were indeed unlocking opportunities for women and girls there. For example, through a partnership with UN Women, a Feminist Knowledge Hub was established to demystify feminism. By extension, the collaboration between WUA and UN Women has strengthened the University's mandate, dismantling systematic patriarchy and enforcing the transformative agenda of gender equality. As a result, such synergies have contributed to an ecosystems approach to tackling gender issues, particularly from the perspective that access to STEM education follows a pipeline, from primary through secondary to tertiary level, which requires the active participation of multiple stakeholders working collaboratively to address systemic barriers and promote inclusive participation. This has culminated in increased uptake of STEM-related disciplines by female students.

In addition, WUA has conducted gender audits, developed gender-mainstreaming strategies and provided gender training to private companies. An interface between any university and companies on gender issues is critical as these companies absorb students for employment after their graduation. Hence, when the workplace infrastructure is not gender responsive, it can deter women from taking up science programmes in universities. Such synergies create a robust ecosystem that increases opportunities for social inclusion and women's participation in science disciplines and careers. At WUA, interfaces between the University and companies are held once every semester to expose new students and graduating students to existing STEM-related opportunities in different companies.

Evidence/Knowledge generation using a gender-audit methodology

Gender transformative education strategies and intervention packages must be informed by a nuanced understanding of the gender roles, gender norms and the underlying power relations specific to a local context. This process requires regular gender audits. A gender audit is a method for gender mainstreaming. It helps institutions identify and understand gender patterns in their composition, structures, processes, organisational cultures and management, as well as in the design and delivery of policies and services (Chingarande et al., 2023). A gender audit helps to understand what works and what doesn't, and how to scale-up workable strategies and intervention packages. This evidence can then be used to advocate for sustained investment. It also calls for revised perspectives on how progress is viewed and measured. This nuanced understanding of progress will require moving beyond learning-outcome assessment and existing gender-equality indicators to measure changes in gender norms and attitudes in universities. For example, progress can be checked by monitoring changes in women and girls' individual agency; tracking community perceptions around the acceptability of females in male-dominated trades and vice versa; measuring female performance in male-dominated disciplines; and analysing deferment levels, drop-outs and shifts in programme enrolment. In addition, leaders within higher education systems need to be equipped to apply gender analysis, and to understand and unpack gender inequality and how it explicitly or implicitly manifests in the education system.

Informed by the above insights, we adopted a gender-audit methodology at WUA, with the intention of understanding the institution's practices and circumstances from a gender perspective, as well as identifying any gaps and strong points. In return, this would enable us to sensitise members of the institution, particularly its management, to the numerous ways in which gender inequality was entrenched at the institution and to inspire positive change towards greater equality. The gender audit was applied to sections and departments of the University. The audit sought information on: women's participation in the University's management and governance; whether curricula fostered a sense of gender accountability and fairness, as assessed through staff interviews; student life on campus, particularly the experiences of students regarding gender and female participation in science-related programmes; and relevant policy reviews, as discussed earlier. The gender policy review looked at whether WUA policies in general protected, respected and fulfilled the rights of women and men to gender equality and non-discrimination. From the findings, recommendations were drawn up and shared with the University management, who then developed an action plan to implement them. Some of the gaps identified through the gender audit were as follows:

- Lack of key policies, including a gender policy, disability policy, an updated anti-sexual harassment policy and gender-responsive policies;
- Limited focus on gender equality in the existing strategic plan;
- Limited science programmes to broaden female students' choices;
- A dormant Gender Equality Committee;
- Uneven knowledge of gender across the various categories of staff, with academic staff more knowledgeable than non-academic staff;
- Limited staff capacity in gender mainstreaming in general, and in gender-responsive pedagogy in particular;
- No budgets to support gender integration at the University;
- Lack of a gender-sensitive culture;
- Lack of gender-responsive infrastructure and facilities;
- Limited participation of female students in science programmes.

WUA went on to activate the dormant Gender Equality Committee to monitor and report on progress in implementing the recommendations. Below is an extract from the action plan.

Table 1: Action plan for the Women in Science Taskforce Committee

Objective: Improve the uptake of science programmes by female students at WUA

Strategies	Indicator	Status
Increase the number of science programmes to choose from	Number of new science programmes introduced	4 (BSc Honours in Health Services, BSc Honours in Nursing Science, MSc in Midwifery Education and MSc in Public Health)
A focal person/department responsible for gender at the University	Focal person or department responsible for gender established	Gender and Diversity Centre established and Director and gender champions in place
Promote gender-sensitive infrastructure development	Infrastructure sensitive to the needs of female students	Toilets with showers for female students and a convenience shop were constructed
Development of a WUA gender policy and gender-mainstreaming strategy	Gender policy and mainstreaming strategy in place	Gender policy and disability policy in place and gender-equality promotion included as a standalone pillar in the University's 2023–2027 strategic plan
Update the University's sexual harassment policy	Updated sexual harassment policy in place	Updated sexual harassment policy in place
Full-fledged gender-audit of the institution	Gender-audit report	In progress

Strategies	Indicator	Status
Training of staff on gender mainstreaming	Improved skills to mainstream gender Positive attitudes towards gender issues More female students in science programmes	Gender-mainstreaming training of all university staff regularly conducted Mandatory 'I Know Gender 1,2,3' course for all new staff
Training of lecturers in gender-responsive pedagogy (GRP)	Participation of women in science disciplines	GRP training of lecturers regularly conducted
Design a simple, specific framework on gender-responsive pedagogy for use by all lecturers	Participation of women in science disciplines	Draft guide was developed
Mentorship programme for female science students	Mentorship programme in place	Mentorship programme in place through the STEM Centre
Partnerships with the private sector on women in science	MoUs in place with the private sector	MoU with STEM Power in place

Staff capacity

One of the major findings at WUA was that although most lecturers showed some gender awareness as stated in the university's mandate – "Addressing gender disparity and fostering equity in university education" – they did not have formal training on gender matters. Male lecturers in science-related programmes still held stereotypical views towards female science students, reflecting a lack of gender competence (Thompson et al., 2022). The lecturers' attitudes were informed by cultural norms (Kuteesa et al., 2024) that stereotype women and girls. Since lecturers are the cornerstone of the higher education system, their very role as educators marks them out as change agents and role models. To make the most of these roles, tertiary institutions need to embark on gender-related capacity-building initiatives. This would include lecturer induction on how to actively promote gender equality in their teaching practices. Lecturers need to be able to examine their own gender prejudices and to identify and challenge inequalities in the lecture hall. This will eventually result in gender-responsive teaching and learning, as evidenced by Chapin and Warne (2020). Once lecturers are capacitated to be gender aware, they are more likely to prepare reformed curricula, including gender-transformative modules and teaching/learning materials. It is equally important to establish peer learning and exchange mechanisms through which lecturers can share experiences, support one another and strengthen transformative teaching practices.

Conclusion

This chapter has outlined several educational pathways that WUA has implemented and continues to implement to unlock the participation of women and girls in science. These pathways include policy, funding, the teaching and learning environment, a multi-stakeholder and ecosystems approach, evidence and knowledge generation, as well as staff capacity-building. Although the transformation of gender norms takes time, there has been a shift in the way the gender business and agenda are being conducted at WUA as a result of the study. This shift has been driven by the political will to support gender transformation. There has been a more deliberate attempt by all the internal stakeholders to foster gender equality at the University. This commitment requires buy-in from the University Council through to management and all staff members across the institution. When gender integration becomes everyone's responsibility – with the strategic plan marking it out as a key pillar and management periodically reporting on progress in this area – the outcomes can be tangible. In addition, the need for staff knowledge, capacity and instruments for gender integration should not be ignored, as these form the foundation for a gender-sensitive university culture. Moving forward, WUA should invest in monitoring and evaluation and the documentation of all gender-related initiatives to measure their successes, understand the challenges and draw lessons for continuous improvement. Tracking of student retention and performance in science programmes is still not done yet is critical. In addition, the University should consider funding for the daycare centre to make access affordable for all female students and staff.

The experiences at WUA can be replicated in other universities that may not yet have a mandate to foster gender equality but recognise the value of gender integration. Drawing on the experience of the Women's University in Africa, it is imperative that institutions of higher learning take internal action to create gender-responsive and gender-friendly educational pathways that attract women and girls to enrol in science programmes.

Acknowledgements

This research was funded by the International Development Research Centre (IDRC) in Canada.

About the Authors

Sunungurai Dominica Chingarande (PhD) is a Professor and Vice-Chancellor at Women's University in Africa, Zimbabwe.

Tenson Muyambo (PhD) is a Research Fellow at the Research Institute for Theology and Religion, College of Human Science, University of South Africa, and a Lecturer at Great Zimbabwe University, Zimbabwe.

Wonder Muchabaiwa (PhD) is a Faculty of Education Coordinator and Lecturer at Midlands State University, Harare Campus, Zimbabwe.

References

Anderson, B., & Naidu, C. (2022). "Fresh meat": First year female students negotiating sexual violence on campus residences. *South African Journal of Higher Education*, 36(1), 41–58. https://dx.doi.org/10.20853/36-1-4800

Anitha, S., & Lewis, R. (2018). Introduction: Some reflections in these promising and challenging times. In S. Anitha & R. Lewis (Eds.), *Gender-based violence in university communities: Policy, prevention and educational interventions in Britain* (pp. 1–20). Policy Press.

Beyene, A. S., Chojenta, C., Roba, H. S., Melka, A. S., & Loxton, D. (2019). Gender-based violence among female youths in educational institutions of sub-Saharan Africa: A systematic review and meta-analysis. *Systematic Reviews*, 8(1), 1–14. https://systematicreviewsjournal.biomedcentral.com/articles/10.1186/s13643-019-0969-9

Breda, T., Grenet, J., Monent, M., & Van Effenterre, C. (2020). *Do female role models reduce the gender gap in science? Evidence from French high schools*. IZA Discussion Paper 13163. IZA Institute of Labor Economics. https://www.iza.org/publications/dp/13163/do-female-role-models-reduce-the-gender-gap-in-science-evidence-from-french-high-schools

Cantor, D., Fisher, B., Chibnall, S., Bruce, C., Townsend, R., Thomas, G., & Lee, H. (2015). *Report on the AAU campus climate survey on sexual assault and sexual misconduct*. The Association of American Universities. https://www.aau.edu/sites/default/files/%40%20Files/Climate%20Survey/AAU_Campus_Climate_Survey_12_14_15.pdf

Caulfield, J. (2023, June 22). How to do thematic analysis: Step by step guide and examples [Blog post]. *Scribbr*. https://www.scribbr.com/methodology/thematic-analysis/

Chapin, J., & Warne, V. (2020). *Gender responsive pedagogy in higher education: A framework*. International Network for Advancing Science and Policy. https://www.inasp.info/sites/default/files/2021-01/Gender%20responsive%20pedagogy%20Framework%20paper.pdf

Chauke, P., Dlamini, N., Kiguwa, P., Mthombeni, A., Nduna, M., & Selebano, N. (2015). Half of the picture: Interrogating common-sense gendered beliefs surrounding sexual harassment practices in higher education. *Agenda*, 29(3), 106–117. https://doi.org/10.1080/10130950.2015.1052678

Chingarande, S. D., Muyambo, T., & Muchabaiwa, W. (2023). *Bridging the gender equality gap in science at the Women's University in Africa*. IDRC Technical Report. https://idl-bnc-idrc.dspacedirect.org/server/api/core/bitstreams/5bdfbe2b-980e-44aa-82f8-9c9f48916a03/content

Dasgupta, N., McManus Scircle, M., & Hunsinger, M. (2015). Female peers in small work groups enhance women's motivation, verbal participation and career aspirations in engineering. *Proceedings of the National Academy of Sciences of the United States of America, 112*(16), 4988–4993. https://doi.org/10.1073/pnas.1422822112

Eble, A., & Hu, F. (2019). *Child beliefs, societal beliefs and teacher-student identity match.* CDEP-CGEG Working Paper No. 43. Center for Development Economics and Policy & Center on Global Economic Governance. https://cgeg.sipa.columbia.edu/sites/cgeg.sipa.columbia.edu/files/content/EbleWP43-2.pdf

Gaidzanwa, R. B. (2007). Academic women: Building human capital at the University of Zimbabwe. In N. T. Assie-Lumumba (Ed.), *Women and higher education in Africa: Reconceptualising gender-based human capabilities and upgrading human rights to knowledge.* CEPARRED Pan Africa Series.

Government of Zimbabwe. (2020). *National Development Strategy 1 (January 2021–December 2025).* https://www.mic.gov.zw/wp-content/uploads/2024/09/NDS1-Final.pdf

Gudyanga, A. (2016). Zimbabwean female participation in physics: Factors of identity formation considered as contributing to developing an orientation to physics by female students. *Journal of Education and Practice, 5*(26), 159–171.

Hervías Parejo, V., & Radulović, B. (2023). Public policies on gender equality. In D. Vujadinović, M. Fröhlich & T. Giegerich (Eds.), *Gender-competent legal education* (pp. 405–428). Springer. https://doi.org/10.1007/978-3-031-14360-1_12

Iwu, R. U., & Azoro, A. V. (2017). A study on the barriers to participation of females in science, mathematics and technology education in Imo State: The way forward. *Educational Research and Reviews, 12*(17), 832–838. https://doi.org/10.5897/ERR2017.3277

How Sweden's support to Makerere University helped mainstream Gender Equality within the Institution. (n.d.). Sweden Abroad. https://www.swedenabroad.se/en/embassies/uganda-kampala/current/news/gender-equality/

Kamwendo, J. C. (2024). Gendering the decision-making positions in higher education: A cross-sectional gender audit in three selected universities in Malawi. *African Journal of Inter/Multidisciplinary Studies, 6*(1), 1–10.

Kofoed, M. S., & McGovney, E. (2019). The effect of same-gender or same-race role models on occupation choice: Evidence from randomly assigned mentors at West Point. *Journal of Human Resources, 54*(2), 430–467. https://doi.org/10.3368/jhr.54.2.0416.7838R1

Kuteesa, K. N., Akpuokwe, C. U., & Udeh, C. A. (2024). Gender equity in education: Addressing challenges and promoting opportunities for social empowerment. *International Journal of Applied Research in Social Sciences, 6*(4), 631–641. https://doi.org/10.51594/ijarss.v6i4.1034

Lim, J., & Meer, J. (2017). The impact of student–teacher gender matches: Random assessment evidence from South Korea. *Journal of Human Resources, 52*(4), 979–997. https://doi.org/10.3368/jhr.52.4.1215-7585R1

Morley, L. (2010). Gender mainstreaming: Myths and measurement in higher education in Ghana and Tanzania. *Compare: A Journal of Comparative and International Education, 40*(4), 533–550. https://doi.org/10.1080/03057925.2010.490377

Mutinta, G. (2022). Gender-based violence among female students and implications for health intervention programmes in public universities in Eastern Cape, South Africa. *Cogent Social Sciences, 8*(1), 2079212. https://doi.org/10.1080/23311886.2022.2079212

Nabbuye, H. (2018). *Gender-sensitive pedagogy: The bridge to girls' quality education in Uganda.* Center for Universal Education, Brookings Institution.

National Science Foundation. (2011). Science and Engineering Indicators. https://ncses.nsf.gov/indicators

Swartz, S., Mahali, A., Arogundade, E., Khalema, E. S., Rule, C., Cooper, A. M., & Naidoo, P. (2017). *Ready or not! Race, education and emancipation: A five-year longitudinal, qualitative study of agency and impasses to success amongst higher education students in a sample of South African universities.* Human Sciences Research Council. http://hdl.handle.net/20.500.11910/11305

Thompson, A., Palmén, R., Seidl, S., Barnard, S., Beranek, S., Dainty, A. R. J., & Hassan, T. M. (2022). Fostering collaborative approaches to gender equality interventions in higher education and research: The case of transnational and multi-institutional communities of practice. *Journal of Gender Studies, 31*(1), 36–54. https://doi.org/10.1080/09589236.2021.1935804

Tizikara, C. (2019). *Investing in women as drivers of growth: A gender-based assessment of the science, technology and innovation ecosystem in Uganda.* RUFORUM. https://www.ruforum.org/sites/default/files/Reports/FAWoVC%20Gender%20Study_Final%20Report.pdf

UNCTAD (United Nations Conference on Trade and Development). (2011). *Applying a gender lens to science, technology and innovation.* UNCTAD. https://unctad.org/publication/applying-gender-lens-science-technology-and-innovation

UNESCO-IESALC (United Nations Educational, Scientific and Cultural Organization, United Nations International Institute for Higher Education in Latin America and the Caribbean). (2021). *Women in higher education: Has the female advantage put an end to gender inequalities?* UNESCO.

Wamboldt, A., Khan, S. R., Mellins, C. A., & Hirsh, J. S. (2018). Friends, strangers and bystanders: Informal practices of sexual assault intervention. *Global Public Health, 14*(1), 53–64. https://doi.org/10.1080/17441692.2018.1472290

Women's University in Africa. (2023–2027). Transformational strategy. Internal document.

World Economic Forum. (2016). *The human capital report.* WEF. https://www.weforum.org/publications/the-human-capital-report-2016/

The "Learning School": A Foundation for Gender Equality and Green Growth in Colombia

Paola Vásquez and Andrea Potes

Introduction

Increasing women's representation in green jobs, especially those requiring skills to design and operate sustainable technologies, not only strengthens women's economic independence but also creates a more diverse workforce. Bringing diverse perspectives to businesses and regions through gender-balanced teams strengthens their innovation and decision-making capabilities, creating more resilient societies in the face of environmental challenges. The Autonomous University of the West, in partnership with Colombia's National Apprenticeship Service's (SENA) Industrial Biotechnology Centre (CBI), sought to support a greater participation of women in the green economy labour market in Colombia.

SENA, created in 1957 under Colombia's Ministry of Labour and Social Security, has the mandate to provide Colombians with free, comprehensive technical and vocational training (TVET). This institution primarily serves vulnerable groups, including single mothers, displaced individuals, victims of armed conflict, rural populations, ethnic communities and low-income youth. In 2023, SENA supported approximately six million apprentices. SENA is the largest public educational institution in Colombia and in the words of Colombians, it is "the most beloved institution in the country". Through 118 centres, covering one or more municipalities, SENA is present in 1 102 of the 1 103 municipalities in Colombia. The project introduced in this chapter was conducted in collaboration with the SENA CBI, a training centre in the south-western part of the country, which acted as the unit of analysis of the case study.

Background and context

Climate crisis and environmental degradation have accelerated a worldwide transition from a linear economy to a green and circular economy (Vidican Auktor, 2020). The latter incentivises taking innovative actions towards sustainable production and consumption that apply the 3Rs: *reduce, reuse* and *recycle* waste and by-products (Manickam & Duraisamy, 2019). The transformation towards more environmentally friendly processes and technologies generates a positive effect on employment generation (Vidican Auktor, 2020). In Latin America and the Caribbean (LAC) alone, between 15 and 22 million green jobs are expected to be created by 2030 (Saget et al., 2020). In LAC, countries face the challenge of achieving a green transition while producing green jobs that offer strong social protection and foster gender equality. A transition that helps to shape the labour market towards inclusion of Latina women, enhancing their employment opportunities in the green economy, is necessary (Bustelo et al., 2023; Organización Internacional del Trabajo y Comisión Europea, Dirección General de Asociaciones Internacionales, 2023).

However, according to the International Labour Organization, more than 80% of the new jobs created for environmental protection and decarbonisation in LAC are concentrated in traditionally male-dominated sectors such as agriculture, energy, manufacturing, transportation and construction (Bustelo et al., 2023). Their environmental transformation requires individuals with skills in Green and Science, Technology, Engineering and Maths (STEM) fields where women are underrepresented (Lathifa, 2023; Steinke et al., 2024). As defined by OECD and Cedefop (2014, p. 16), green skills are "the skills needed by the workforce, in all sectors and at all levels, in order to help the adaptation of products, services and processes to the transformations due to climate change and to environmental requirements and regulations". These include technical knowledge, values, attitudes and abilities to develop cleaner services and production processes and operate green technologies that protect ecosystems and biodiversity, preserve environmental quality and support a sustainable and resource-efficient society (Ibrahim et al., 2020; LinkedIn Economic Graph, 2022).

Minority women, including Latinas, African descendants and indigenous women, face greater barriers to enrol, persevere and advance in Green-STEM careers (Armstrong & Jovanovic, 2015; Miles et al., 2022). One of the most common barriers is gender stereotypes that influence individual, family and cultural perceptions about which STEM green jobs are acceptable for women (UN Women, 2021). These barriers widen the green skills gender gap (LinkedIn Economic Graph, 2022).

Currently, women constitute less than 25% of graduates in fields of study required for the green economy and are underrepresented in sectors with green job potential (OECD, 2023). In LAC, women are almost absent in sectors such as gas, water and energy (Sevilla, 2021); in the energy sector specifically, women make up less than 20% of the workforce (Sacristán & Tatto, 2021). In Colombia, only 32% of students entering undergraduate STEM programmes in 2023 were women (Mineducación, 2023).

Against this backdrop, special attention must be paid to addressing gender inequalities in LAC contexts by equipping women with crucial STEM skills to advance in the sustainability sector (Islam & Jirattikorn, 2024). Any alternative risks rendering the green transition in the region gender-blind (Kolovich et al., 2024). Green skills acquisition can help prevent women's stagnation in low-productivity jobs, facilitate their advancement into high-productivity, eco-friendly roles and help them stay competitive in the sustainable economy (ILO, 2015; LinkedIn Economic Graph, 2022). Specifically, technical and vocational education and training (TVET), understood as "education and training given to the learners to acquire skills, knowledge and attitude needed in the world of work and necessary for employment in ones' chosen occupation" (Ejiofor & Ali, 2015, p. 2), is of great relevance to prepare women for the current and future needs of the labour market, economy and environment (UN Women, 2021).

Nevertheless, the TVET landscape in several countries remains anchored to gender and patriarchal structures (Wignall et al., 2023), especially in highly masculinised STEM programmes, leading to low female representation (Atsu & Lartey, 2018; Chauke, 2022). Although several projects and initiatives have made progress in promoting gender equity in TVET STEM-related education, few have done so in the framework of green growth and in LAC contexts. Further, these initiatives are limited in scope and tend to lack a systemic vision to address the educational institution as a whole. As a result, they focus on specific academic programmes or areas, prioritise the implementation of isolated actions (e.g. highlighting women scientists only on International Women's Day), propose strategies to achieve gender balance without addressing the root causes of inequity within the organisation and place greater emphasis on developing individual rather than organisational capacities. This approach fails to permeate the various levels of the organisational structure or foster comprehensive transformations that lead to sustainable impact. It prioritises the transfer of new knowledge around gender equity in environmental STEM fields to trainees, without altering the organisational DNA.

Organisational learning provides an approach to advancing gender equity in a way that addresses the above constraints (Andersson & Johansson, 2022; Buzzanell, 2018; Posselt et al., 2018). Organisational learning processes are essential to fostering a culture that supports women's advancement into scientific and technical roles, including green jobs. However, very few initiatives for gender equality in green science and technology in LAC assume organisational learning approaches, focusing efforts on transferring knowledge and skills so that the organisation internalises gender equity in its values, behaviours, policies, processes and organisational routines (Crossan et al., 1999). When internalisation fails, that is, when it does not reach the heart of organisations, they easily revert to old practices and habits (Ørberg Jensen et al., 2013). In our case, this would imply returning to an organisational culture that favours inequity, accentuates sexist stereotypes and limits the personal and professional growth of women in vocational careers with an environmental STEM focus. Therefore, we sought to answer the following questions:

1. How, from an organisational learning approach, can educational institutions more effectively encourage female students' participation in Green-STEM fields?
2. How do educational institutions integrate and internalise gender equity in STEM to promote inclusive green growth from educational processes?

Theoretical tools of the study

The study adopted a gender-transformative approach, which seeks to constructively, and in a context-driven way, transform power relations and socially accepted norms that reinforce gendered inequalities (Hillenbrand et al., 2015; McDougall et al., 2021). Here, removing structural barriers is the starting point for changing habits, relations, norms, beliefs, stereotypes, laws, policies, practices and harmful behaviours that perpetuate gender gaps (Bilimoria et al., 2008).

In line with this, organisational learning is conceived as a means to achieve the desired change (Bianchi et al., 2022); in this case, the desired change was to reduce discrimination in STEM disciplines with an environmental focus in TVET education. Organisational learning studies show how an organisation learns and adapts to change (Huber, 1991). It is a complex process of developing new knowledge that has the potential to generate behavioural and cognitive changes through action (Škerlavaj et al., 2007).

We used the 5i Learning Framework for Gender Equity in STEM proposed by Jones and Macpherson (2006) to guide organisational learning processes around gender equity in Green-STEM fields within SENA CBI (i.e. the TVET institution analysed in the research study).

Jones and Macpherson outline five sub-processes (the 5is) for developing and internalising new knowledge: intuiting, interpreting, integrating, institutionalising and inter-organisation. *Intuiting* involves recognising new ideas for organisational change, often inspired by external actors (Huber, 1991). *Interpreting* analyses these ideas individually or in groups, with communication key to achieving collective understanding. *Integrating* implements the analysed ideas. And *Institutionalising* embeds the new knowledge into the organisation's routines, which include the procedures, strategies, technologies, beliefs, cultural norms and behavioural codes developed by organisations (Levit & March, 1988). *Inter-organisational learning* occurs when organisations collaborate on shared interests with external providers such as universities, consultants and researchers. These actors help develop and institutionalise knowledge, driving strategic renewal towards a culture of equity in STEM (Andersson & Johansson, 2022; Jones & Macpherson, 2006).

In this light, the study developed a new framework based on the 5is to guide education institutions towards more inclusive Green-STEM education processes (Figure 1). Integrating organisational learning and gender-transformative principles, the framework defines key actions for internal and external actors leading this transition. It frames the shift to a more equitable STEM pedagogy as a dynamic learning process, structured around five sub-processes (5is) and outlines specific actions for each phase.

It is not clear from existing research and practice how to integrate gender mainstreaming and organisational learning to achieve equity (Andersson & Johansson, 2022; see Chapter 3 for a discussion of the importance of gender mainstreaming and gender transformation in institutions and organisations). Therefore, our proposed model closes this gap by addressing gender balance in science and technology through the integration of organisational learning and gender transformative approaches. This approach can be used to plan, implement and evaluate initiatives that seek to increase the representation of women in STEM in higher education.

Figure 1: The 5i Learning Framework for Gender Equity in STEM

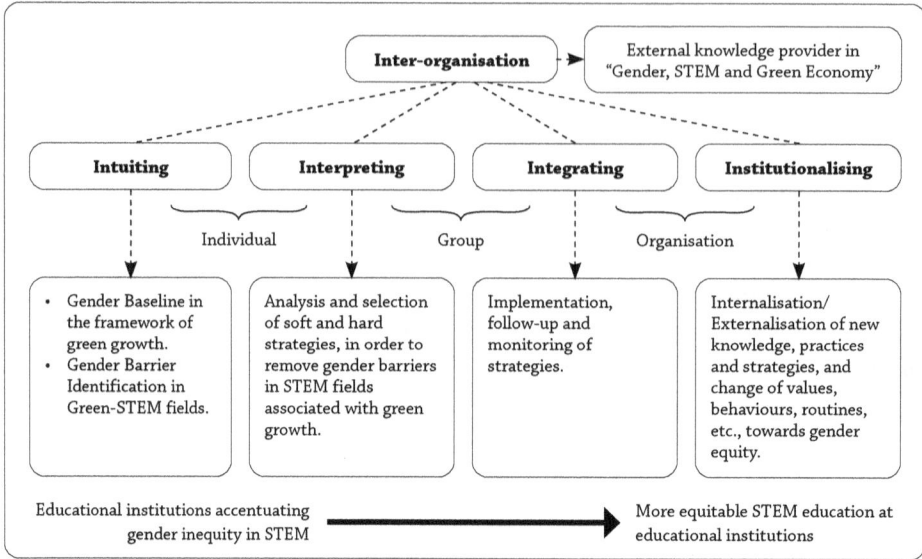

Adapted from Jones and Macpherson (2006)

Methodology

The research adopted the 5i Learning Framework for Gender Equity in STEM to guide the development of a single case study, with SENA CBI as the unit of analysis. The case study method, incorporating both descriptive and explanatory approaches, enables a deeper understanding of specific phenomena (Pereira et al., 2023). Widely used in social sciences and education (Schoch, 2020), the case study method has proven effective in various contexts, such as evaluating higher education institutions' information systems (Pereira et al., 2023), analysing student and teacher perceptions of active learning methodologies (Carvalho et al., 2021) and assessing the impact of problem-based learning on the practical skills and clinical experience of future physicians (Korniichuk et al., 2021). Both qualitative and quantitative data were collected to ensure triangulation, providing a comprehensive understanding of the research phenomenon and enhancing the validity and reliability of the findings. This mixed-methods approach allowed for a more robust analysis by cross-verifying results from different data sources.

Seven STEM-focused TVET programmes with high environmental potential were selected for this study. These included Environmental Monitoring, Biotechnological Processes Applied to Industry, Environmental Management and Sustainable Use of Biodiversity. The invitation to participate in the survey was shared through institutional emails, SENA's digital platforms where a video encouraging participation was published and social media channels such as Facebook. The invitation message included the study's objectives, the eligibility criteria for participants and the survey link. Out of 1 002 apprentices, 121 responded to the online survey, ensuring a high degree of representativeness of the target population. In addition, 17 semi-structured interviews were conducted in person with instructors and academic coordinators who represented the entire group of educators involved in the seven prioritised programmes. To further explore specific topics, focus group discussions were also held with 134 apprentices, some of whom had already completed the survey. Participation in all data collection formats was voluntary. While only female apprentices were invited to participate, both male and female educators took part in the interviews.

Findings

Intuiting

The case study was developed progressively, following the phases of the 5i Learning Framework for Gender Equity in STEM. Throughout this process, researchers worked to enable members of the SENA CBI community (learners, instructors and academic coordinators) to gradually gain the knowledge and skills necessary to independently implement, replicate and refine each phase according to their roles within the institution.

The first phase focused on strengthening the capacity of SENA CBI to *intuit* (recognise) alternatives that promote gender balance in TVET careers with an environmental STEM focus. Recognising that effective solutions cannot be proposed without a deep understanding of the problem and its causes, a gender baseline was established, primarily aimed at identifying the root causes of inequity that may serve as barriers to the advancement of female learners in science and green technology fields.

Through an extensive literature review and the collection of primary data from the SENA CBI community, the gender baseline was constructed. The review mainly focused on scientific articles and studies on gender barriers in STEM in developing countries. However, limited information was available on this topic in Latin America, particularly within the context of vocational education.

Based on the barriers identified in the literature, qualitative and quantitative tools were developed to collect primary data. The participation of instructors and coordinators from SENA CBI in designing surveys and interviews provided them with the opportunity to engage in research processes. This involvement also allowed instructors and coordinators to understand the project's objectives from the outset, fostering a stronger connection and ownership from the very beginning. Their engagement enriched the analysis of the barriers. Instructors' close relationships with learners enabled them to understand the learners' realities first-hand, facilitating a deeper understanding of the identified barriers and their causes. These connections deepened researchers' understanding of the identified barriers and their underlying causes, facilitated the analysis of their interrelationships, validating them within the project's context and scope, and ultimately selecting the key barriers to address in the next phase (Table 1).

Table 1: **Main gender barriers in environment-focused TVET-STEM careers**

Barrier	Description
B1	There are insufficient and/or undisclosed female referents in STEM fields, at the academic and occupational levels, and in the green industry field.
B2	Sexist and gender stereotypes, which establish the skills, roles and careers suitable for women and men, limit the participation of women in STEM careers in academia and the workplace.
B3	Lack of self-confidence in girls in mathematics, induced by the social and school environment.
B4	Women may be fearful of entering male-dominated academic environments, considering these environments hostile to them.
B5	Stereotypes that exclude women from STEM careers are reinforced in families.
B6	Managers, instructors or the trainees themselves may limit women's participation in practical activities considered masculine, which are specific to the career or job position.
B7	Women's technical skills are underestimated throughout their academic training and in the workplace, with men being preferred for the performance of some activities.
B8	When the majority of partners are men, women may feel intimidated or harassed by inappropriate comments, attitudes or practices towards them.
B9	There is a lack of training for women in technical subjects associated with green industries to help them move into leadership positions.

In particular, the interviews and focus groups were essential for enriching our understanding of women apprentices' experiences. The one-on-one and small group interactions fostered trust, facilitating the exchange of sensitive information. The semi-structured formats allowed for real-time adaptation of questions to delve deeper into specific or emerging aspects. In these spaces, the apprentices highlighted the persistence of social and family prejudices that question their ability to study and work in male-dominated fields such as industry, construction and the sciences. Apprentices reported hearing comments from peers that underestimated their mental and physical capabilities to perform in these fields.

These stereotypes perpetuate the misconception that certain areas of the green industry, such as sustainable construction and renewable energy, are incompatible with the characteristics associated with femininity or societal expectations of women. This may be due to the persistent collective mindset that men should handle physically demanding labour (e.g. installing and maintaining solar panels, working at heights).

In this regard, an academic coordinator commented that companies often prefer male apprentices for internships in logistics, arguing that men have the technical skills and physical strength to carry boxes. For one coordinator, this is a misguided perception, as

> [o]ur logistics programme is not based on physical strength. Our apprentices are capable of efficiently organising storage systems and inventory management, preventing product expiration and loss, which reduces waste and its negative environmental impact while improving the company's productivity. However, these green skills of our female apprentices are not recognised by those employers with outdated views on TVET careers and the role of women in them.

Similar situations were observed with some companies that reported a preference for hiring men in production plants or manufacturing areas related to STEM competencies, arguing that "They prefer not to hire women in agro-industrial production farms because these spaces are considered unsafe for women," as an instructor stated. Thus, gender biases end up excluding women or limiting their access to green jobs that require technical and/or physical skills, by deeming them supposedly incapable. However, the apprentices stated that women have the capacity to work in the sustainability field, often proposing innovative environmental solutions that their male counterparts have not identified. Additionally, some trainees who are already engaged in internships at companies shared: "Women have to fight to keep our jobs, not let ourselves be sidelined, and never lower our heads." This reveals that they perceive the workplace as a constant struggle to earn both technical and personal respect, simply because they are women.

Findings show that women apprentices face gender bias before, during and after their STEM training, compounded by factors such as age, ethnic background, educational level and geographic origin. At SENA, this is particularly prevalent due to the large heterogeneity of apprentices entering TVET education, which includes individuals with continuous schooling, others who have been out of education for 10 to 15 years, members of minority groups such as Indigenous or Afro-descendant people, women from conflict-affected areas and older individuals, among other profiles. While universities primarily attract young graduates, TVET education attracts individuals of all ages, mostly with economic limitations, interested in learning a trade quickly to meet personal and family needs.

Interviews highlight that Afro-descendant apprentices at SENA CBI are particularly vulnerable, facing not only socio-economic difficulties but also racial and cultural discrimination. An academic coordinator shared how an instructor expressed biases based on both the skin colour and gender of an apprentice, attributing her low academic performance to these factors with comments such as:

> Well, since that girl is from XXX city and is Afro-descendant, I have to help her because she can't keep up with the rest of the apprentices; I'm sure the education in her town isn't good, and here she's overwhelmed with so much information, especially with math.

Another instructor remarked: "*Some apprentices criticise the hairstyles of their Afro-descendant peers and discriminate against them.*" On the other hand, older apprentices expressed feeling intimidated by their younger peers, questioning their ability to finish the programme: "*I'm so old, will I be able to finish this career? Who will hire me?*" In these cases, female instructors have been crucial, offering support and motivation to help them continue. Additionally, apprentices value the high presence of female instructors in some programmes, as it builds their confidence and facilitates interaction during their training.

Apprentices highlighted sexual harassment as a challenge that can occur in all spaces, from educational environments to the streets and workplaces. Apprentices shared experiences such as: "*In the company, since there are more men, when you ask for a favour as an apprentice, they make inappropriate insinuations.*" Unfortunately, many companies still lack guidelines, policies or mechanisms to implement a gender perspective or prevent gender-based violence, which hinders women's progress in STEM careers. As one instructor mentioned, in one company, the solution to prevent harassment of a SENA apprentice was to place a sign saying, "*No flirting with the SENA apprentice – Prohibited*", which is insufficient in addressing the harassment issue.

The ongoing involvement of SENA instructors and coordinators in designing, collecting and analysing field data strengthened and developed their knowledge and skills to identify weaknesses and opportunities for promoting women apprentices in the green economy. Their participation in training sessions, reflection spaces and informal dialogues about gender equality in green jobs strengthened their knowledge to drive a green, just and equitable transition from the TVET institution. These reflections focused on how to promote environmentally sustainable economies without leaving anyone behind, ensuring inclusion through STEM environmental education processes that equip both men and women with the tools needed to access decent green jobs. Particular attention was given to actions taken by researchers, academic actors and governments in other countries, highlighting the resulting benefits in strengthening the role of women in STEM. This dialogue aimed to broaden the perspective on effective solutions that are sometimes overlooked or unfamiliar in the local context.

In addition, through the various activities, instructors reaffirmed their roles as professionals contributing to science and technology beyond their teaching duties, gained recognition as STEM experts from trainees and validated their impact as female role models inspiring young women. At the same time, trainees deepened their understanding of concepts such as STEM, gender equity and gender transformation, recognising that women scientists can thrive in Latin America. Thus, during the *Intuition* stage, the topic of inclusiveness in STEM careers started to be approached in a much more open way within SENA CBI. This stage was also key for introducing concepts and tools like the Gender Equality Continuum, which guides strategies and programmes to transition from gender-blind to gender-transformative approaches, advancing gender equity in STEM.

Interpreting

Once the SENA CBI community strengthened its ability to *intuit* (recognise) the causes and potential alternatives to reduce the gender gap in TVET-STEM careers with an environmental focus, the next phase began. This stage focused on enhancing their capacity to *interpret* (understand) these alternatives or solutions aimed at achieving gender parity. *Interpretation*, as a group exercise, allows for the collective analysis of alternatives in depth and the selection of the most suitable ones for later implementation, considering the project's objectives, context and scope. Thus, between external researchers and the SENA CBI team, it was concluded that two types of strategies were necessary: (1) soft strategies focused on raising awareness and highlighting female leadership in the fields of science and green technology, aiming to inspire and motivate women to take a more active role in the green economy; and (2) hard strategies focused on transferring and/or strengthening new knowledge (mainly of a technical nature) and developing Green-STEM skills through practice. To this end, the use of active learning environments was proposed, in which environmental actions would be implemented under a practical learning approach. Table 2 consolidates the main strategies, which were built so that each one contributed to the removal of multiple barriers to maximise their impact.

Table 2: Consolidated strategies and related barriers

Strategy	Soft	Barrier to remove
S.1	Recognising women's leadership in STEM fields.	B1, B2, B4, B5, B8
S.2	Inspiring women in STEM.	
	Hard	
S.3	Green pilots for experiential environmental training with a gender perspective (on-campus).	B1, B2, B3, B4, B6, B7, B9
S.4	Green pilots for experiential environmental training with a gender perspective and in real environments, including natural and business settings (off-campus).	

The combination of soft and hard strategies is essential, as they complement and reinforce one another, facilitating the development of a wide range of skills and promoting comprehensive learning. While soft strategies create the emotional and theoretical foundation that inspires and prepares apprentices, hands-on learning spaces strengthen that knowledge and transform it into applicable green technical skills for solving real environmental problems.

Integrating

Actively involving the SENA CBI instructors during this stage allowed them to *interpret* (understand) each of the strategies, including their scope and objectives, expected benefits and novel elements, among other aspects. Additionally, as part of the *Interpretation* phase, the researchers and the SENA CBI team collaboratively reflected on the activities necessary to implement the strategies, that is, to *integrate* them into the TVET educational institution. In order to facilitate their integration and long-term sustainability, activities were prioritised based on the following criteria: easy to implement at low or moderate cost; adaptable or replicable across multiple training programmes; promote learning-by-doing methods, teamwork, innovation and inclusion; involve low-complexity technologies, processes and practices that align with the academic or theoretical foundations guiding the selected training programmes;

and focus on Green-STEM topics of increasing relevance in both national and global labour markets. Internal and external stakeholders from various social and STEM disciplines played a key role in the *integration* of the strategies at SENA CBI. Their contributions are reflected in the activities carried out to put these strategies into action, as outlined below.

Recognising and inspiring female leadership in Green-STEM fields (S1 & S2)

Through a workshop called "My Favourite Scientist", trainees and instructors (both female and male) recognised the experiences and leadership of Latin American women in science and technology fields. The workshop began by presenting data about gender inequality in STEM in the world and Colombia. Then groups of trainees analysed the biographies of Latin American women scientists recognised for their contribution to science and the socio-environmental impact of their work. On a billboard, using comics and magazine clippings, trainees captured information such as the place and date of birth of the scientists, characteristics of their work, field of knowledge and curiosities of their biography. Finally, each group presented their work and reflections to their peers.

The workshop helped to break down false beliefs among the trainees. When students recognise women scientists living in the same region, who have overcome similar barriers, they understand that pursuing and excelling in the field of science is a real possibility for them.

> *When we asked the trainees to name their favourite scientist, the answer alluded to the 'dead men's fair', as they only named Einstein and Newton, but now they recognise that Colombian and Latin women are also doing science nowadays.* (SENA CBI Instructor)

> *It has been very inspiring for me to learn about the lives of these women and the obstacles they have faced. It encourages me to keep going forward, regardless of my age, and to continue to better myself every day.* (SENA CBI Apprentice)

Although the first workshops were led by an external practitioner from the gender area, SENA CBI instructors were always invited to co-lead this activity. This co-leadership approach eased the transfer of the necessary pedagogical and methodological elements for the development of the workshop; thus, instructors learned the details of the activity, were able to adjust or complement it according to the particularities of each group of trainees and helped to guide and develop the activity on the ground. In other words, the instructors' abilities to integrate this strategy into the training cycle were strengthened, especially increasing their knowledge to promote gender balance in STEM with simple actions in the classroom.

The workshops were frequently accompanied by panels and live talks featuring successful local women in STEM fields, providing the apprentices with the opportunity to engage face-to-face with renowned scientists and engineers. These sessions allowed the trainees to explore both the personal and professional aspects of these women's journeys, learn about the strategies that led to their success and discover the technological advancements they are leading to protect the planet. The fact that these stories were local, referencing regions, customs and challenges familiar to the apprentices, facilitated a deeper connection.

By hearing stories they could relate to, as they had experienced similar situations, the apprentices found inspiration, feeling empowered to overcome obstacles in their own paths. Female engineers shared anecdotes that reflected the reality of many Colombian families and demonstrated that achieving great things is possible, motivating apprentices to excel:

> In my family, we were four siblings. We walked to school under the scorching sun in Cali, and sometimes the only thing we ate all day was water with panela [a block of brown sugar] and royal bread [the cheapest bread in Colombian bakeries]. Now, I manage the circular economy department at a government agency, and ... I have my own car.

These workshops were effective; opportunities to hear from women role models are rarely provided in formal education contexts, where technical training often takes precedence. No matter how proficient apprentices become in technical skills or advanced technologies, if we do not inspire them, help them see themselves as STEM leaders and ignite their confidence and passion for science, our impact will remain limited.

Green pilots for experiential environmental training with a gender perspective (S3)

To guide active learning towards developing apprentices' problem-solving skills in their local environment, the project team decided to select a theme that would resonate with them: sustainable urban agriculture.

Active learning began with theoretical sessions to introduce the concepts and principles of agroecology, preparing apprentices before transitioning to practical activities. SENA instructors and external experts in resource efficiency and sustainable agriculture supported the pedagogical cycle, covering the design, construction and management of the experimental garden, built on approximately 170 m^2, as well as the harvesting and post-harvesting processes.

Apprentice groups were assigned specific responsibilities (i.e. watering, measuring plant growth, identifying pests, etc.) that enabled them to develop key skills, such as teamwork, critical analysis and decision-making. Additionally, the project team ensured that both male and female apprentices actively participated, making sure everyone had direct contact with the land and engaged in tasks that required numerical calculations or technical analysis. This approach allowed them to develop better agricultural skills and prevented women from being relegated to passive roles, such as taking notes, as has occurred in other cases.

The experience helped male apprentices break gender stereotypes, with many expressing pride in seeing their female peers working side by side, recognising their ability to perform tasks that require both physical and cognitive effort. On one occasion, an attempt to exclude women arose, despite the gender training prior to the activity. An external agroecology expert suggested that only men should till the land and measure environmental parameters due to their greater physical strength, prompting corrective action by the project team. This highlights the need, at times, to re-educate team members to question and reshape deeply ingrained gender beliefs within STEM disciplines.

Overall, the active participation of SENA CBI instructors was crucial in guiding the pedagogical sessions and identifying key areas for improvement in each selected training programme using the pilot garden. This involvement also highlighted the technical skills of the female instructors, who worked alongside external experts, showcasing to the apprentices the value of female leadership within their own institution. This engagement allowed the SENA CBI community to become more familiar with the garden, fostering a deeper connection with the environmental pilot, enhancing their ability to manage it and expanding its potential as a learning platform on a larger scale within the TVET institution.

Green pilots for experiential environmental training with a gender perspective and in real environments, including natural and business settings (S4)

The implementation of environmental pilots in community contexts brought the trainees closer to real environmental challenges, involving them in a practical and reflective way in the search for innovative and sustainable solutions in collaboration with the local community. The apprentices, together with experts and instructors in STEM fields, took part in the installation of vermicomposting systems in 13 rural small businesses led by women, who make up a legally constituted Association of Rural Women Producers (Corpobarranco). The association is made up of women in agriculture, who are mainly involved in growing grapes, corn, bananas, fruit trees and raising small livestock (e.g. chickens and fish).

By working with a women-led organisation, apprentices gained appreciation for the role of women in the green economy, and the opportunity benefited the female farmers and their work.

Through the activity, female apprentices and female farmers interacted with each other and women from various STEM backgrounds to learn about the vermicomposting systems. The experiential learning process was supported by theoretical sessions to introduce key concepts before field activities. Participants then conducted exercises to validate parameters of the vermicomposting system. They also learned to monitor key variables like temperature and pH and apply corrective measures when necessary.

Vermicomposting systems were successfully implemented and operated by female farmers, producing high-quality bio-compost. All participants demonstrated the knowledge and skills needed for running the types of processes that promote rural circularity, tackling environmental challenges collaboratively. Notably, the apprentices recognised the effort and learning capacity of these women, viewing them as role models in technological and environmental transformations. The rural women's diverse ages, from very young to elderly, and their generally low educational levels, motivated the apprentices to excel in Green-STEM fields, following their example. This experience allowed trainees to explore intersectionality in the green economy and understand how to transfer knowledge to rural communities, witnessing that science can be successfully applied by rural women. Finally, on-site observation helped to constantly identify weaknesses in the transfer of STEM knowledge, from which actions were taken to strengthen the learning process for both female farmers and apprentices.

Institutionalising

To ensure the long-term sustainability of the strategies developed in the project, a programme was created as part of the *Institutionalising* (internalisation) phase. The programme consolidates the different strategies and defines the application route for them within SENA CBI, to guide their ongoing implementation, even after the project team leaves. Protocols, guidelines, booklets and pedagogical material were provided to guide the use of the technological prototypes and the development of the soft strategies, with a view to sustaining them over time. Instructors and coordinators were involved in creating these materials and received training in key aspects to maintain the progress made. This approach modified pedagogical processes and practices, bringing the SENA CBI community closer to real-world environmental business transformation in enterprises and rural associations led by women, while promoting female leadership in STEM fields across various contexts.

An observation process supported by evaluation criteria showed that SENA CBI developed internalisation capabilities by effectively replicating the strategies internally with other groups of trainees from different training programmes. SENA CBI initiated the scaling up of strategies to other SENA centres not covered during the project in other cities in Colombia. Critically, sharing and externalising the knowledge acquired demonstrates a high level of internalisation. SENA CBI staff are also analysing the possibility of converting some of the soft strategies into pedagogical courses on gender equity to be included in the training programmes led by the SENA School of Instructors. In turn, SENA CBI has begun to lead gender equity initiatives in Green-STEM fields in schools that are affiliated with this institution, which also demonstrates its capacity to transfer the knowledge acquired to other types of educational entities.

Inter-organisationalising

Finally, as demonstrated in the case description, the *Inter-organisational* approach brought together various stakeholders who supported the learning process. (1) The UAO University, with its researchers and experts, contributed specialised technical and scientific knowledge; (2) Corpobarranco, a rural women's association, shared valuable empirical knowledge on small-scale food production; and (3) rural small businesses led by women served as STEM laboratories, where different areas of expertise were integrated to foster environmental improvements. These collaborations connected the SENA CBI community with the dynamics and challenges of the local context, providing a platform for developing both green-technical and life skills.

Conclusions

To address climate change and ensure environmental sustainability, we need to move from unsustainable industries to ones that promote green and inclusive growth. Yet, because of the inequities in STEM programmes and careers in Colombia, there are not as many women prepared to enter this sustainable labour market as their male counterparts. This case study demonstrated how the most important and recognised TVET institution in the country could address issues of gender inequity in training programmes with an environmental STEM focus by using an organisational learning approach. The organisational learning approach was crucial to modifying behaviours, attitudes and pedagogical practices that may have been reinforcing the gender gap in STEM.

Change towards a more equitable TVET institution was possible via a gradual learning process, through the stages of Intuition, Interpretation, Integration, Institutionalisation and Inter-organisation. In our case, it was essential that the project team actively involved the TVET institution and dedicated sufficient time to ensure that it acquires the knowledge and skills necessary to develop and continue to improve each stage of the learning cycle on its own. Efforts were directed towards achieving integration and internalisation levels, as this allows progress to be made in modifying the organisational processes, routines and policies in favour of greater participation of women in the green science and technology sectors.

Equally important was the combination of soft and hard strategies and their gradual implementation, as they enable the development of a wide range of skills, from motivation to the application of technical concepts across various productive sectors. Starting with soft strategies facilitated a smoother and more natural transition to hard strategies. This combination proved to be key to breaking down barriers such as the lack of female referents in the green industry, bringing female instructors and trainees closer to environmental practices and technologies in real scenarios, facilitating the processes of interpretation and integration of new STEM knowledge through innovative educational strategies outside the classroom. The selection of easy-to-apply strategies, which can be replicated and sustained over time with the technical, human and financial resources of the TVET institution, should be given priority.

Constant dialogue and communication between external knowledge providers and TVET institution staff allowed for the creation and application of innovative strategies to remove gender barriers in STEM. Spaces for joint reflection enabled the sharing of knowledge, and adjusting, redesigning or maturing strategies, based on a process of co-creation and feedback between external and internal actors (see Chapter 7 for another example of stakeholder engagement and co-creation).

Finally, SENA CBI proved to be a 'learning organisation' that developed multiple capabilities to more effectively address gender equity issues in STEM through inclusive TVET training. Moving forward, it is crucial that companies of all sizes (micro, small, medium and large) also engage in these learning processes, strengthening their capacity to welcome and empower women, allowing them to take on leadership roles in the transition of productive sectors to green technologies. Until this happens, the efforts made by the TVET institution to empower its apprentices in environmental STEM careers will be in vain, as women shall continue to face barriers in the industrial sector that hinder their progress in Green-STEM fields. Although this chapter has focused on the TVET system in one country in Latin America, it will be important to explore if and how it can be used to facilitate gender equity in Green-STEM programmes of study in other educational contexts.

Acknowledgements

This research was funded by the International Development Research Centre (IDRC) in Canada.

About the Authors

Paola Vásquez is an Associate Professor at Universidad Autónoma de Occidente in Colombia.

Andrea Potes is an Academic Coordinator at SENA CBI in Colombia.

References

Armstrong, M. A., & Jovanovic, J. (2015). Starting at the crossroads: Intersectional approaches to institutionally supporting underrepresented minority women STEM faculty. *Journal of Women and Minorities in Science and Engineering, 21*(2), 141–157. https://doi.org/10.1615/JWomenMinorScienEng.2015011275

Andersson, E., & Johansson, K. (2022). Organisational learning in gender mainstreaming: Openings and barriers for implementation and change. *International Journal of Learning and Change, 14*(3), 339–355. https://doi.org/10.1504/IJLC.2021.10034732

Atsu, A. M., & Lartey, R. L. (2018). Enhancing participation of girls in Technical and Vocational Education and Training (TVET): The case of Tamale Technical University. *EPH – International Journal of Education Research, 2*(1), 1–8.

Bianchi, G., Testa, F., Boiral, O., & Iraldo, F. (2022). Organizational learning for environmental sustainability: Internalizing lifecycle management. *Organization and Environment, 35*(1), 103–129. https://doi.org/10.1177/1086026621998744

Bilimoria, D., Joy, S., & Liang, X. (2008). Breaking barriers and creating inclusiveness: Lessons of organizational transformation to advance women faculty in academic science and engineering. *Human Resource
Management, 47*(3), 423–441. https://doi.org/10.1002/hrm.20225

Bustelo, M., Martinez, K., González, S., & Suaya, A. (2023). *Género e inclusión en la agenda verde: Dónde esta-
mos y cómo avanzar?* [Resumen de políticas No. IDB-PB-00390]. División de Género y Diversidad, Banco
Interamericano de Desarrollo.

Buzzanell, P. M. (2018). Introduction to special issue: Learning organization/organizational learning and
gender issues. *The Learning Organization, 25*(1), 2–9. https://doi.org/10.1108/TLO-11-2017-0107

Carvalho, A., Teixeira, S. J., Olim, L., Campanella, S. D., & Costa, T. (2021). Pedagogical innovation in higher
education and active learning methodologies – A case study. *Education + Training, 63*(2), 195–213.
https://doi.org/10.1108/ET-05-2020-0141

Chauke, T. A. (2022). Gender differences in determinants of students' interest in STEM education. *Social
Sciences, 11*(11), 534. https://doi.org/10.3390/socsci11110534

Crossan, M., Lane, H., & White, R. (1999). An organizational learning framework: From intuition to institution. *Academy of Management Review, 24*(3), 522–537. http://dx.doi.org/10.2307/259140

Ejiofor, T. E., & Ali, C. C. (2015). Linking TVET institutions and industries for national development:
Challenges and strategies in Nigeria. *Nigeria Vocational Association Journal (NVA), 20*(1), 166–173.

Hillenbrand, E., Karim, N., Mohanraj, P., & Wu, D. (2015). *Measuring gender-transformative change: A review of
literature and promising practices.* Working Paper. CARE USA. https://hdl.handle.net/20.500.12348/248

Huber, G. P. (1991). Organizational learning: The contributing processes and the literatures. *Organization
Science, 2*(1), 88–115. https://doi.org/10.1287/orsc.2.1.88

Ibrahim, Z., Lai, C. S., Zaime, A. F., Lee, M. F., & Othman, N. M. (2020). Green skills in knowledge and attitude dimensions from the industrial perspective. *IOP conference series: Materials science and engineering*
(Vol. 917). IOP Publishing. https://doi.org/10.1088/1757-899X/917/1/012025

ILO (International Labour Organization). (2015). *Gender equality and green jobs.* Policy Brief. ILO. https://
www.ilo.org/publications/gender-equality-and-green-jobs

ILO. (2019). *Skills for a greener future: A global view.* International Labour Office, ILO. https://www.ilo.org/
publications/skills-greener-future-global-view

Islam, N., & Jirattikorn, A. (2024). Breaking gender barriers in STEM education for achieving the SDG of
quality education in Bangladesh. *Development in Practice, 34*(1), 129–135. https://doi.org/10.1080/0961
4524.2023.2229965

Jones, O., & Macpherson, A. (2006). Inter-organizational learning and strategic renewal in SMEs. Extending
the 4I framework. *Long Range Planning, 39*(2), 155–175. https://doi.org/10.1016/j.lrp.2005.02.012

Kolovich, L. L., Newiak, M., & Ruiz Abril, E. (2024). Gender and the green economy: What conditions for a
gender-transformative transition to the green economy in Africa? In L. Kolovich & M. Newiak (Eds.),
Gender equality and economic development in sub-Saharan Africa (pp. 363–378). International Monetary
Fund. https://www.elibrary.imf.org/display/book/9798400246968/CH020.xml

Korniichuk, O. Y., Bambyzov, L. M., Kosenko, V. M., Spaska, A. M., & Tsekhmister, Y. V. (2021). Application of
the case study method in medical education. *International Journal of Learning, Teaching and Educational
Research, 20*(7), 175–191. https://doi.org/10.26803/IJLTER.20.7.10

Lathifa, Z. (2023). Factors contributing to the underrepresentation of women and minority students in
STEM fields. *Sage Science Review of Educational Technology, 6*(1), 39–47. https://journals.sagescience.
org/index.php/ssret/article/view/58/56

LEE (Laboratorio de Economía de la Educación de la Pontificia Universidad Javeriana). (2022). *Informe 67:
Las mujeres son minoría en las carreras STEM.* https://lee.javeriana.edu.co/w/lee-informe-67

Levitt, B., & March, J. G. (1988). Organizational learning. *Annual Review of Sociology, 14,* 319–340. https://
doi.org/10.1146/annurev.so.14.080188.001535

LinkedIn Economic Graph. (2022). *Global green skills report 2022.* https://economicgraph.linkedin.com/con-
tent/dam/me/economicgraph/en-us/global-green-skills-report/global-green-skills-report-pdf/
li-green-economy-report-2022-annex.pdf

Manickam, P., & Duraisamy, G. (2019). 3Rs and circular economy. In S. S. Muthu (Ed.), *Circular economy in textiles and apparel: Processing, manufacturing and design* (pp. 77–93). Woodhead Publishing.

McDougall, C., Badstue, L., Mulema, A., Fischer, G., Najjar, D., Pyburn, R., Elias, M., Joshi, D., & Vos, A. (2021). Toward structural change: Gender transformative approaches. In R. Pyburn & A. van Eerdewijk (Eds.), *Advancing gender equality through agricultural and environmental research: Past, present and future* (pp. 365–402). International Food Policy Research Institute.

Miles, M. L., Agger, C. A., Roby, R. S., & Morton, T. R. (2022). Who's who: How "women of color" are (or are not) represented in STEM education research. *Science Education, 106*(2), 229–256. https://doi.org/10.1002/sce.21694

Mineducación (Ministerio de Educación Nacional). (2023, marzo 7). STEM: una lucha en clave de género. *Educación.* https://www.mineducaion.gov.co/portal/micrositios-institucionales/Dia-de-la-Mujer-2023/414325:STEM-una-lucha-en-clave-de-genero

OECD (Organisation for Economic Co-operation and Development). (2023). *Job creation and local economic development 2023: Bridging the great green divide.* OECD Publishing. https://doi.org/10.1787/21db61c1-en

OECD & Cedefop (European Centre for the Development of Vocational Training). (2014). *Greener skills and jobs.* OECD Publishing. http://dx.doi.org/10.1787/9789264208704-en

Ørberg Jensen, P. D., Larsen, M. M., & Pedersen, T. (2013). The organizational design of offshoring: Taking stock and moving forward. *Journal of International Management, 19*(4), 315–323. https://doi.org/10.1016/j.intman.2013.03.012

Organización Internacional del Trabajo y Comisión Europea, Dirección General de Asociaciones Internacionales. (2023). Maria Elena, V. *Empleos verdes, una oportunidad para las mujeres en América Latina.* Programa EUROCLIMA+.

Pereira, R. H., de Carvalho, J. V., & Rocha, Á. (2023). Architecture of a maturity model for information systems in higher education institutions: Multiple case study for dimensions identification. *Computational and Mathematical Organization Theory, 29*(4), 526–541. https://doi.org/10.1007/s10588-021-09342-z

Posselt, J., Porter, K., & Kamimura, A. (2018). Organizational pathways toward gender equity in doctoral education: Chemistry and civil engineering compared. *American Journal of Education, 124*(4). https://doi.org/10.1086/698457

Sacristán, G., & Tatto, P. (2021, Noviembre 11). La mujer, motor de la transición energética. *BID Invest.* https://idbinvest.org/es/blog/genero/la-mujer-motor-de-la-transicion-energetica

Saget, C., Vogt-Schlib, A., & Luu, T. (2020). *Jobs in a net-zero emissions future in Latin America and the Caribbean.* IDB. http://dx.doi.org/10.18235/0002509

Schoch, K. (2020). Case study research. In G. J. Burkholder, K. A. Cox, L. M. Crawford & J. H. Hitchcock (Eds.), *Research design and methods: An applied guide for the scholar-practitioner* (pp. 245–258). Sage.

Sevilla, M. (2021). *La educación técnico-profesional y su potencial para mejorar la trayectoria educativa y laboral de las mujeres en las áreas de ciencia, tecnología, ingeniería y matemáticas: una revisión regional.* Gender Affairs series, No. 160 (LC/TS.2021/155). Economic Commission for Latin America and the Caribbean (ECLAC).

Škerlavaj, M., Štemberger, M. I., Skrinjar, R., & Dimovski, V. (2007). Organizational learning culture – The missing link between business process change and organizational performance. *International Journal of Production Economics, 106*(2), 346–367. https://doi.org/10.1016/j.ijpe.2006.07.009

Steinke, J., Baumel, K., & Turner, M. M. (2024). Cultivating authenticity as role models: Women in STEM influencers on Instagram. *Science Communication, 46*(5), 543–583. https://doi.org/10.1177/10755470241239942

UN Women. (2021). *Green jobs for women in Africa: Opportunities and policy intervention.* Policy Brief. UN Women. https://africa.unwomen.org/sites/default/files/Field%20Office%20Africa/Attachments/Publications/2021/11/20211206_UN%20Woman_Green%20Jobs_policy%20brief_ENG_webpages.pdf

Vidican Auktor, G. (2020). *Green industrial skills for a sustainable future*. United Nations Industrial
Development Organization. https://www.unido.org/sites/default/files/files/2021-02/LKDForum-2020_
Green-Skills-for-a-Sustainable-Future.pdf

Wignall, R., Piquard, B., & Joel, E. (2023). Up-skilling women or de-skilling patriarchy? How TVET can drive
wider gender transformation and the decent work agenda in sub-Saharan Africa. *International Journal of
Educational Development, 102*, 102850. https://doi.org/10.1016/j.ijedudev.2023.102850

Gender Policies and Gender Transformation within the African Research Universities Alliance

Roseanne Diab, Muthise Bulani and Phyllis Kalele

Introduction

Globally, gender transformation within organisations is receiving much attention. Universities are prime examples of organisations striving towards gender equality across many fronts. An important focus is on the gender gap in senior academic leadership (e.g. O'Keefe & Courtois, 2019). While the world average for women faculty representation in tertiary education institutions has increased from 33.6% in 1990 to 43.2% in 2020 (THE & UNESCO, 2022), women remain underrepresented in leadership roles. Only around a quarter of the top 200 universities in the Times Higher Education (THE) World University Rankings have a female leader (THE, 2025). Blackmore (2014) described the dearth of female academics in leadership positions at higher education institutions (HEIs) as a global systemic problem, which has stubbornly persisted.

Indeed, HEIs worldwide are still dominated by male academics (Wotipka et al., 2018), with women comprising on average only 40% of academics (Bello et al., 2021). The gender gap that exists at lower academic levels is exacerbated by the intersection with precarity (O'Keefe & Courtois, 2019), leading to the term gendered precarity. Gendered precarity refers to gendered differences in job security; women across all academic disciplines are more likely than men to hold fixed-term or contract positions and as a result, women are more likely to end up in insecure career pathways, which ultimately affects their productivity and career progression (OECD, 2021). Gender gaps also dominate in certain disciplines. Generally, women are underrepresented in Science, Technology, Engineering and Mathematics (STEM) disciplines (e.g. Casad et al., 2020).

As universities strive for gender equality in terms of numbers, they are also under pressure to transform in other important ways; to change their gendered institutional cultures (Howe-Walsh & Turnbull, 2016) and to address formal and informal gendered practices, including conscious and unconscious bias. Gender transformation involves so much more than addressing the unequal representation of men and women in terms of numbers. It involves changing the gender and social norms, such as stereotypes and gender roles, and unequal power relations that disadvantage women and prevent them from being fully integrated. Yallew and Maruza (2020) emphasise that "transforming and creating equitable systems and institutions goes beyond ensuring quantitative representation and demographic parity. Representation is only one dimension of equity and does not, in and of itself, mean much if the underlying norms and rules of engagement remain untransformed."

In other words, through gender transformative policies, institutions can go beyond increasing the number or visibility of women academics and work towards dismantling gender stereotypes within their systems that make women's participation difficult. Therefore, by evaluating gender policies, we can gain further understanding of institutional aspirations for gender equality and equity.

We conducted research on gender equality at African research-intensive universities as part of a large mixed-methods project in which the analysis of gender policies and their role in gender transformation was but one objective. While this contribution diverts from the overarching theme of the collection in its lack of STEM focus, we highlight the value of considering research-intensive universities in discussions around gender equality in STEM given the emphasis many research-intensive universities place on STEM (for an alternative approach to examining the relationship between policies and gender equality, see Chapter 8, which takes a field- and country-specific approach).

One of the surprising findings that emerged from the policy analysis was the absence of standalone gender policies at some universities, and yet simultaneously, an acute institutional awareness of the imperative of gender equality. This unexpected finding led us to interrogate the circumstances and to analyse what was driving the aspiration towards gender equality. It raised many questions about the role of policy and whether there were any shortcomings to not having an institutional gender policy in place. We also bring the issue of intersectionality to bear in our analysis as this emerged as a major theme in our investigation.

African research-intensive universities

The study sample comprised 16 African research-intensive universities across nine African nations, which made up the African Research Universities Alliance (ARUA) at the time of the study. ARUA was founded in March 2015 with the aim of expanding and enhancing quality research in Africa by Africans. The vision is "to make African researchers and institutions globally competitive while contributing to the generation of knowledge for socio-economic transformation in Africa" (ARUA, n.d., p. 6).

The 16 universities comprising the ARUA network are as follows: Addis Ababa University (AAU), Ethiopia; University of Cape Town (UCT), South Africa; University Cheikh Anta Diop (UCAD), Senegal; University of Dar es Salaam (UDSM), Tanzania; University of Ghana (UG), Ghana; University of Ibadan (UI), Nigeria; University of KwaZulu-Natal (UKZN), South Africa; University of Lagos (ULAG), Nigeria; Makerere University (MU), Uganda; University of Nairobi (UoN), Kenya; Obafemi Awolowo University (OAU), Nigeria; University of Pretoria (UP), South Africa; Rhodes University (RU), South Africa; University of Rwanda (UR), Rwanda; Stellenbosch University (SU), South Africa; and University of the Witwatersrand (Wits), South Africa.

ARUA is governed by a Board of Directors made up of the Vice-Chancellors (VCs) of member universities, who meet annually to address concerns of policy, oversight of programmes and operations, as well as leading the development of strategic objectives in their respective universities. Of the 16 VCs at the time of the study, six (four of whom represent the sub-regions of ARUA universities) form an Executive Committee that meets quarterly and is responsible for carrying out the Board's responsibilities on a more regular basis. The daily affairs of ARUA are run by the Secretariat, which is currently located in Accra, Ghana and supported by the Secretariat at Wits in South Africa.

ARUA's strategic objectives are to:

- Increase Africa's research contribution from 1% to 5% over a 10-year period;
- Increase the number of African universities in the top 200 from one to at least 10 over a 10-year period;
- Increase the number of faculty members with PhDs from 45% to 75% over a 10-year period;

- Contribute to the development of good quality PhDs for other African universities;
- Develop strong links between research universities and industry;
- Become strong and effective advocates for research funding by national governments and international agencies (ARUA, n.d.).

These objectives, together with the current priority areas – collaborative research, training and support for PhDs, capacity-building for research management and research advocacy – all contribute to the realisation of the vision and mission of ARUA.

For our study on gender transformation at African universities, we reasoned that as some of Africa's best resourced universities, ARUA institutions would likely be trailblazers when it came to addressing gender equality issues and that some best practice examples could be identified and shared to benefit other institutions across Africa.

Methodology

The methodology was qualitative using quantitative elements, comprising both desktop research and primary data collection. University websites were valuable sources of information on gender-related policies and strategies, as well as relevant gender-related structures. We were able to access information for 15 of the 16 universities. UCAD in Senegal was excluded from the policy analysis because of the lack of information on its website.

We obtained ethical clearance to conduct research at eight of the 16 institutions, viz. AAU, UCT, UG, UKZN, RU, UR, SU and Wits, of which five were in South Africa, one in Ethiopia, one in Ghana and one in Rwanda. Ultimately, we were compelled to exclude the other eight institutions from the primary data collection due to extensive delays caused by the COVID-19 pandemic.

An online survey instrument was distributed to both men and women in senior leadership positions at the eight universities where ethics approval was obtained. A total of 46 responses, 24 men, 21 women and one other from six universities were received. A full analysis of this component of the study is reported by Diab et al. (2023). The questions were wide-ranging but mainly targeted factors that played a role in women's accession to leadership positions.

Key informant interviews were conducted at the same eight universities using two semi-structured questionnaires (one targeting VCs and a second targeting other senior university leaders from Dean and above). A total of 64 interviews were conducted.

The majority of the chapter will focus specifically on policies; however, in the case of survey responses, where policies were mentioned as relevant in assisting women to achieve leadership positions or to overcome career advancement barriers, the responses are analysed here. In the case of interviews, where we received relevant inputs on gender policies, excerpts from these contributions have been included in our analysis.

Status of gender policies at ARUA institutions

Table 1 summarises the status of policies and structures at 15 ARUA institutions. Eight institutions (53%) are listed as having gender policies; however, we were only able to access information on six of them. UCT's policy is under development and was not made available to us, and the policy at UDSM was under review and hence not accessible at the time of our investigation.

Table 1: Status of gender policies and structures at ARUA institutions

Institution	Country	Relevant policy	Relevant structure(s)
AAU	Ethiopia	Gender Policy	Women's, Children's and Youth Affairs Office
UCT	South Africa	Gender Policy[a]	Office for Inclusivity and Change (OIC)
UDSM	Tanzania	Gender Policy[b]	–
UG	Ghana	Gender Policy	Equal Opportunities Board (OEB)
UI	Nigeria	Gender Policy	Gender Mainstreaming Office (GMO)
UKZN	South Africa	–	–
ULAG	Nigeria	–	–
MU	Uganda	Gender Equality Policy	Gender Mainstreaming Division (later becoming a Directorate)
UoN	Kenya	Gender Policy	Gender Mainstreaming Division
OAU	Nigeria	–	Centre for Gender and Social Policy Studies
UP	South Africa	–	Transformation Office (TO)
RU	South Africa	–	Equity and Institutional Culture Office and Harassment and Discrimination Office
UR	Rwanda	Gender Policy	–
SU	South Africa	–	Equality Unit (EqU) and Transformation Office (TO)
Wits	South Africa	–	Gender Equity Office (GEO) and Transformation and Employment Equity Office (TEEO)

Notes
[a] UCT has a Gender Policy under development, which was not made available.
[b] UDSM's Gender Policy was undergoing revisions and was not accessible.

There is much variation in the gender-related structures that exist. Some have a dedicated 'gender office', which goes by various names, for example Gender Mainstreaming Office (UI), Gender Mainstreaming Directorate (MU) and Gender Equity Office (Wits). AAU had a Gender Office, but in 2019 changed its name to Women's, Children's and Youth Affairs Office, which could be construed as a retrogressive step for various reasons. First, the term gender is inclusive of both men and women. Second, the broadened responsibility detracts from a gender focus, and third, the linking of women and children entrenches traditional female roles. Many of the South African universities have units/offices that have a broader mandate extending to transformation, inclusivity and institutional culture (e.g. Office for Inclusivity and Change at UCT), which dilutes the focus on gender. Others (e.g. UDSM, OAU) have research centres that take responsibility for gender matters, which may include developing gender-sensitive policies, gender mainstreaming within the university, raising awareness and outreach programmes. The dual functions of research and implementation of university policy are not ideally co-located. A research centre is an academic unit situated in a faculty and reporting to a Dean, whereas implementation of university policy is an administrative function more appropriately reporting to a member of the university executive. Most of the gender offices or equivalent are located in the office of the VC or Deputy VC, signalling the importance attached to the functions of the offices. We turn now to an analysis of the gender policies at each of the six institutions from which we were able to source information.

Addis Ababa University (AAU)

The AAU's Gender Policy[1] is framed within national legislation that promotes gender equality. It acknowledges the gender gaps that exist in academic staff appointments, promotion, leadership, research and publication, as well as gender gaps in student enrolment, performance and retention. The policy aims to address these gaps and to promote gender justice by mainstreaming gender in all aspects of the university's activities. It also refers to a demand for a gender-responsive environment and an institutional culture that promotes gender equality.

It is a comprehensive policy with wide-ranging objectives, including, among other things, the creation of a conducive environment for women/girls, awareness-raising, ensuring women's/girls' access to institutional resources and increasing participation in decision-making bodies. The policy also seeks to integrate gender issues into curricula so that all students at the university understand gender issues. Responsibility for adhering to and implementing the gender policy rests with every person who is part of the university. The university commits to various strategies to achieve its objectives – for example, the

---

1 https://www.scribd.com/document/382275495/AAU-Gender-Policy-Edited-Nov-17-2015-pdf

collection of gender-disaggregated data and gender budgeting – engendering the curriculum and gender-responsive action plans in all departments.

University of Ghana (UG)

UG's Gender Policy[2] recognises the inequality that exists between men and women in the greater society as well as within the university, and how discrimination constitutes a barrier to progress. It mentions the Constitution of the Republic of Ghana, which acknowledges that those who are discriminated against based on sex are disadvantaged.

The policy strives to assist the university in achieving gender equality in "critical spheres of decision-making" and it applies to all members of the university community. It includes mention of, inter alia, gender equity, gender mainstreaming, gender gap, gender-based violence (GBV) and sexual harassment, which it acknowledges can occur between individuals of different and same sex. The responsibility for ensuring compliance is placed on the University Council and the VC.

The policy mentions an Equal Opportunities Board (EOB), which is responsible for its full implementation. It consists of 13 members drawn from both internal and external university communities, with a secretariat located at the Centre for Gender Studies and Advocacy (CEGENSA). CEGENSA is expected to play a role in supporting the EOB in its mandate to implement the policy.

There is a commitment in the policy to publish an annual Gender Equality Report, to evaluate the impact of the gender policy every four years and to conduct annual gender audits.

University of Ibadan (UI)

The Gender Policy at UI[3] which applies to both staff and students, was developed after a process of sensitisation, advocacy and consensus building. It is referred to as a flagship document that signals the university's commitment to being "a beacon of innovation and transformation in Nigeria and Africa". Further, it is referred to as "a benchmark for the measurement of institutional and national advancement, and the vanguard for engineering positive societal change and transformation". The policy commits the university to "[fostering] healthy identities, [and] a community characterised by equity, a sense of self-worth and

---

2 https://cegensa.ug.edu.gh/sites/default/files/downloads/GENDER_POLICY.pdf
3 https://gmo.ui.edu.ng/ui-gender-policy

fulfilment". In addition, it refers to fairness in accessing resources and opportunities and ensuring equal rewards for equal work.

The vision stated in UI's policy is "to be a world-class university where gender equity is institutionalised, and students and staff integrate gender friendly perspectives into personal and professional dealings in achieving the aims and goals of the university". It acknowledges that when the University College Ibadan was established in 1948, it was part of a highly patriarchal society, with no commitment to gender equity. This has changed substantially since the development of the gender policy, which is far-reaching in its objectives. It commits to gender budgeting, engendering the curriculum, ensuring gender equity in decision-making bodies, the incorporation of gender perspectives in research and innovation, and monitoring the effectiveness of the policy.

The UI has had a longstanding focus on gender and is regarded as being at the forefront of gender research and advocacy in Nigeria and Africa. A Women's Research and Documentation Centre was established in 1986 in response to the Beijing Platform of Action as a multidisciplinary centre located in the Institute of African Studies. The Association of African Universities selected UI as the pilot centre for its training modules on gender mainstreaming in African universities.

A Gender Mainstreaming Programme was initiated at UI in 2007 with funding aid from the MacArthur Foundation. This included the development of both the gender policy and the sexual harassment policy, and the Gender Mainstreaming Office.

Makerere University (MU)

The Gender Equality Policy at MU[4] has a focus on 'gender justice', which sets it apart from other university policies that do not mention the term. It commits the university to ensuring human and financial capacity and resources in its pursuit of gender justice. It also embraces management and prevention of gender violence, discrimination and injustice. The policy is framed within the national and international policy context, emphasising particularly that gender equality is central to sustainable development (SDG 5), where everyone is treated with respect and dignity and given equal opportunity to realise their full potential.

The policy openly acknowledges that many gender gaps still exist within the university. It draws attention to the fact that policy formulation is still gender blind; that despite MU having instituted affirmative action in 1990 in favour of female student applicants (1.5 points scheme, where women seeking admission

---

4 https://policies.mak.ac.ug/policy/gender-equality-policy

are allocated an extra 1.5 points), the enrolment of female students is still below target; gender gaps persist in decision-making positions; and planning units have not embraced gender mainstreaming in their planning, budgeting and implementation processes.

Gender mainstreaming is given prominence through the creation of the Gender Mainstreaming Division (now Directorate) in 2002. The policy states that: "The integration of gender in programme planning and implementation is seen as integral to solving many institutional and societal problems." The example is given of the HIV/AIDS pandemic, which has remained a challenge because insufficient attention has been given to the underlying gender dimension. Furthermore, in the 10-year university strategic plan 2020/2030 and those prior, gender mainstreaming was listed as one of four strategic priorities.[5]

MU plans to integrate gender as a cross-cutting issue into all its functions. It acknowledges that there are other issues that intersect with gender and lists specifically, disability, social class and age. It recognises that men and women are not part of homogeneous groups, but does not refer to sexual diversity per se. However, this is perhaps the beginning of an awareness around sexual diversity. It acknowledges that the needs and aspirations of both men and women must be considered and that the organisational culture is a critical part of gender equality. It commits to engendering the curriculum and creating a gender-friendly and inclusive secure environment; supporting affirmative action programmes aimed at addressing gender gaps in student enrolment (particularly science-based programmes); investing in infrastructure and resources to improve gender balance in recruitment, promotion, retention and performance of staff; and undertaking gender budgeting, where policies are backed by budgets.

MU has been praised in many quarters (e.g. Kigotho, 2021) as a leader in promoting gender equality and gender empowerment, and universities have been encouraged to emulate it. The university has a long history relating to gender justice, dating to 1945, when the first six female students were admitted. At the time, the university had a male culture with the motto, "Let's be Men". The motto was subsequently changed to "We Build for the Future". This early recognition provided the foundation for a broader gender agenda that was to follow in the 1990s. MU was also singled out as a leader on the continent in promoting gender equality by a key informant from a South African university.

In 1990, the Department of Women and Gender Studies was established as an academic unit, becoming a school in 2010. According to a report published by the Swedish Embassy in 2021, "the School is at the forefront of academic

5 https://www.mak.ac.ug/about/strategic-plan

and community initiatives to address gender and development issues from an African perspective" (Kabonesa, 2021). It also offers training programmes up to PhD level and undertakes research.

University of Nairobi (UoN)

The Gender Policy at the UoN[6] was developed after an extensive consultative process instituted by the then VC in 2005. The goal of the policy is "to sustain a fair and just academic environment where men and women have equal opportunities, voice, rights and access to resources so that they can realise their potential and contribution in a community of scholars characterised by a culture of mutual respect".

The policy commits the university to gender-responsive management and gender sensitivity in curriculum design, content and delivery. It establishes a Gender Mainstreaming Division in the office of the VC, which is indicative of the value attached to the implementation of the policy. The functions of the Division include, inter alia: awareness-raising; promotion of a gender-sensitive, inclusive and secure environment; promotion of gender equality in student enrolment and staff recruitment, training and promotion; gender research; and monitoring and evaluation. There is a responsibility to reach out to schools, with specific mention of boys and girls from poor backgrounds, rural areas and slums to enable access to university education.

The policy also addresses sexual harassment, with the Gender Mainstreaming Division responsible for receiving and addressing complaints. It acknowledges that sexual harassment occurs against men and women. According to Kameri-Mbote et al. (2018), it lacks a provision prohibiting student–lecturer relationships. They note that universities face problems with respect to sexual harassment because of the power dynamics between lecturers and students.

University of Rwanda (UR)

UR has a comprehensive Gender Policy[7] that is endorsed personally by the VC. The policy was developed by the Centre for Gender Studies with funding from the Swedish International Development Agency (Sida). It was developed in the context of the Rwandan national government's vision and commitment, in the post-1994 genocide era, to build a society free of gender-based discrimination

---

6 https://uonbi.ac.ke/sites/default/files/UONGenderPolicyJune2008.pdf
7 https://ur.ac.rw/documents/UR%20Gender%20Policy.compressed.pdf

and where men and women participate fully and equitably in all developmental processes.

The policy commits the university to taking concrete actions to promote gender equality and equity in all its operations, and to prevent GBV and discrimination, including other forms of injustice, within its community.

The policy openly acknowledges many shortcomings and gender gaps in the university and explicitly states its intentions to mainstream gender in all its operations. Examples of shortcomings include:

- Gender gaps in student enrolment and completion rates and staffing;
- University policies that are gender blind;
- The need for capacity-building to ensure the generation of sex-disaggregated statistics;
- The lack of a gender mainstreaming unit or department;
- The lack of a GBV and sexual harassment policy, as well as the absence of reporting procedures and awareness-raising efforts.

Furthermore, the policy displays an understanding of intersectionality issues and lists vulnerable groups that in some cases are unique to Rwanda. Examples include the very poor, those living with disabilities, orphans and victims of genocide. It is also noted that gender mainstreaming has been undertaken in many research projects, most of which are funded by Sida, and which have consequently responded to Sida's gender-mainstreaming requirements.

The vision of the UR gender policy is "to promote a diverse staff, student and stakeholder community, in which all people are valued, respected and treated equally and equitably in terms of gender". It commits the university to increase female staff to at least 50% parity, to gender equality in student enrolment, performance and completion, to the production of sex-disaggregated statistics, engendering of the curriculum, to ensuring a secure environment free from sexual and gender-based violence (SGBV), and the mainstreaming of gender.

Analysis of gender policies

Gender policy for ARUA

Although our focus was on gender policies at individual ARUA institutions, we note that ARUA does not have a gender policy, nor does it include a statement on its website[8] about advancing gender equality or consider it in its latest

---

8 https://arua.org.za

2022–2027 strategic plan. This is a serious omission that should be addressed to signal ARUA's role in advancing gender equality on the continent particularly in research and amongst African researchers in line with African Union (AU) strategies and statements, and actions of the Association of African Universities.

The AU Strategy for Gender Equality and Women's Empowerment (GEWE) 2018–2028 (AU, 2019), which was launched at the AU Summit in February 2019, is a key and relevant policy document for ARUA. It builds on the earlier 2009 Gender Policy and is a framework document that aims to mitigate or eliminate major constraints that are hampering gender equality and the full participation of women and girls. It supports Agenda 2063 (AU, 2015), which sets out the vision of an Africa that is non-sexist and where girls and boys can reach their full potential, and where men and women can contribute equally to the development of their societies.

The Association of African Universities has also sought to advance gender equality amongst its members. They were involved in a collaborative venture to mainstream gender in higher education institutions across Africa, resulting in a gender-mainstreaming toolkit.[9] They have also been responsible for focusing attention on the STEM disciplines as key to empowering women.

The absence of a gender focus for ARUA stands in stark contrast to the situation at the League of European Research Universities (LERU), which consists of 23 prominent research-intensive universities across 12 countries in Europe.[10] They have a Policy Group on Equity, Diversity and Inclusion (EDI), which has produced four policy papers, each one with an explicit gender focus. The group has also published each university's Gender Equality Plan on the LERU website, and they regularly host conferences with gender as a theme.

It is noted that ARUA has a Centre of Excellence for Inequality Research (ACEIR), one of the 13 Centres of Excellence of ARUA. Configured as a hub-and-spoke model, with the hub and the South African node hosted by UCT and the Ghana and Kenya nodes hosted by UG and UoN, respectively, gender inequality is one of the focus areas of the centre. It is recommended that ACEIR could take responsibility for developing a gender policy for ARUA.

Gender policies vs anti-discrimination policies

Of the eight universities with gender policies, only one is in South Africa (UCT) (Table 1: Status of gender policies and structures at ARUA institutions), despite

---

9 https://www.aau.org/wp-content/uploads/sites/9/2019/07/Toolkit-module1.pdf
10 https://www.leru.org

South Africa's dominance in terms of ARUA membership. The other seven are spread across seven countries, viz. Ethiopia, Ghana, Kenya, Nigeria, Rwanda, Tanzania and Uganda. Of the universities with no gender policy in place, they included two in Nigeria (ULAG and OAU) and five universities (UKZN, UP, RU, SU and Wits) in South Africa. This was a surprising finding, particularly for South African universities, given their considerable awareness of gender issues as evidenced by other gender-related policies such as those on sexual harassment and sexual orientation, structures in place and public statements made by university leaders. It seems that for South African institutions this was not an oversight but a deliberate strategy. All have umbrella anti-discrimination policies, which focus predominantly on race but include gender as a key element.

Probing why South African institutions have opted for anti-discrimination policies rather than standalone gender policies, reasons included the country's unique apartheid history and a consequent deliberate intersectional approach. One key informant stated, *"[it is] because of our fractured past, and the need to focus on grounds in the Constitution, where race is at the forefront"*. Another stated,

> *I can see advantages of having a gender specific policy, but I'm inclined more to the intersectional approach because ... of the complexity [and] especially the history of universities [in South Africa] ... You might find that any measures to promote gender equality, often would benefit white women and not black women ... because of the racial dynamics of that university.*

The same respondent noted, *"discrimination doesn't just happen in terms of single attributes like gender, race, sexual orientation, religion or political views"*. Another point raised was *"the minute you [have] a gender policy ... [then people would ask] ... where is the standalone race policy?"*

A concern raised with some of the senior South African university leaders about an anti-discrimination policy being focused on the negative or what one must not do, was allayed as it was emphasised that it needed to be viewed in conjunction with the national Employment Equity Act (No. 55 of 1998), which explicitly promotes equality in terms of gender, race and disability. Notwithstanding this point, it is critical to note that the focus of the Employment Equity Act is on achieving numerical targets or quotas; gender mainstreaming is not addressed.

Importantly, the lack of a standalone gender policy means that there is no aspirational policy to address elements such as gender mainstreaming, the collection of gender-disaggregated data, gender budgeting, engendering the curriculum and the application of a gender lens in research, etc. Aspirations to increase women faculty member numbers and the setting of targets are addressed through statutory institutional Employment Equity Plans, but the other gender elements mentioned above are excluded. This is regarded as a major flaw and a missed opportunity to change the gendered attitudes and social norms. However, it should be noted that UKZN, although it does not have a gender policy, introduced a compulsory module for all first-year students titled Critical Social Justice and Citizenship. The module will address "social injustices of gender-based violence (GBV), racism, xenophobia and homophobia" (UKZN, 2024).

The purpose of a gender policy is to advance gender equality by setting out the intent of an organisation and enabling the organisation to set targets, spell out aspirations and put in place strategies to meet the targets. Generally, such a document would identify the status of gender equality, barriers to gender equality and the gender-related challenges faced by the organisation and would articulate how it planned to address these in practical ways. The gender policy hence provides the framework for conceptualising and implementing a gender programme at a particular institution.

Gender policy and gender transformation

Turning to our key question on the relationship between policy and gender transformation, we argue that a gender policy is a prerequisite for gender transformation. The emphasis here is on the term 'transformation' as opposed to gender awareness or gender sensitivity. According to the World Health Organization's Gender Responsiveness Assessment Scale (WHO, 2011), there are five levels of gender responsiveness, ranging from gender-unequal, to gender-blind, gender-sensitive, gender-specific to gender-transformative. Applying this scale to universities, we note that a gender-sensitive organisation is one that is gender aware but does not address the inequality created by unequal gender norms, roles and relations. To be gender-transformative, an organisation is required to commit explicitly to promoting gender equality, to change harmful gender norms, roles and practices, and to introduce strategies to address unequal power relations between men and women. A gender-sensitive organisation displays awareness but does not take any remedial action, whereas a gender-specific organisation intentionally targets men or women to meet their respective group needs (WHO, 2011).

Based on these descriptors of gender responsiveness, we categorise the South African institutions with anti-discrimination policies but not gender policies as gender specific. They have all recognised the need, for example, to tackle the problem of sexual harassment and have introduced one or more policies to address it. They fall short, however, when it comes to addressing the root causes of unequal power relations between men and women, having no policy in place to address this. In summary, a gender-transformative university needs to be more than just aware of the importance of gender equality and needs to go beyond addressing equality in terms of just numbers but also address equal participation. Our conclusion is that there are many more actions that need to be taken and that a gender policy is a prerequisite to inform transformative actions. Juxtaposed to this, the six ARUA institutions with gender policies as outlined above, have laid the foundations to become gender-transformative institutions. All their gender policies contain important statements about gender mainstreaming, a key element of gender transformation. Further analysis would be necessary to determine the extent to which these institutions have achieved the goal of tackling the root causes of gender inequality.

Conclusion

Our research focused on gender policies and structures at African research-intensive universities, with a view towards investigating the relationship between gender policies and gender transformation. ARUA, a network of 16 at the time of study (now 23 at the time of publication) universities across nine African nations, comprised the sample for the study. University websites were valuable sources of information on gender-related policies and strategies, as well as relevant gender-related structures. Information for 15 of the 16 universities was accessible; UCAD in Senegal was excluded from the policy analysis because of the lack of information on its website.

A key finding was the absence of a gender policy for ARUA itself. ARUA should lead by example; the absence of a gender policy is regarded as a serious omission that should be addressed to signal ARUA's role in advancing gender equality on the continent in line with AU strategies and statements, and actions of the Association of African Universities. We have recommended that the ARUA Centre of Excellence for Inequality in Research take responsibility for developing a gender policy for ARUA.

Of the eight universities with gender policies, only one is in South Africa (UCT). The other seven are spread across seven countries, viz. Ethiopia, Ghana, Kenya, Nigeria, Rwanda, Tanzania and Uganda. Of the universities with no gender policy in place, they included two in Nigeria (ULAG and OAU) and five universities (UKZN, UP, RU, SU and Wits) in South Africa. This was a surprising finding given their considerable awareness of gender issues as evidenced by other gender-related policies such as those on sexual harassment, structures in place and public statements made by university leaders. For South African institutions this was a deliberate strategy. All South African universities have umbrella anti-discrimination policies, which focus predominantly on race but include gender as a key element.

As mentioned, the lack of a standalone gender policy means that there is no aspirational policy to address elements such as gender mainstreaming, the collection of gender-disaggregated data, gender budgeting, engendering the curriculum and the application of a gender lens in research, etc. Aspirations to increase the number of women faculty members and the setting of targets are addressed through statutory institutional Employment Equity Plans, but the other gender elements mentioned above are excluded. This is a major flaw.

Finnemore and Jurkovich (2020) highlight the importance of aspirational work for social activism and driving change. The authors argue that successful organisations and governments are built on shared aspirations and cite UNESCO's Sustainable Development Goals as an example. The benefits of articulating and recording shared goals are provided as concrete examples of the value of aspirations.

Based on the WHO's classification of gender responsiveness, we find the South African institutions with anti-discrimination policies but not gender policies to be categorised as gender specific not gender transformative. They fall short when it comes to addressing the root causes of unequal power relations between men and women and going beyond addressing equality in terms of just numbers. A gender policy is a prerequisite for the attainment of gender transformation at a university.

Therefore, we conclude that ARUA universities and their policies vary in their gender responsiveness. We highlight the importance of an overarching ARUA policy to serve as a unifying and guiding framework for individual member institutions. Further, we emphasise the importance of developing gender-specific policies for those universities that do not currently have them.

Given the recent global movement towards gender-transformative policies and practices, we hope that the current chapter provides a basis for evaluating gender responsiveness in individual HEIs and broader networks like ARUA. Future work should interrogate the extent of gender transformation by including its key elements at the outset of the evaluation.

It is important to bear in mind that gender transformation moves beyond individual self-improvement among women and girls by tackling the root causes of gender inequality. It aims to change gender norms – including gender roles, expectations, stereotypes, harmful attitudes, and customs and practices – to address imbalances of power and privilege between men and women. Gender transformation goes beyond a focus on an increase in numbers. It aims to strengthen women's agency and visibility and generally reshape unequal power relations.

Acknowledgements

This research was funded by the International Development Research Centre (IDRC) in Canada under Grant No. 109199-001. The Academy of Science of South Africa (ASSAf) administered the project, with the Gender in Science, Innovation, Technology and Engineering (GenderInSITE) Africa focal point as a partner in the project. The support of the ARUA Secretariat is acknowledged. Country focal points in Ghana and Rwanda are thanked for facilitating ethical clearances and interviews at their institutions. All respondents who participated in the online survey and/or key informant interviews are thanked for their willingness to contribute and for sharing their insights and knowledge.

About the Authors

Roseanne Diab is Emeritus Professor at the University of KwaZulu-Natal, Durban, South Africa, and at the time of this study was Director of GenderInSITE, based in Trieste, Italy.

Muthise Bulani is a Scientist at the South African Medical Research Council. She was a Project Administrator and Researcher at the Academy of Science of South Africa at the time of this study.

Phyllis Kalele is a Science Diplomat and at the time of the study was Senior Liaison Officer at the Academy of Science of South Africa.

References

AU (African Union). (2015). *African Union Agenda 2063: The Africa we want*. Framework document. African Union Commission. https://au.int/sites/default/files/documents/33126-doc-framework_document_book.pdf

AU (2019). *African Union strategy for gender equality and women's empowerment*. African Union Commission. https://au.int/en/documents/20190320/au-strategy-gender-equality-womens-empowerment-2018-2028

ARUA (African Research Universities Alliance). (n.d.). *The concept*. ARUA. https://arua.org.za/wp-content/uploads/ARUA-Concept.pdf

Bello, A., Blowers, T., Schneegans, S., & Straza, T. (2021). To be smart, the digital revolution will need to be inclusive. In *UNESCO science report: The race against time for smarter development* (pp. 109–135). https://unesdoc.unesco.org/ark:/48223/pf0000377456

Blackmore, J. (2014). Wasting talent? Gender and the problematics of academic disenchantment and disengagement with leadership. *Higher Education Research and Development, 33*(1), 86–99. https://doi.org/10.1080/07294360.2013.864616

Casad, B. J., Franks, J. E., Garasky, C. E., Kittleman, M. M., Roesler, A. C., Hall, D. Y., & Petzel, Z. W. (2020). Gender inequality in academia: Problems and solutions for women faculty in STEM. *Journal of Neuroscience Research, 99*(1), 13–23. https://doi.org/10.1002/jnr.24631

Diab, R. D., Kalele, P., Bulani, M., Boateng, F. K., & Mukeshimana, M. (2023). Gender perspectives on academic leadership at African universities. *International Journal of African Higher Education, 10*(2), 138–159. https://doi.org/10.6017/ijahe.v10i2.17619

Finnemore, M., & Jurkovich, M. (2020). The politics of aspiration. *International Studies Quarterly, 64*(4), 759–769. https://doi.org/10.1093/isq/sqaa052

Howe-Walsh, L., & Turnbull, S. (2016). Barriers to women leaders in academia: Tales from science and technology. *Studies in Higher Education, 41*(3), 415–428. https://doi.org/10.1080/03075079.2014.929102

Kabonesa, C. (2021, March 5). How Sweden's support to Makerere University helped mainstream gender equality within public universities in Uganda [Blog post]. *Sweden Abroad.* https://www.swedenabroad.se/en/embassies/uganda-kampala/current/news/gender-equality/

Kameri-Mbote, P., Kinyanjui, S., & Gadaffi, Y. (2018). Sexual harassment in the workplace in Kenya. *East African Law Journal,* 184–209. https://www.ielrc.org/content/a1802.pdf

Kigotho, W. (2021, November 4). Makerere's gender equality efforts are paying off. *University World News – Africa Edition.* https://www.universityworldnews.com/post.php?story=2021110214143835

O'Keefe, T., & Courtois, A. (2019). 'Not one of the family': Gender and precarious work in the neoliberal university. *Gender, Work and Organization, 20*(4), 463–479. https://doi.org/10.1111/gwao.12346

OECD (Organisation for Economic Co-operation and Development). (2021). *Reducing the precarity of academic research careers.* OECD Science, Technology and Industry Policy Papers, No. 113. OECD Publishing. https://doi.org/10.1787/0f8bd468-en

THE (Times Higher Education). (2025, March 5). International Women's Day: Top universities led by women. *Times Higher Education.* https://www.timeshighereducation.com/student/best-universities/top-10-universities-led-women

THE & UNESCO-IESALC (International Institute for Higher Education in Latin America and the Caribbean). (2022). *Gender equality: How global universities are performing, Part 1* [Programme and meeting document]. THE and UNESCO-IESALC. https://unesdoc.unesco.org/ark:/48223/pf0000380987

UKZN (University of KwaZulu-Natal). (2024, February 20). First-year students set to benefit from new critical social justice and citizenship module [Blog post]. https://ukzn.ac.za/news/first-year-students-set-to-benefit-from-new-critical-social-justice-and-citizenship-module/

WHO (World Health Organization). (2011). *Gender mainstreaming for health managers: A practical approach.* Department of Gender, Women and Health, World Health Organization. https://www.who.int/publications/i/item/9789241501057

Wotipka, C. M., Nakagawa, M., & Svec, J. (2018). Global linkages, the higher education pipeline, and national contexts: The worldwide growth of women faculty, 1970–2012. *International Journal of Comparative Sociology, 59*(3), 212–238. https://doi.org/10.1177/0020715218780475

Yallew, A. T., & Maruza, F. (2020, November 5). A call to study the gendered dimension of intellectual cultures. *University World News – Africa Edition.* https://www.universityworldnews.com/post.php?story=20201104040052337

Gender Inequalities in STEM: Focusing on Agricultural Science in West African Public Universities and Research Units

Christine Ajokè Ouinsavi, Charlemagne Dossou Sèblodo Judes Gbemavo,
Bienvenue N. Sourou Kuiga, Adigla Appolinaire Wédjangnon,
Béatrice Adépo-Gourène, Hadiza Kiari Fougou, Salamatou Abdourahamane Iliassou,
Ali Mahamane, Alice Ouattara Coulibaly, Yao Alexis N'go, Alexis Abodohoui
and Yvette Onibon Doubogan

Introduction

Agroforestry systems improve agriculture's resilience, enhance local farmers' livelihoods and contribute to balancing global ecosystems. However, women in West Africa are discouraged from engaging in agroforestry and face challenges accessing technologies tailored to their needs (Kiptot & Franzel, 2012). A pervasive gender bias has historically kept the agricultural sector male-dominated in West African countries, underscoring the importance of achieving gender equality in agricultural research to foster sustainable development in the region. This study builds on previous research indicating gender biases affect women's participation and leadership in Science, Technology, Engineering and Mathematics (STEM) fields, focusing on applied agricultural research and sciences in West Africa (Fakoya et al., 2010; FAO, 2021; Kiptot & Franzel, 2012). Specifically, we aim to better understand gender biases in both agricultural work and research.

Despite the attention to gender accorded by various programmes implemented in West Africa and international actors (e.g. the Agricultural

Productivity Programme in West Africa, Women in Climate Resilience Agriculture in West and Central Africa, Economic Community of West Africa agricultural policy), women continue to be underrepresented in agricultural research and development communities in West Africa (Hagège & Condon, 2021). In agricultural science, women make up 36% of the global workforce (FAO, 2023) and face barriers limiting their productivity and earnings (FAO, 2021). Research and initiatives in agricultural science should prioritise addressing gender-based barriers, considering the experiences and concerns of both men and women (Ayinde et al., 2013). While some progress has been made in improving gender balance in universities and research teams in sub-Saharan countries (e.g. Benin) (Direnberger & Onibon Doubogan, 2022), further efforts are necessary to address gender bias in agricultural sciences and applied agriculture research.

Women's participation in agricultural science is critical to ensuring the representation of diverse perspectives. One contributor to gender inequality in agricultural research is the lack of an appropriate research methodology in survey design and data analysis, which leads to biased results that marginalise women farmers' opinions (Savran Al-Haik, 2016); more women in agricultural science, designing research and analysing data can help address this issue. Involving farmers, especially women farmers, in research and technology development is crucial to ensuring that the technologies being developed meet their needs, yet existing research methods may not accurately reflect farmers' realities due to gender biases. To truly include women farmers, researchers must understand the social norms, roles and constraints that shape their daily lives and work. A gender-sensitive approach, one that considers the diverse identities of both farmers and researchers, is essential to producing fair, accurate and relevant agricultural science.

To better understand the current landscape surrounding gender equality in agricultural science in West Africa, the current chapter addresses the following three questions.

1. What is the state of gender-based inequalities in agricultural science in West Africa?
2. Do student-enrolment trends in West African universities suggest progress towards gender equality in agricultural science?
3. What factors are associated with gender-based inequalities in (a) agricultural work and (b) agricultural research in West Africa?

In Question 3, we seek to focus on both agricultural work and agricultural research, because we argue that for researchers to effectively address gender inequalities in their research, they must also have a better understanding of the gender inequalities faced by workers themselves. Further, by better understanding the norms around agricultural work, researchers can be more sensitive to such norms in their data collection and analyses.

All three of these research questions were investigated by focusing on three Francophone West African countries: Benin, Côte d'Ivoire and Niger. These countries share a similar education system and organisation of universities as members of the African and Malagasy Council for Higher Education, therefore are comparable to a degree, yet different socio-cultural norms mean they offer a broader view of gender inclusion in agricultural research across the region. Our research aimed to go beyond simply presenting gender statistics and instead focuses on understanding factors related to gender disparities in agricultural work and research, and considering how to address these factors.

Methodological approach

The data collection was conducted in three ways: (1) a survey of staff in training institutions using a questionnaire for quantitative and qualitative data collection; (2) a meta-analysis of published research; and (3) the participatory rural appraisal (Chambers, 1994) method used to more deeply explain the factors associated with gender-based inequalities in agricultural research.

For interviews with staff in research institutions, the consent of the participants was obtained. This consent was established by completing the survey questionnaire, agreeing to disclose their identity and signing attendance lists during the interviews. The research activities were approved and authorised by the respective local ethics committees for the scientific research of each project partner (University of Parakou, Nangui Abrogoua University and University of Diffa).

Survey of training and research institutions

To better understand gender inequalities in agriculture and move towards gender equality, we collected both quantitative and qualitative data.

Quantitative data covered the numbers, by gender, of students enrolled and trained in agricultural training courses over the last three decades (1990–2020); teaching staff and research team members; managers in training and research structures; and the number of research projects submitted and funded by gender (Question 2).

Qualitative data focused on sociological constraints and sexist stereotypes affecting the consideration of women's concerns in agricultural research, methodological approaches in the agricultural sciences and possible solutions to strengthen the inclusion of women in agricultural research (Questions 1 and 3).

Data were collected via surveys of managers and other administrative human resources personnel in public universities (a total of 10 universities), research centres (a total of 6 research centres) and university research laboratories (a total of 40 laboratories) in Benin, Côte d'Ivoire and Niger.

The data collected were managed in the ACCESS relational database management system, then extracted for statistical analysis. Prior to highlighting agricultural research participation across the three countries, we conducted a statistical inference (Chi-square homogeneity test) to test whether there is a significant difference in the distribution of male and female staff within the agricultural science training structures of public universities in Benin, Niger and Côte d'Ivoire. We found no significant differences in gender distributions across the three countries (see statistics below); this lack of difference further motivated investigating the three contexts in one study. The enrolment and qualification data for universities in the three countries were described through descriptive statistics (relative frequency calculation). Graphs (e.g. histograms, curves) were also constructed to better describe the data. All data analysis and graphics were performed using R software (R Core Team, 2024). Notably, due to the country's socio-political and security contingencies, data could not be obtained on all metrics for institutions in Niger; therefore, some of the presented results include only data from Benin and Côte d'Ivoire.

Meta-analysis

To better understand the factors associated with gender-based inequality in agricultural research (Question 3), we searched for agricultural studies (i.e. studies in agricultural production systems, including land management, agri-environment, crop and livestock production, rural economics and sociology, farm management and financing, and food processing) published in West Africa between January 2012 and December 2021. The PRISMA (Preferred Reporting Items for Systematic Reviews and Meta-Analyses) method facilitated study selection and data extraction. A data matrix – "Inclusion or non-inclusion of gender crossed with sampling type" – was extracted from the raw database before data selection. Fisher's exact test was applied to assess the relationship between gender inclusion and sampling type (Poitevineau, 2004). The selected studies were statistically summarised through meta-analysis to estimate the proportion of women in the survey samples, with the goal of assessing the hypothesis of gender inequality in the study sampling. Univariate meta-analyses were conducted to explore the factors linked to this inequality. The analyses were performed in R software (R Core Team, 2022).

Case study using participatory rural appraisal

To answer Question 3 in more detail and to identify possible endogenous approaches to reducing gender inequalities in agricultural study samples and developing an inclusive, gender-sensitive methodology, a case study based on participatory research was carried out in Benin, one of the three focal countries. Using the participatory rural appraisal (Chambers, 1994) method, data collection took place in Benin. Participatory rural appraisal (PRA) refers to a set of flexible, low-cost and efficient methods used to enable workers to collect and analyse information about rural communities. It helps workers understand the past, present and future conditions of these areas. By doing so, PRA provides a complete view of challenges, opportunities, resources and solutions within rural settings. This approach aims to achieve specific goals within a set time-frame by involving the community in planning and decision-making processes (Chandra, 2010; see Chapter 11 for another example of the use of participatory research methods).

PRA enables researchers to gather insights directly from local people and encourages their active participation in searching for solutions to their problems and decision-making processes. This approach was used to engage both female and male farmers in understanding and analysing the gender-based bias in agricultural research. Farmers were interviewed in three groups: a women-only group, a men-only group and a mixed group including the participants in both previous groups. Interviews were conducted simultaneously in each locality. Through discussions with each group, valuable insights were gathered regarding gender roles in agricultural data collection and the reasons for gender disparities in respondent selection for agricultural surveys. Various data collection methods, including observation, interviews, diagrams, games and workshops, were utilised to gather information.

Results

Gender inequalities are prevalent in agricultural science in West Africa

To address Question 1, we investigate the proportions of women and men across a variety of institutions in the three focal countries. We start by presenting the proportion of female teachers in agricultural science courses at public universities and private research institutions. Proportions of women were below 25% in all public universities (15.36% in Benin, 17.19% in Niger and 22.22% in Côte d'Ivoire, see Figure 1). The proportions of women in STEM focusing on agricultural science training in public universities are not statistically different across the three countries (χ^2 : 5.4344, df: 2; p-value = 0.06606); this suggests, as anticipated, that there are similarities in gender disparities across the three countries.

Figure 1: Gendered distribution of teachers in agricultural science training structures in public universities in Benin, Niger and Côte d'Ivoire

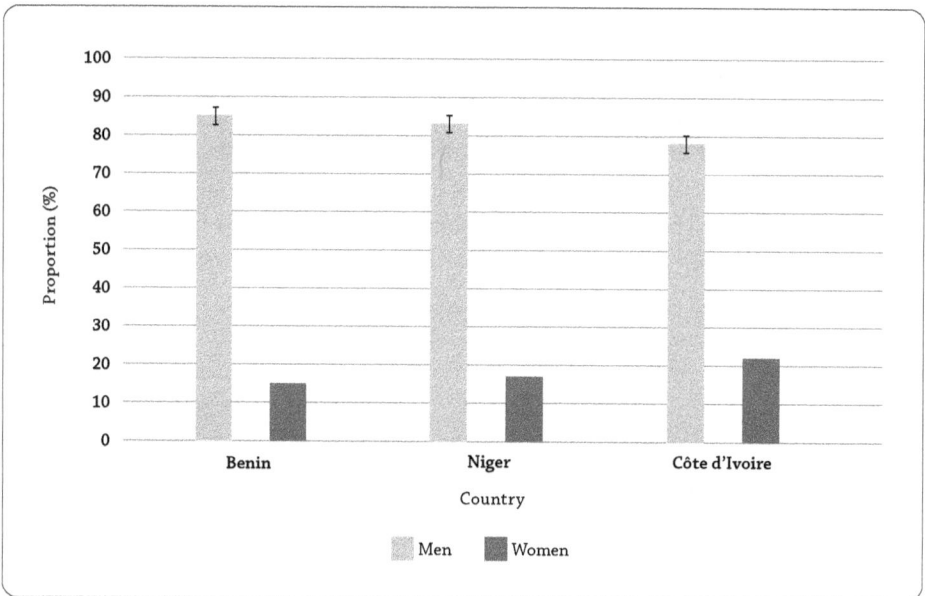

Like the public universities, agricultural science research centres (public research institutions that are not universities) also showed low rates of women representation, at 27.76% in Benin and 20.50% in Côte d'Ivoire (Figure 2).

Figure 2: Gendered distribution of researchers in agricultural science research centres in Benin and Côte d'Ivoire

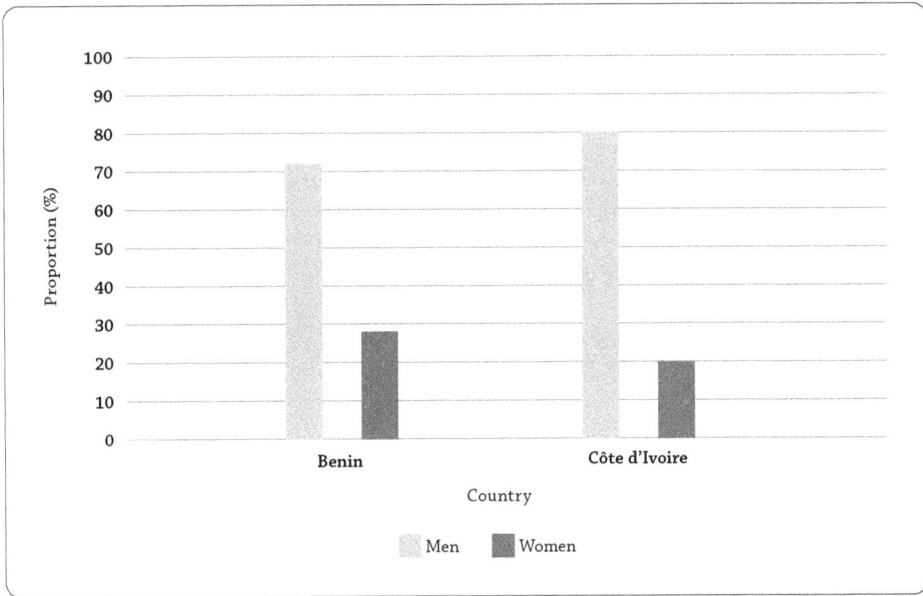

Gender statistics of the research team staff

In the field of agricultural science, in 2023, women represented 16.46% of members of research teams in public universities in Benin and 21.15% in the public universities of Côte d'Ivoire, that is a representation average of 19% for the two countries (Table 1).

Table 1: Statistics on research team personnel

Country	Men		Women	
	Number	Rate (%)	Number	Rate (%)
Benin	82	78.85	22	21.15
Côte d'Ivoire	137	83.54	27	16.46

Periodic gender-disaggregated data for lead investigators on research proposals submitted and funded research projects

In the field of STEM focusing on agricultural science, research proposals were submitted for funding by a minority of women and did not exceed 31% in the public universities of Benin, Niger and Côte d'Ivoire (Table 2). The proportion of women teacher–researchers who submitted research proposals to research teams was between 15% and 30% for the three countries represented (Table 2).

Table 2: Periodic statistics on research proposals submitted by gender in STEM focusing on agricultural science research teams in public universities in Benin, Niger and Côte d'Ivoire

Country (period)	Men		Women	
	Number	Rate (%)	Number	Rate (%)
Benin (2018–2021)	27	72.97	10	27.03
Côte d'Ivoire (2007–2021)	34	69.39	15	30.61
Niger (2016–2021)	11	84.62	2	15.38

In the field of agricultural science, the rate of women teacher-researchers with funded research projects was 9.09% (2018–2021 period), 20% (2016–2021 period) and 33.33% (2007–2021 period) respectively in the public universities of Benin, Niger and Côte d'Ivoire (Table 3).

Table 3: Periodic statistics on projects funded by gender in agricultural science research teams in public universities in Benin, Niger and Côte d'Ivoire

Country	Men		Women	
	Number	Rate (%)	Number	Rate (%)
Benin	10	90.91	1	9.09
Côte d'Ivoire	20	66.67	10	33.33
Niger	8	80.00	2	20.00

Gender statistics on access to management positions

We then investigated university governance based on gender. We find university governance in Benin and Côte d'Ivoire is dominated by men (Figure 4). The proportion of women research professors in management positions in agricultural science schools, faculties or training units was 6.25% in Benin's public universities in 2023. This rate was 20% for all public universities in Côte d'Ivoire (Figure 4).

Figure 4: Gender distribution of the heads of training structures in public universities in Benin and Côte d'Ivoire in 2023

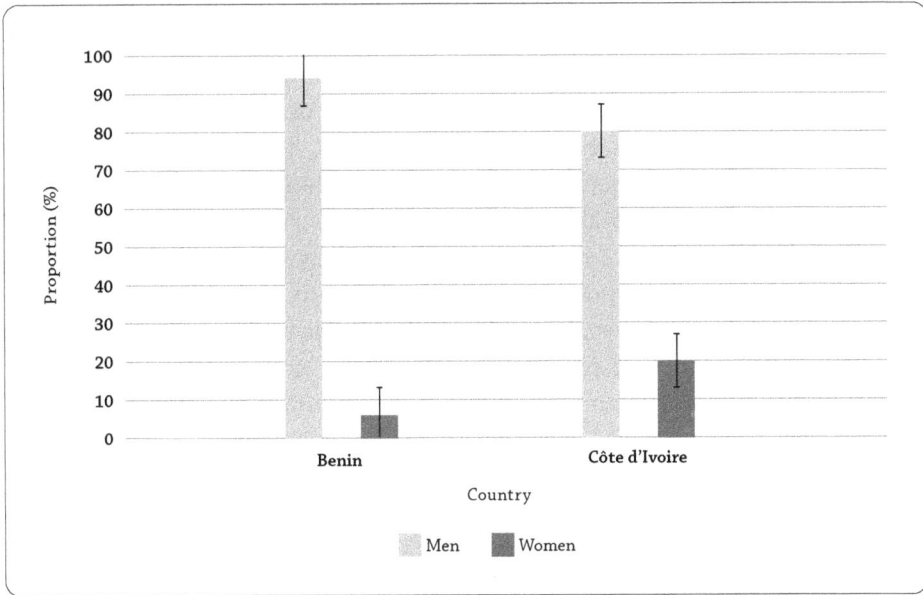

In the West African sub-region, efforts by leaders to reduce gender disparities (e.g. free education for girls in primary and secondary education, creation of the women's institute to support women in the school system and administration) are still insufficient, as revealed by statistics drawn from the figures presented in this document. Overall, women are underrepresented in higher education, with women representing less than 25% of the students enrolled in schools, faculties or training units dedicated to STEM focusing on agricultural sciences in 2023, in the public universities of Benin, Niger and Côte d'Ivoire.

Gender dynamics of enrolment and alumni suggest some progress towards gender equality in agricultural science in West Africa

To investigate whether enrolment and alumni trends show progress towards gender equality, we investigate trends over periods of six years or more (years vary based on country) for all three countries.

Over the period from 2005 to 2021, 14 701 female students were enrolled in agricultural science in Benin's public universities, compared with 60 586 male students. Women thus accounted for 19.53% of the total enrolment of 75 287. In Côte d'Ivoire's public universities, between 2012 and 2022, 1 083 female students were enrolled in agricultural science, compared with 2 966 male students. Women, therefore, accounted for 25.37% of the 39 750 enrolments. In Niger public universities, between 2015 and 2023, 839 female students were enrolled in agricultural science, compared with 4 346 male students. Women represent 16.18 % of the total student registration during this period.

Overall, female students were less represented than male students in agricultural science courses at public universities in Benin, Côte d'Ivoire and Niger. In Benin's public universities, from 2005 to 2011, the enrolment rate of female students in the bachelor's programme was higher than in the engineering, master's and PhD programmes (Figure 5). On the other hand, in the universities of Côte d'Ivoire, from 2012 to 2022, female student enrolment rates in the bachelor's and master's programmes were almost the same and higher than those in the engineer, DEA (Diplôme d'Études Approfondie) and PhD programmes (Figure 6). However, in Niger's universities from 2015 to 2023, female enrolment rates were higher for bachelor's degrees than for master's programmes (Figure 7).

Academic degrees in the African and Malagasy Council for Higher Education system refer to the number of years of formal study completed since obtaining the BAC (high degree certificate) qualification. Thus, there are Bachelor (BAC + 3 years of formal study), Master (BAC + 5 years of formal study) and PhD (BAC + 8 years of formal study) in the current system. In a former system, there were Bachelor (BAC + 3 years of formal study), Master 1 (BAC + 4 years of formal study), DEA/Engineer (BAC + 5 years of formal study) and PhD (BAC + 8 years of formal study).

Figure 8 shows the evolution of the gender parity index (number of female enrolments compared to male enrolment in a year) in public universities in Benin, Côte d'Ivoire and Niger. There has been a clear improvement in the ratio of female to male student enrolment per year in the bachelor's, master's and doctoral cycles for the 2018–2019 academic year in Benin's universities (Figure 8a). On the other hand, in the public universities of Côte d'Ivoire, this ratio varied between 2005 and 2011 for all training programmes, indicating variability and an imbalance to the detriment of female enrolment (Figure 8b). In public universities in Niger, the data show a significant gap in the gender parity index over time for two levels of study, with higher values for the bachelor's level. The enrolment of women at the master's level is very low (Figure 8c).

Figure 5: Proportion of women students enrolled in Benin universities in STEM focusing on agricultural science (Master = BAC + 5 and Master 1 = BAC + 4)

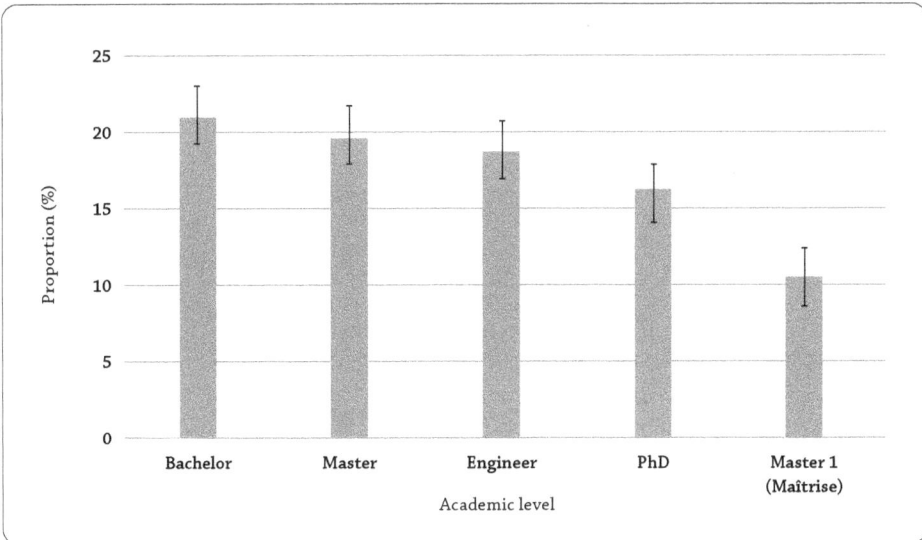

Figure 6: Proportion of women students enrolled in Côte d'Ivoire's universities in STEM focusing on agricultural science

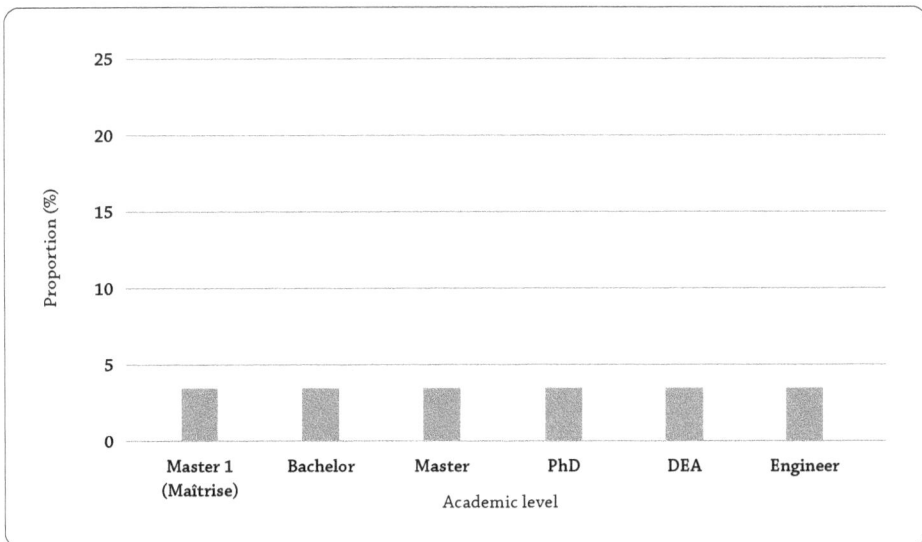

Figure 7: Proportion of women students enrolled in Niger's universities in STEM focusing on agricultural science

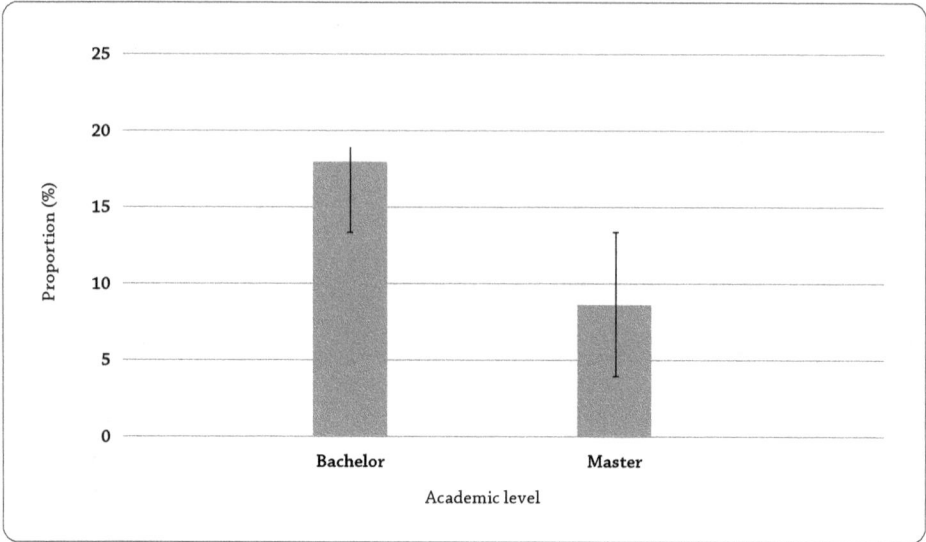

Figure 8 (a): Temporal evolution of the gender parity index of enrolment in Benin's national universities in agricultural science

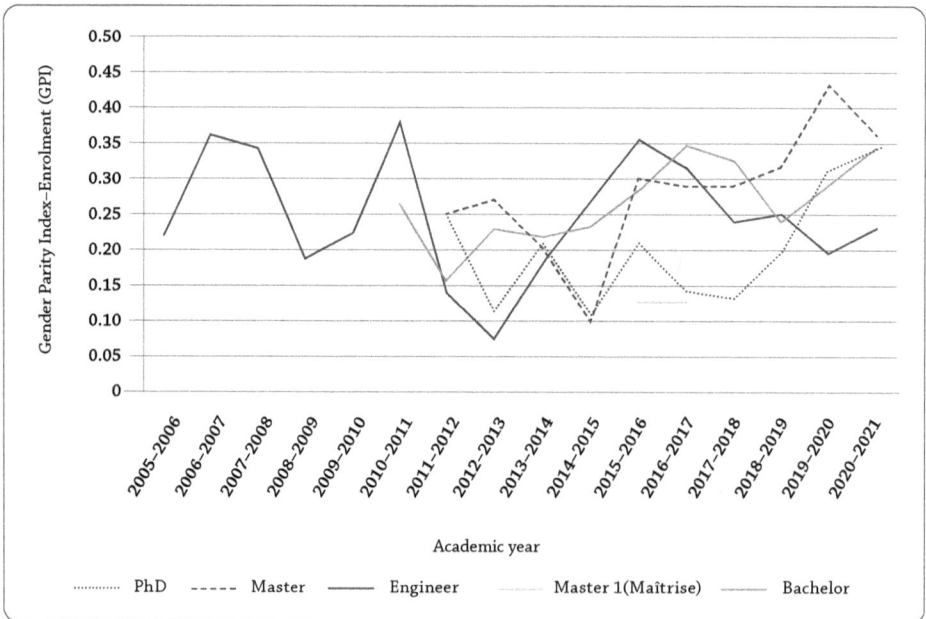

Figure 8 (b): Temporal evolution of the gender parity index of enrolment in Côte d'Ivoire's national universities in agricultural science

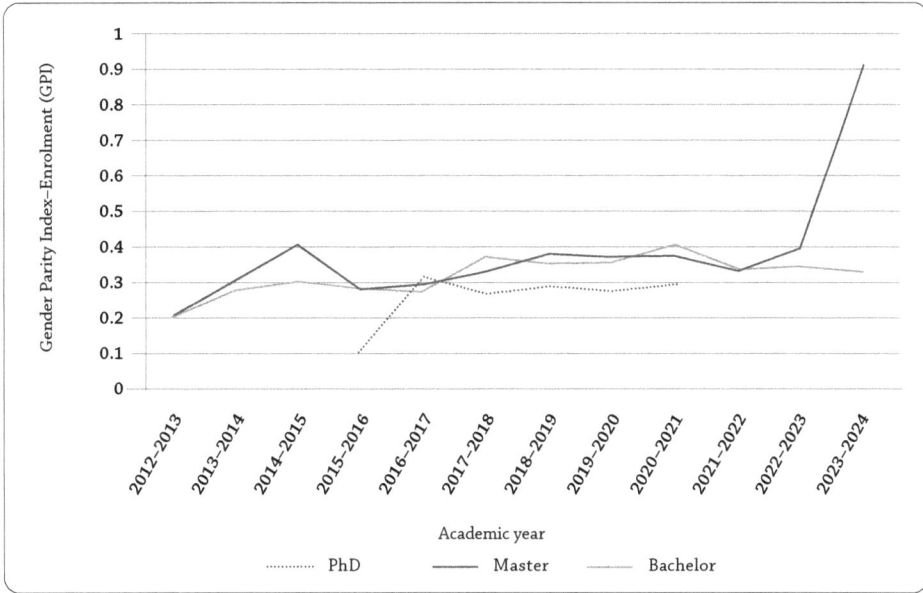

Figure 8 (c): Temporal evolution of the gender parity index of enrolment in Niger's national universities in agricultural science

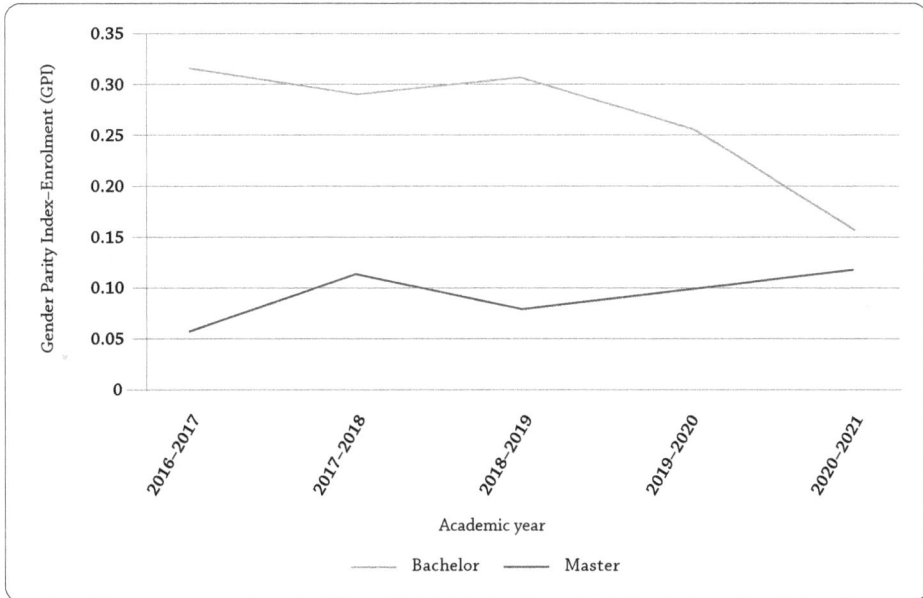

Distribution and gender dynamics of alumni

Over the period from 2005 to 2021, 7 996 female students versus 28 939 male students were trained in agricultural science in Benin's public universities. Women accounted for 21.65% of the total of 36 935 students. In Côte d'Ivoire's public universities, from 2012 to 2022, 3 507 female versus 7 945 male students were trained in agricultural sciences, representing a proportion of 30.62% of women of a total of 11 452 students. In Niger's public universities, between 2016 and 2023, 346 female students versus 1 200 male students were qualifying in agricultural science. Women represent 23.83 % of the total number of students qualifying during this period.

In Benin's public universities, from 2005 to 2011, more female students were trained in the master's cycle than in the bachelor's, master's, engineer and doctorate cycles (Figure 9a). This could be explained by the fact that, in Benin, this period (2005–2011) corresponds with the first years of the creation of most of the master's programmes in agricultural sciences, which would have led to an engulfment not only of students in the normal programme, but also, and above all, of former undergraduates. On the other hand, in the universities of Côte d'Ivoire, from 2012 to 2022, the percentage of female undergraduate students was higher than that of female postgraduate students (Figure 9b). In the national universities of Niger, the qualification rate of females is higher for the bachelor's level than the master's level between the period from 2016 to 2023 (Figure 9c).

Figure 10 shows the evolution over time of the annual ratio of female student alumni to male student alumni, known as the gender parity index, in the public universities of Benin and Côte d'Ivoire. In Benin's universities, since the 2016–2017 academic year, there has been a clear improvement in the number of female students trained compared with male students each year in the bachelor's, master's and doctoral cycles (Figure 10a). In Côte d'Ivoire's public universities, on the other hand, this improvement has been noticeable since the 2021–2022 academic year. An opposite trend is observed in public universities in Niger, with a higher female presence at the bachelor's level than at the master's level over time. The trend observed in Benin can be explained by the free education for girls in primary and secondary education offered in 2006 for nursery and primary education, and in 2010 for secondary education, by the Benin government.

Figure 9 (a): Propotion of women students qualified in agricultural science in Benin's national universities

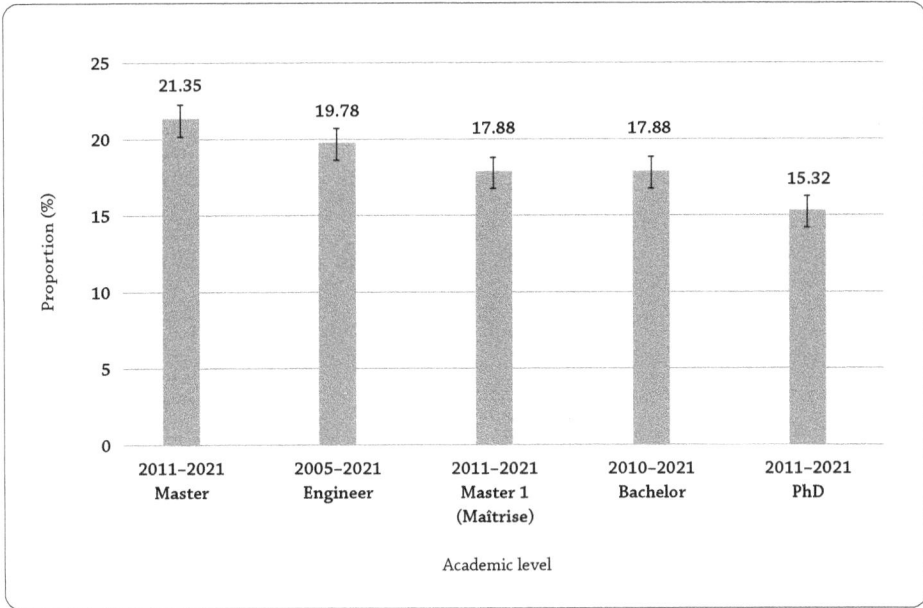

Figure 9 (b): Propotion of women students qualified in agricultural science in Côte d'Ivoire's national universities

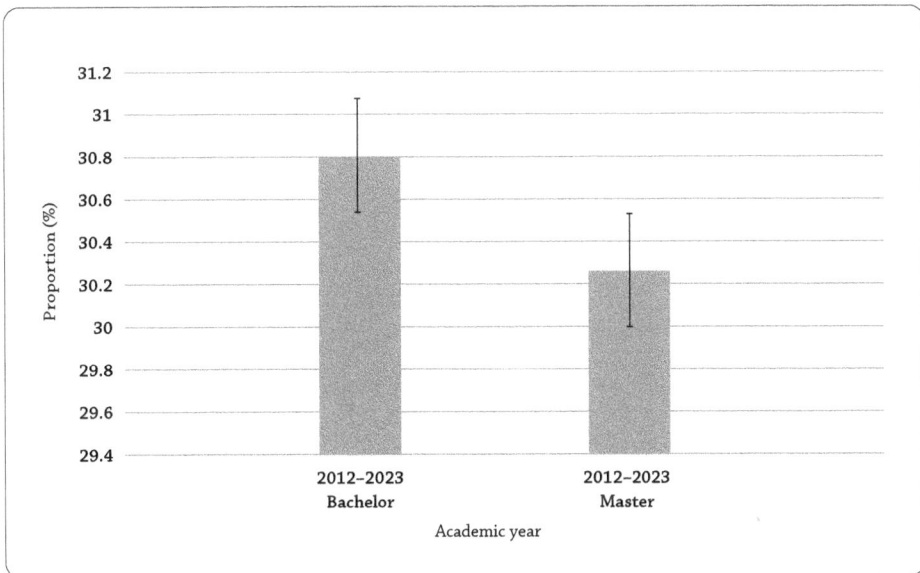

Figure 9 (c): Propotion of women students qualified in agricultural science in Niger's national universities

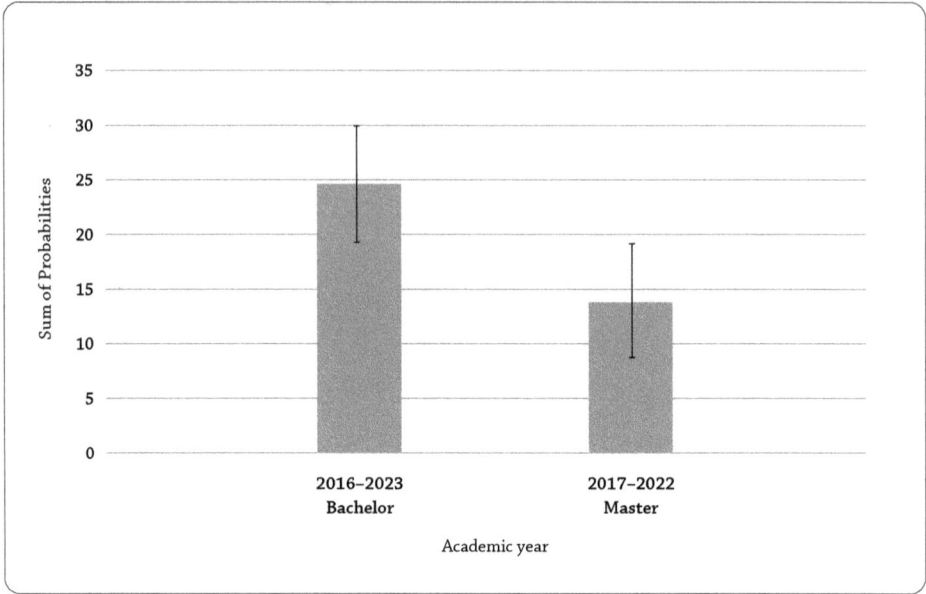

Figure 10 (a): Temporal evolution of the gender parity index of qualification in Benin's national universities in agricultural science

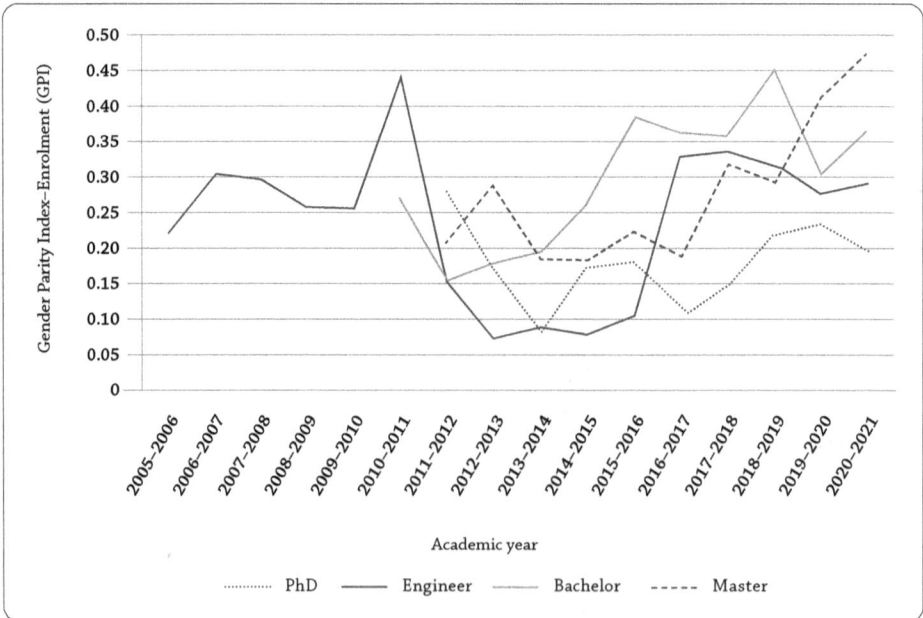

Figure 10 (b): Temporal evolution of the gender parity index of qualification in Côte d'Ivoire's national universities in agricultural science

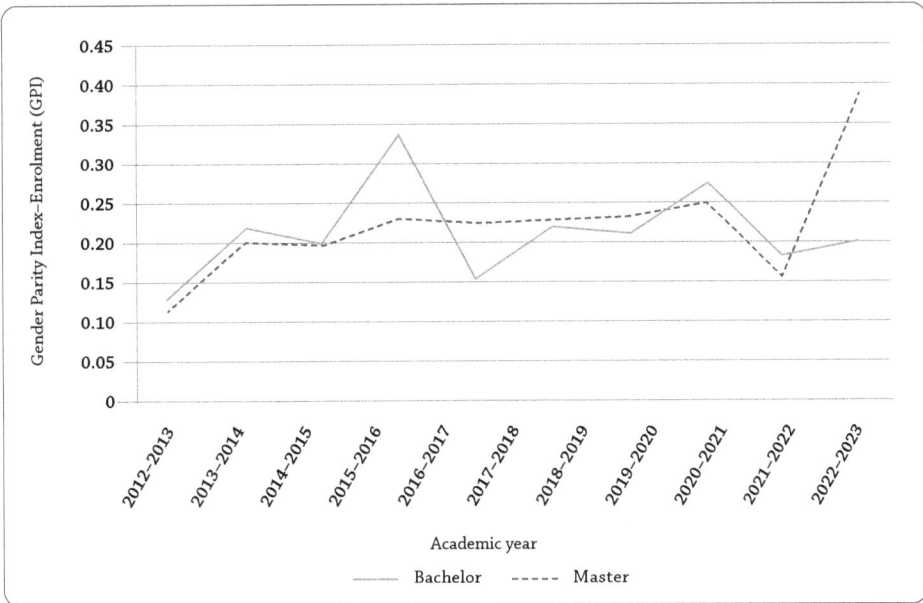

Figure 10 (c): Temporal evolution of the gender parity index of qualification in Niger's national universities in agricultural science

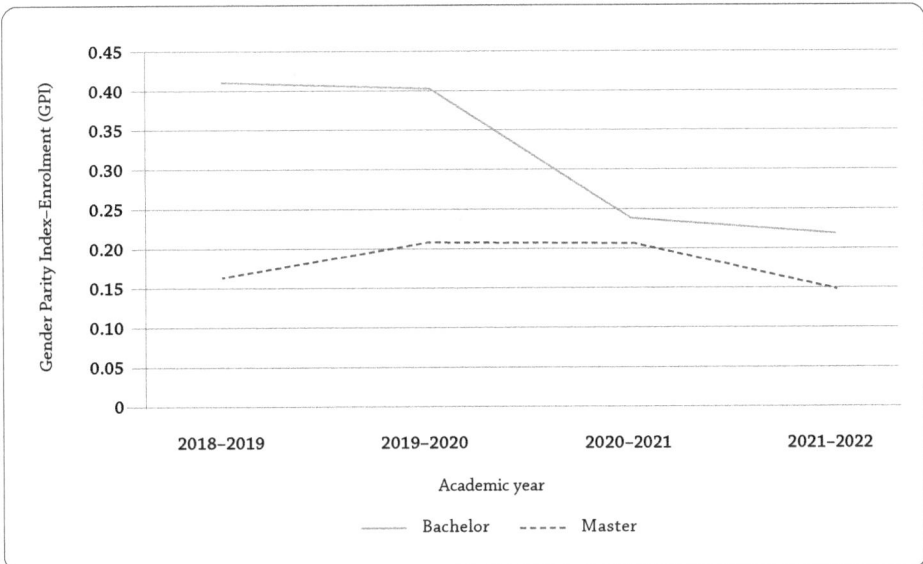

A range of complex factors are related to gender disparities in work and research

Gender disparities in work

To address Question 3a, we investigate gender disparities in agricultural work. While this question does not focus on agricultural research specifically, we argue that understanding gender disparities in agricultural work helps to ensure that researchers adequately consider gender in their research designs and data collection procedures. We further suggest that addressing inequalities in agricultural work may contribute to creating more inclusive environments, which could, in turn, encourage greater participation of women in agricultural research.

Women play crucial roles in processing and adding value to agricultural products, underscoring the importance of including both men and women in comprehensive agricultural data collection. However, biases may arise if interviewers lack an understanding of local socio-cultural norms, impacting the quality of responses obtained from farmers. Women's participation in data collection interviews is contingent upon the behaviour of data collectors and their adherence to socio-cultural norms, influencing men's decisions on allowing women to participate. As such, we highlight the most prevalent barriers to gender equality in agricultural work as shared by agricultural workers themselves. These include:

- **Land ownership disparity:** Women typically possess a limited share of land, ranging from 0.5 to 1 hectare, within their husbands' agricultural holdings. Moreover, men frequently assign infertile land to women following an extended period of farming. This is supported by the following statement made by a Benin woman and endorsed by others: *"my husband allowed me to farm one of his small plots which he has stopped using, it is less than a hectare in size and my harvests are often poor"*. Despite empirical evidence indicating that equalising women's access to agricultural resources vis-à-vis men can lead to a significant 30% increase in agricultural yields (Doss et al., 2018), this unequal land distribution persists.
- **Women's fragility:** To the question "Do women perform all the tasks on their farms in the same way as men?" one male participant from Benin answered: *"There are certain activities that my wife can't do, such as ploughing, clearing land and applying pesticides. I often help her if I have the time, or*

she calls on the services of young people." Most of the other men agreed with these comments, as did most of the women.

These words show that women have historically been perceived as fragile individuals, often deemed incapable of engaging in various agricultural tasks such as ploughing, mowing, clearing, and applying herbicides and pesticides. Consequently, women were typically relegated to roles centred around harvesting, processing and trading agricultural products. This perception of women's fragility perpetuated by men has served as the foundation for the myriad challenges and obstacles women face in agriculture. Their empowerment becomes compromised when they rely on men to fulfil their basic livelihood requirements.

- **Socio-cultural factors linked to gender:** In response to the same question about women's fragility, some women from Benin assert:

  In our locality, tradition forbids women to carry out agricultural activities that keep them bent over for long periods, or that favour the passage of sand through their legs ... If a woman doesn't respect this prohibition, she risks losing her fertility, and most of us here believe in this.

  This answer clearly reveals that, in some traditions, engaging in agricultural tasks that involve prolonged bending can potentially lead to health issues for women, as it is believed that this posture may cause the accumulation of air in the uterus, contributing to certain diseases. Additionally, there is cautionary advice for women to avoid allowing sand to pass through their legs.
- **Perceptions of pregnancy and maternity:** Women's biological condition is often viewed as a hindrance to engaging in agricultural activities, with men doubting their ability to manage large farms effectively.
- **Marital dynamics:** Traditional practices in various African countries, including Benin, dictate that married women relocate to their husbands' homes, leading to the belief that women cannot independently own farms. Inheritance for young women is often seen as a gift from their husbands, and any land they possess is considered the husband's property.
- **Limited access to farm labour and equipment:** To increase their labour for competitive production, women sometimes need to hire male labourers for some strenuous tasks like land clearing and ploughing, but men may not always provide satisfactory services. This leads to neglect of women's needs and potential exploitation.

- **Influence of tradition (patriarchal system):** Embedded in a patriarchal system, married women are expected to be subservient to their husbands in all aspects, including agricultural activities. Men may view women's agricultural pursuits as a challenge to their authority and may resist supporting them.

Limitations in research approaches contribute to gender-based inequalities in research

The participatory research synthesis (community-based research) also examined the potential sources of gender inequalities prevalent in agricultural science studies. Despite the lack of statistical correlation with sampling methods or obvious techniques well-known in the meta-analysis results, the process highlighted the complexities surrounding this issue. By carefully analysing the data, possible explanations and solutions gradually emerged, offering a roadmap for addressing these persistent disparities in the field. Through this deliberate exploration, a clearer understanding emerged, underscoring the importance of unpacking the underlying factors contributing to gender imbalances in agricultural science research.

Interviews with male and female farmers identified several factors associated with gender disparities in agricultural research and gathered approaches to solving these factors. These factors and their solutions are summarised below.

- **Patriarchal norms influence expression:** The patriarchal system often marginalises women's voices in public settings, leading to situations where women may be excluded from interviews without their input being sought. As a solution, questionnaires and data collection tools should explicitly require women's presence to provide their perspectives, and arrangements should be made to involve both farmers and their wives in household surveys.
- **Scope of surveys:** Some surveys tend to focus solely on household heads, neglecting the roles and insights of other household members. Potential solutions include appointments scheduled with both producers and their spouses for household surveys; questionnaires incorporating gender-related queries to capture diverse viewpoints; training programmes should sensitise investigators on the socio-cultural norms prevailing in the target communities before fieldwork commences; and efforts should be made to engage local data collectors familiar with the community context.

- **Education disparity:** The perception that women have higher illiteracy rates often leads to the biased selection of male participants for agricultural surveys, as reported by men. To overcome this challenge, the participation of both women and men farmers should be a key criterion in household selection for data collection, ensuring a more inclusive and representative data-gathering process.
- **Communication barriers:** Women often feel hesitant to speak openly in the presence of their husbands and may decline engagement with researchers. To face this challenge, initiatives should focus on raising awareness among women about the importance of their participation.
- **Selection of interviewers:** Interviewers sometimes overlook engaging with women, perceiving them as incapable or lacking knowledge of farming activities. As a solution, the involvement of both women and men should be a key criterion in selecting households for data collection.
- **Religious and gender considerations:** In certain religious contexts, interactions between men (especially strangers) and women may be restricted. It is therefore advisable to have female data collectors engage with women and male collectors with men during the acquisition of agricultural data, respecting religious norms and ensuring ease of communication.
- **Scheduling interviews:** Women's availability for interviews is often limited due to domestic responsibilities. In this case, data collectors could schedule interviews at times convenient for women, facilitating their active participation in data-collection processes.

Suggestions from farmers for gender-inclusive research methodology

Based on this case study, which has enabled us to gain a deeper understanding of the roots of gender disparities in agricultural research, several suggestions have been made directly by stakeholders in the agricultural world and beneficiaries of agricultural research results (i.e. farmers themselves) and are worthy of mention.

Proper structuring of questionnaires and data collection forms should mandate the presence of women to address specific inquiries. To emphasise the significance of women's involvement, data collectors should refrain from posing identical questions to both men and women. Biases in surveys incorporating gender aspects often stem from question formulation and the language used by data collectors to convey messages. Furthermore, farmers have highlighted their sensitivity towards gender-related topics, underscoring the importance for researchers to carefully select appropriate wording when crafting question-naires for gender-inclusive research.

Discussion

The various statistical results obtained relating to the gender distribution of teaching and research staff, positions of responsibility in training and research structures, and the composition of research teams and financed projects show a persistent disparity in the three West African countries, disadvantaging girls and women. This suggests that in Benin, Côte d'Ivoire and Niger, the issue of gender-based inequalities in agricultural sciences remains a major challenge (Question 1).

When considering the evolutionary dynamics of students enrolled and trained in the various fields of agricultural sciences at public universities, the results reveal a relative increase in girls/women statistics, albeit slight, between 2005 and 2021 in Benin, and between 2012 and 2023 in Côte d'Ivoire. This trend in the dynamics of the statistics suggests slight progress towards gender equality in the enrolment and training of female students in the agri-cultural sciences in these two West African countries (Question 2). This could be explained, in part, by the efforts of the governments of both countries to provide free nursery, primary and lower-secondary education.

Based on our findings, it is evident that gender inequalities in agricul-tural research and development in West Africa are shaped by a complex set of structural and cultural barriers (Question 3). Understanding these barriers is essential not only for promoting equality in agricultural work but also for informing more inclusive and context-sensitive research practices. Through our investigation, we have gained insights into barriers to equality in agricultural work as well as research. Though not the primary focus of this study, we want to emphasise the importance of increasing equality in agricultural work.

It is imperative to ensure that women have equal access to and ownership rights over agricultural land. This objective can be pursued through legal reforms and awareness campaigns that challenge the traditional notion of land ownership as a male prerogative. Furthermore, it is crucial to address the perception of women as fragile and incapable of engaging in specific agricul-tural tasks.

Training programmes should be established to equip women with the neces-sary skills and knowledge to participate in a broader spectrum of agricultural activities. Cultural beliefs and practices that hinder women's involvement in agriculture must be confronted. This can be achieved through community dialogues, awareness campaigns and educational initiatives that challenge these entrenched norms and promote gender equality. To promote equal participation, women should have equal access to farm labour, equipment and agricultural services such as training, credit and extension support. This can be achieved through targeted programmes that address the specific needs and challenges faced by women in agriculture. Additionally, men should be educated about the benefits of gender equality and encouraged to support and empower women in agricultural endeavours. Finally, data-collection processes by researchers in agricultural science must be inclusive, capturing the experiences and perspectives of both men and women. Data collectors should be trained to be sensitive to gender issues, ensuring that women's voices are adequately represented in the research and development process.

Farmers' observations of these inequalities have highlighted notable biases in the sampling methodologies that are commonly employed in agricultural studies, which frequently lead to the exclusion of certain gender groups from the resulting research outcomes and from the dissemination of agricultural technology innovations. The gender of the researcher or data collector, as well as the process of gathering agricultural data from farmers, introduces additional sources of bias into data collection and subsequent analysis. Societal norms often impede access for male data collectors to obtain information from female farmers during surveys, necessitating respectful adherence to local socio-cultural norms and practices throughout the research process. Addressing the identified disparities voiced by both male and female farmers, proposed solutions centre on five key points: (1) structuring questionnaires and data collection forms to mandate women's participation is explicitly required in specific responses; (2) scheduling household surveys to include both farmers and their spouses to capture a more complete household perspective; (3) incorporating local individuals among data collectors to improve familiarity and trust within communities; (4) facilitating gender-congruent interactions in agricultural data collection by pairing women farmers with female data collectors and male farmers with male counterparts; and (5) coordinating interview timings based on women's availability to enhance their engagement and provide equitable opportunities to participate.

The solutions advocated by farmers call for the implementation of tailored approaches in designing agricultural research protocols and the execution of field surveys. These strategies encompass the adoption of statistically robust sampling techniques to ensure the inclusive representation of women, men and all marginalised groups among the target populations in research endeavours, thereby supporting more accurate, equitable and applicable findings across the agricultural sector.

Conclusion

Women are still underrepresented in agricultural sciences in Benin, Côte d'Ivoire and Niger, with some variations in the statistics from one country to another. This underrepresentation is quite pronounced in both the categories of registered learners and graduates. The same is true for teaching staff in public universities, in the governance of universities and their structures, within research teams, and for leadership in drafting and coordinating research projects. It should be noted, however, that the lack of a database on the gender distribution of disaggregated statistics in several universities and research centres in West Africa may be a limitation in assessing the evolutionary trend of these statistics.

Gender disparities serve as substantial impediments to progress and development within societies. As a result, it is imperative that scientific investigations, often utilised to devise solutions and innovations, are meticulously structured to mitigate any inherent gender biases in their methodological frameworks. To facilitate the attainment of research outcomes conducive to establishing comprehensive and participatory solutions and technologies, this study has elucidated various facets of agricultural research that contribute to gender inequalities, pinpointing the associated factors and strategies for curtailing such biases. The disparities identified within agricultural research encompass socio-demographic considerations, such as cultural norms and land ownership practices, biological elements including pregnancy and maternity concerns, and organisational or institutional factors like the structuring of surveys, survey design and the recruitment of interviewers. By considering these barriers and implementing these recommendations, researchers are encouraged to critically engage with and reduce gender bias in their work, ensuring that gender perspectives are meaningfully integrated, an essential step towards fostering inclusive and sustainable development.

Acknowledgements

The authors are grateful to Canada's International Development Research Centre (IDRC), which funded this work under project 109799-001, "Strengthening Gender Inclusion in Agricultural Research for More Promising Results in West Africa (RIGRA)". We are also grateful to all Head of Records' services within universities and research institutions from Benin, Côte d'Ivoire and Niger, for their open minds and collaboration.

About the Authors

Christine Ouinsavi is a Professor of Silviculture and Natural Resources Management at the University of Parakou, Parakou, Benin.

Charlemagne Dossou Sèblodo Judes Gbemavo is an Associate Professor of Biostatistics at the National University of Sciences, Technologies, Engineering and Mathematics, Abomey, Benin.

Bienvenue N. Sourou Kuiga is a Postdoctoral Researcher in Environmental Sciences at the Laboratoire d'Etudes et de Recherches Forestières, University of Parakou, Parakou, Benin.

Adigla Appolinaire Wédjangnon is a Postdoctoral Researcher in Environmental Sciences at the Laboratoire d'Etudes et de Recherches Forestières, University of Parakou, Parakou, Benin.

Béatrice Adépo-Gourène is a Professor of Population Genetics at the Nangui Abrogoua University, Abidjan, Côte d'Ivoire.

Hadiza Kiari Fougou is an Associate Professor of Geography at the University of Diffa, Niger.

Salamatou Abdourahamane Illiassou is an Associate Professor of Ecology and Geography at the University of Diffa, Niger.

Ali Mahamane is a Professor of Botany and Ecology at the Department of Biology, Faculty of Sciences and Technologies, Abdou Moumouni University, Niamey, Niger.

Alice Ouattara Coulibaly is an Associate Researcher in Population Genetics and Hydrobiology at the Oceanological Research Centre in Abidjan, Côte d'Ivoire.

Yao Alexis N'go is an Associate Professor of Environmental Sciences at the Nangui Abrogoua University, Abidjan, Côte d'Ivoire.

Alexis Abodohoui is an Associate Professor of Economy at the University of Parakou, Parakou, Benin.

Yvette Onibon Doubogan is a Professor of Sociology of Development at the University of Parakou, Parakou, Benin.

References

Ayinde, O. E., Abduolaye, T., Olaoye, G., & Akangbe, J. A. (2013). Gender and innovation in agriculture: A case study of farmers' varietal preference of drought tolerant maize in southern Guinea Savannah Region of Nigeria. *Albanian Journal of Agricultural Sciences*, 12(4), 617–625. https://hdl.handle.net/10568/76667

Chambers, R. (1994). Participatory rural appraisal (PRA): Analysis of experience. *World Development*, 22(9), 1253–1268. https://doi.org/10.1016/0305-750X(94)90003-5

Chandra, G. (2010). Participatory rural appraisal. In P. Kaitha, K. K. Vass, A. P. Sharma, U. Bhaumik & G. Chandra (Eds.), *Issues and tools for social science research in inland fisheries* (pp. 286–302). Central Inland Fisheries Research Institute.

Direnberger, L., & Onibon Doubogan, Y. (2022). Les universitaires béninoises face aux hiérarchies dans la production des savoirs francophones sur le genre. *Genre, sexualité et société*, 27. https://doi.org/10.4000/gss.7245

Doss, C., Meinzen-Dick, R., Quisumbing, A., & Theis, S. (2018). Women in agriculture: Four myths. *Global Food Security*, 16, 69–74. https://doi.org/10.1016/j.gfs.2017.10.001

Fakoya, E. O., Ajayi, M. T., Oloruntoba, A. A., & Bolarinwa, K. K. (2010). Gender involvement in Fadama farming for sustainable food security in Ogun state, Nigeria. *OIDA International Journal of Sustainable Development*, 2(1), 89–95. https://ssrn.com/abstract=1695791

FAO (Food and Agriculture Organization of the United Nations). (2021). *Climate-smart agriculture case studies 2021: Projects from around the world*. FAO. https://openknowledge.fao.org/server/api/core/bitstreams/1a3714ba-5e7e-407d-acf2-1faa4d07a160/content

FAO (2023). *The status of women in agrifood systems – Overview*. FAO. https://openknowledge.fao.org/items/1b87f67b-57b2-4951-903f-b872f0ef021c

Hagège, M., & Condon, S. (2021). Enquêtes statistiques et approches intersectionnelles : considérations pour l'élaboration d'une enquête sur les violences de genre dans les Outre-mer. *Terrains & travaux*, 36-37(1), 183–204. https://stm.cairn.info/article/TT_036_0183

Kiptot, E., & Franzel, S. (2012). Gender and agroforestry in Africa: A review of women's participation. *Agroforestry Systems*, 84(1), 35–58. https://doi.org/10.1007/s10457-011-9419-y

Poitevineau, J. (2004). L'usage des tests statistiques par les chercheurs en psychologie : aspect normatif, descriptif et prescriptif. *Mathématique & sciences humaines / Mathematics & Social Sciences*, 167(3), 5–25. https://doi.org/10.4000/msh.2900

R Core Team (2022). *R: A language and environment for statistical computing* [Computer software]. R Foundation for Statistical Computing. https://www.R-project.org/

R Core Team (2024). *R Foundation for Statistical Computing* [Computer software].. https://www.R-project.org/

Savran Al-Haik, H. (2016). Exploring women farmers' experiences: A case study of gender inequality on small Turkish farms. Unpublished doctoral dissertation, Virginia Polytechnic Institute and State University.

CHAPTER 5

Uncovering Indigenous Women in STEM: A First Approach from Mexico

David Navarrete G.

Introduction

The Programa de Apoyo a Mujeres Indígenas en Ciencia, Tecnología, Ingeniería y Matemáticas (PEPMI) was launched in 2018.[1] This was the first programme of its kind in the history of Mexico due to three articulated components: (1) its target population (indigenous women with PhDs); (2) the level of training at which it operated (postdoctoral); and (3) its focus on Science, Technology, Engineering and Mathematics (STEM) fields. Furthermore, the programme included a range of supplementary supports for the fellows that is not typically encompassed in conventional scholarship schemes, providing them not only with a living stipend but also significant resources to carry out their research.

PEPMI lasted five years (2018–2022). Its main objective was to support indigenous women in the initial stage of their scientific careers by linking them to the country's research sector through a three-year postdoctoral stay. A second objective was to provide indigenous women with the opportunity to strengthen their skills and expertise for the generation of scientific knowledge in their areas of specialisation. Thirdly, it was expected that the enhanced scientific skills and expertise would facilitate the fellows' ability to contribute to the development of their communities and the country as a whole. At the end of the programme, it was expected that the fellows would have the necessary

---

1 Programme to Support Indigenous Women in Science, Technology, Engineering and Mathematics.

attributes to serve as role models to encourage greater participation of indigenous women in STEM fields, where they are particularly underrepresented.

A research study evaluating the academic experiences of PEPMI grantees ran parallel to the operation of PEPMI. The central purpose of the study
was to document the academic profile of the grantees, their postdoctoral
research experiences and the main academic results obtained at the end of
the programme. As part of the data collection process, remote questionnaires
were administered and visits were made to grantees at their research centres.
Individual semi-structured interviews were also conducted, both in person and
online, at various points during the postdoctoral period. Additionally, focus
groups were conducted to gather further perspectives on the grantees' personal
and research experiences. The study provided original information on the target
population and useful data for partner institutions to assess the final results of
PEPMI. It also served to identify the niche occupied by the programme and to
raise awareness of its existence and relevance among scholarly circles.

Via PEPMI, a total of 12 young indigenous women scientists from different
states and ethnic groups in Mexico were awarded scholarships. In addition to
the significant benefits PEPMI brought to the grantees, the programme yielded
knowledge and insights about a set of relevant topics that were not initially
anticipated. Insights gained included the educational and professional barriers
and opportunities for young indigenous women wishing to pursue scientific
careers, as well as the policy and practical conditions in public research centres
to host innovative programmes that foster social inclusion. This chapter seeks
to shed light on the experiences of indigenous women who have reached the
highest levels of academic training in STEM disciplines by highlighting additional knowledge and insights not covered in the original evaluation of PEPMI
(Navarrete G. et al., 2023). Subsequently, the chapter aims to contribute to an
understanding of the different challenges and opportunities of minority and
disadvantaged sub-groups of women, and to the development of more effective
strategies to address the specific gender gaps that affect them.

In the opening section, I examine the context in which PEPMI operated and
the design components that made it stand out as an innovative programme,
shedding light on the statistically small but socially relevant segment of the
country's young indigenous women with the interest and preparation to pursue
a scientific career.

Based on the information gathered in the evaluative research study on the
academic trajectories and postdoctoral research projects of the grantees, the
second section of the chapter reflects on the contribution that programmes
such as PEPMI can make to advancing our knowledge of the personal capacities

and contextual factors that enable women from historically marginalised indigenous communities in Mexico to advance in their academic and professional pursuits. The second section also draws attention to the value of supporting and promoting the work of young indigenous women engaged in cutting-edge research. The project's emphasis on supporting and promoting fellows made a significant contribution to challenging and reshaping prevailing negative stereotypes and prejudices about indigenous women in Mexico, particularly regarding their capabilities in science and participation in STEM fields.

Part three presents a reflection on the scope and limitations of PEPMI by addressing the question: Are postdoctoral fellowships an appropriate way to support and promote the professional development of indigenous women scientists, particularly in STEM fields, and are investments at the individual level an effective strategy to advance broader social and gender equity goals in the Mexican scientific system? As will be demonstrated in the following sections, the PEPMI results provide a positive answer to both questions.

Through the discussion of the context surrounding PEPMI, the value of the programme for grantees and a broader understanding of the experiences of indigenous women scientists in Mexico and the limitations of PEPMI, the chapter aims to provide an overview of the programme, including successes and areas for future improvement. In all, through reflection, the chapter aims to provide insights for those looking to better understand the challenges faced by indigenous women scientists and those looking to implement programmes to support them.

An innovative programme: The context and rationale surrounding PEPMI

Recruiting indigenous women with PhDs in STEM fields was one of the first challenges that the PEPMI coordinator and her team at the Centro de Investigaciones y Estudios Superiores en Antropología Social (CIESAS) faced when starting the programme in the spring of 2018. At the invitation of the coordinator, I participated in several working meetings where the topic was discussed. It was difficult to find candidates, given the specific requirements of the programme.

The solid experience of CIESAS in operating postgraduate scholarship programmes for indigenous peoples offered valuable information about indigenous women with doctorates (Navarrete G. & Gallart, 2018).[2] The landscape

---

2 CIESAS has operated two different postgraduate scholarship programmes for indigenous people but articulated sequentially and in their design and objectives. The first, the Programa Internacional

was very different from twenty years prior, when practically nothing was known about indigenous women with doctorates (Navarrete G., 2013). CIESAS's extensive network of contacts, including indigenous fellows and alumni of the scholarship programmes, together with the relationships established over twenty years with the institutions and graduate programmes where they have studied, has proved a useful resource. However, it was insufficient for the specific outreach required for PEPMI. While previous indigenous-focused postgraduate fellowship programmes were open to candidates from all disciplines of knowledge, the stipulation that applicants have a robust history of practical work and social commitment meant previous scholarships were in social sciences and humanities fields. PEPMI's focus on STEM disciplines was uncharted territory.

Resources and expertise from CONACYT (Mexico's National Council of Science and Technology), PEPMI's funding partner institution, together with the International Development Research Centre (IDRC) were also leveraged in the effort to identify eligible candidates for PEPMI. Created in the 1970s, CONACYT was the public institution responsible for drawing up the country's science and technology policies and for promoting and strengthening its scientific and technological development.[3] It was also the main public body that awarded scholarships for postgraduate studies. CONACYT therefore had an extensive database of its scholarship recipients, although only in recent years has it begun to record their ethnicity. Despite its utility, the information in question lacked sufficient consistency and was not frequently updated. The distribution of the initial PEPMI call for applications to the email inboxes of the former PhD fellows with whom CONACYT had a record-keeping relationship yielded modest results. The two rounds of grants were also publicised through

---

de Becas de Posgrado para Indígenas (IFP Mexico, for its acronym in English), began in 2001 and concluded in 2013 (Navarrete G., 2013). Funded by the Ford Foundation, it was the first master's and doctoral scholarship programme aimed at the indigenous population in Mexico. Shortly before the conclusion of this programme, which yielded successful results, and with the aim of providing continuity to a type of intervention that continued to be relevant and necessary, in 2012 CIESAS managed to attract the interest and funding of CONACYT, giving rise to the Programa de Becas de Posgrado para Indígenas (PROBEPI). This programme continues to date. For an introduction to PROBEPI, see http://becasindigenas.ciesas.edu.mx.

3 In May 2023, the General Law on Humanities, Sciences, Technologies and Innovation was enacted, which introduced changes in the functioning and name of CONACYT, which became the Consejo Nacional de Humanidades, Ciencias y Tecnologías (CONAHCYT, National Council for Humanities, Sciences and Technologies). In November 2024, CONAHCYT disappeared, being replaced by the Ministry of Science, Humanities, Technology and Innovation (SECIHTI, for its acronym in Spanish). The acronym CONACYT, which was in force during the implementation of PEPMI, will be used in this text.

other media; these included the websites of CIESAS, CONACYT and other higher education institutions offering STEM degrees.

Despite these resources, the number of applications received was lower than expected. The result can be attributed to several factors. It is not uncommon for the inaugural calls of new fellowship programmes to attract a smaller number of applications than those received in subsequent promotions, when the existence of the programme and the opportunities it offers have become more widely known. Further, the number of scholarships on offer – 10 in each PEPMI call – may have discouraged some applicants from applying because they assumed that their chances of obtaining a scholarship would be low. Eligibility criteria for scholarship applicants, which included having to carry out the postdoctoral stay in a public research centre and the requirement to develop a project aligned with CONACYT-prioritised lines of knowledge generation and application, may have limited the number of applicants as well.[4]

Critically, the programme's target population, indigenous women holding doctoral degrees in STEM disciplines, is limited in size, and there are no precise data on the population, as scant attention has been devoted to the matter. It is nevertheless acknowledged that their number is very limited, which is partly related to the number of indigenous women entering university and those who manage to study at the doctoral level.

The following data overview establishes population characteristics. In 2020, the mean level of schooling among women aged 15 and over who speak an indigenous language was 5.8 years (INEGI, 2022).[5] As might be anticipated, indigenous women represent only a small minority of those pursuing higher education. In the 2021–2022 academic year, only 33 106 women speakers of indigenous languages (MHLI)[6] were registered as pursuing a bachelor's degree, representing 0.7% of the total national enrolment at this level of education. In the same academic cycle, there were 593 MHLI enrolled in master's programmes

---

4 The CONACYT System of Public Centres – under the SECIHTI since 2024 – comprises 26 scientific research and specialised human resources training institutions. Spread across the country, these scientific institutes develop different research lines. Ten centres specialise in exact and natural sciences, eight in technological development and eight in social sciences research (https://secihti.mx/cp/). They represent a significant and influential element of Mexico's scientific system, which encompasses a broader array of research institutions, including those affiliated with the country's public and, to a lesser extent, private universities.

5 The National Commission for the Development of Indigenous Peoples shared data based on a 2015 census that 51.1% women and 48.9% men in the overall population of the country are indigenous (Gobierno de México, 2018). This figure represents just under 6% of the total population of the country.

6 MHLI is the Spanish abbreviation for Mujeres Hablantes de Lenguas Indígenas.

(0.19% of the national master's enrolment) and 104 enrolled in doctoral programmes (0.18% of the national doctoral enrolment) (ANUIES, 2022).[7]

In general, Mexico's indigenous population faces low levels of access to higher education. The limited rates of indigenous peoples in higher education can be attributed to a number of factors, including poverty, difficulties in accessing university education services due to geographic isolation, the low quality of education received at previous levels, and, until recently, a dearth of institutional support for higher education.[8] Despite the longstanding awareness of the educational disparities between indigenous and non-indigenous individuals and the adverse implications of this for Mexican society, the most significant legal reforms and institutional initiatives exclusively targeting indigenous students' access to higher education date to the early 2000s (Didou, 2011; Navarrete G., 2017). Prior to that, disadvantageous competition with students from more fortunate socio-economic sectors and with superior academic preparation was the norm for indigenous students in pursuit of scholarships.

For indigenous women, the problems described above were compounded by several additional difficulties. The dominant patriarchal culture of most indigenous groups, the reproductive role assigned to women, their family responsibilities centred on child-rearing and housework and stereotypes characterising them as less competent are all factors that hinder their formal educational progression (Navarrete G. et al., 2023).

Barriers for women in STEM fields are similar to those reported in Mexico and in Latin America for women in general (Andrade Baena, 2023; Bello & Estébanez, 2022; IPADE & Movimiento STEM, 2020; ONU Mujeres, 2020). For most indigenous women, poverty and racial discrimination are two important additional factors. Women are not a homogeneous group, nor are their barriers and opportunities to access and participate in these disciplines. However, intersectionality, or an understanding of how an individual's multiple identities impact their experiences, is often overlooked. In her recent study on the gender gap in STEM in Latin America, Assorbi (2023) found that 120 out of 154 recent gender-sensitive STEM education initiatives in 17 Latin American countries,

---

7 No information was located on self-identified indigenous women pursuing university studies. Self-ascription is another legally recognised criterion for the classification of the indigenous population in Mexico. The average level of education among these women is 9.9 years (INEGI, 2022), higher than those who speak an indigenous language. However, few are likely to go on to study for a doctorate. In Mexico, about 1% of the population has a doctorate.

8 Numerous reports, research and empirical studies have highlighted the importance of these factors among the various barriers to greater participation by indigenous people in higher education. See Carnoy et al. (2002); González Girón and Martínez García (2022). These limitations help explain the low percentage of the indigenous language-speaking population with higher education: 4.7% in 2015 (CDI, 2015).

including Mexico, do not have an intersectional perspective at all, "targeting only girls and women in general, regardless of other socio-economic characteristics that may be related to their exclusion from access". To develop effective programmes and policies aimed at reversing inequalities and discrimination, it is essential to design them with intersectionality in mind.

It was in this context that PEPMI was launched and implemented. However, it must be stressed that this did not occur in isolation. Over the last 20 years, numerous organisations and institutions in Mexico have developed proposals and initiatives at different levels with the objective of reducing gender-based gaps and promoting women's scientific vocations in STEM fields.[9] However, none of these actions targeted indigenous women. The implementation of PEPMI, with its additional focus on the post-doctoral level, made this population group and its specific needs in the final stage of the lifecycle visible.[10] It also provided a first insight into the challenges and opportunities encountered by young indigenous women in their pursuit of research positions and involvement in scientific and technological production within STEM fields.

The duration of the scholarships was three years, which was one year longer than the standard duration for a postdoctoral fellowship in Mexico at the time. In addition to the support provided by CONACYT for postdoctoral fellowships (including a monthly stipend for the fellows' expenses, a lump sum for relocation and installation expenses, and medical services in the public health system), IDRC's participation injected funding for research and dissemination, as well as a seed fund for community projects or activities. Research funding was 'demand-driven' or 'tailor-made', allowing each grantee to define what she needed for her research project. Grantees were also eligible for funding to improve their English language skills.

In accordance with the agreement between the programme partners, the postdoctoral stays were to be carried out in one of the 26 public research centres (CPI) of CONACYT. The host research institution provided an experienced researcher and subject matter expert as a tutor for each postdoctoral fellow. The tutors offered guidance on the design and development of research projects, including financial aspects, which were often unfamiliar to the post-docs. They also aided with training of specialised programmes and laboratory equipment, the planning and implementation of human resources training

---

9 For an overview of the main proposals and actions implemented, see Andrade Baena (2023); Ramírez Hernández et al. (2022).

10 I adopt the concept of 'lifecycle' as employed by numerous scholars to signify the various stages women traverse in their relationship with science. These include the early years of childhood and primary education, followed by secondary education, higher education, and finally, research positions and scientific and technological production.

activities (including teaching and thesis direction) and the dissemination of the results of the grantees' research.

The physical and human research infrastructure provided by each CPI, and the importance of the tutor in supporting and facilitating the work of the fellows in the abovementioned aspects, illustrate the value and formative benefits that postdoctoral periods can have. This highlights the necessity for institutional support for this purpose. Although the postdoctoral period is typically regarded as a time dedicated to advancing research in one's chosen field, for young indigenous scholars who have recently completed their doctoral studies, it is more than just an academic experience. It also provides an opportunity to expand their personal and professional networks and to develop self-confidence.

A further noteworthy aspect of the PEPMI design was the incorporation of the aforementioned research study. Despite the proven value of these types of studies accompanying the development of fellowship programmes, it is not a common practice to allocate funding for the purpose of evaluating a fellowship programme. This component guaranteed the availability of comprehensive documentation of the academic experiences of the fellows during their tenure at the conclusion of PEPMI. Furthermore, the analytical component of the study enabled the programme's projections to be extended beyond their internal dimension and disseminated in specialist forums.

The innovative nature of PEPMI was also evident in the institutional spaces where it was implemented. The presence of indigenous postdocs and the existence of a programme specific to their gender and ethnic identity was a novel phenomenon in the CPIs where the grantees carried out their stays. In most of these scientific institutes, research has been conducted *on* indigenous communities. These communities and their members tend to be seen as research subjects rather than actors in their own development.

This perception changed among many of those who had the opportunity to interact with the grantees and gain insight into their scientific research capabilities. The research team also conducted interviews with senior CPI staff and fellows' tutors, which served as a further catalyst for challenging these stereotypes. These discussions, in conjunction with the questionnaires distributed to the tutors at the outset and conclusion of the postdoctoral fellows' tenures, and participation of several tutors in select collective work meetings convened by the Programme Coordination with grantees, compelled the tutors to engage in more profound reflection concerning the ethnic and gendered attributes of the postdocs and how these attributes influenced their research projects. Furthermore, the tutors were encouraged to consider broader issues, such as the lack of social inclusion policies and the systematic underrepresentation of indigenous women in the country's scientific institutions.

Dismantling stereotypes and biases: Twelve young indigenous women scientists

Additional PEPMI eligibility criteria included having obtained a PhD within a period of no more than five years (i.e. in 2013 or later) and having a high-quality academic profile and production. Applicants were also required to have been accepted to engage in research pertaining to a specific line of knowledge generation and application, as developed within a CONACYT CPI.

Two calls for applications with national coverage were made, one in 2018 and the other in 2019. The applications were evaluated by CONACYT, which selected a group of 12 indigenous women from the centre and south of the country, belonging to seven different ethnic groups (see Table 1). The first cohort of six postdoctoral researchers commenced their tenure in 2018 and concluded in 2021, while the second group's tenure was from 2019 to 2022.

The grantees were between 31 and 49 years old, with the majority (8) falling within the 31–37 age range. Six were single, five were married and one was divorced. Four of the married women had one child and one had two children. The grantees were born in localities in central and southern Mexico, where the highest percentage of the country's indigenous population is located: four of them were born in Yucatan, four in Oaxaca, two in Chiapas and two in the State of Mexico (Figure 1). The grantees belong to the following indigenous groups: Mayan (4), Zapotec (2), Mixtec (1), Mazatec (1), Mam (1), Tseltal (1) and Otomi (2).

The research study identified the educational and professional profiles of the grantees. It also identified the motivations and circumstances that enabled them to pursue their formal studies to doctoral level. From the findings common elements and experiences emerged that speak to the personal capacities and contextual factors that enabled women from indigenous communities in Mexico to progress academically and professionally.[11] This cohort is characterised by its ability to recognise and seize opportunities at hand, even in the face of constraints.

The group of indigenous women recruited and supported by PEPMI had outstanding knowledge capital and skills for study and scientific work. At the same time, they lacked certain tools and needed to strengthen other skills

---

11 The following reflections are based on the data contained in Navarrete G. and García Martínez's (2023) unpublished report.

Figure 1: Map of grantees' places of origin

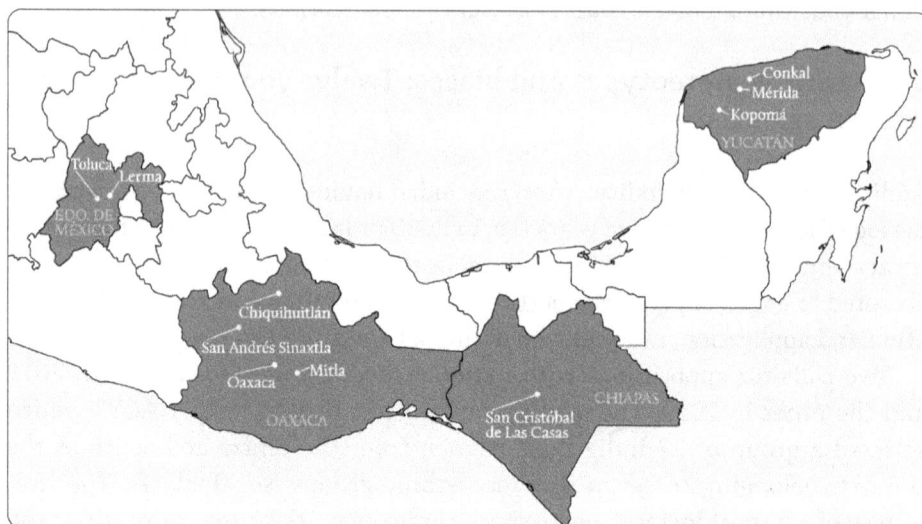

that were important for their long-term success in STEM (e.g. networking, technical laboratory skills and English language skills). The clarity provided by the research study on these issues facilitated a more precise allocation of programme resources and support.

A primary commonality among grantees is that they are of recent generations of indigenous people who continue to contend with social inequity yet have witnessed partial improvements in their living conditions compared to older generations, in part due to the implementation of various public programmes and policies over recent decades (CONEVAL, 2019). It is also noteworthy that, in comparison to other states with sizeable indigenous populations, the number of higher education institutions in the states of origin of the fellows – Oaxaca, Yucatán, Chiapas and the State of Mexico – has increased in the present century, thus facilitating greater availability of educational opportunities for the indigenous population.[12]

A further common experience among the fellows is that they received their entire education, from elementary level through to postgraduate studies,

---

12 Notwithstanding the considerable obstacles faced by indigenous women, the educational trajectory of PEPMI grantees illustrates that educational opportunities are gradually expanding. Furthermore, although not exceeding the narrow range of MHLI pursuing a postgraduate degree noted in the previous section, a recent investigation revealed that the number of MHLI engaged in master's degree studies increased twofold between 2016 and 2022 (outnumbering men in the latter year), while the number of those pursuing a doctorate rose threefold over the same period (approaching parity with men) (Romero-López & Anell-Parra, 2023).

within the public education system. This underscores the importance of free public education in Mexico for a vast array of socio-economic groups, including indigenous women. Additionally, several of the postdocs highlighted the significance of having received a publicly financed scholarship (at the state or national level) during one or more stages of their pre-university education. The recipients of those scholarships attested that the scholarships were essential to continuing their studies. This is also the case regarding their postgraduate studies (master's and doctorate), for which all the grantees received a grant from the federal government through CONACYT.

At the time of applying for the scholarship, most grantees had already gained work experience in areas related to their interests and specialisations. One was a laboratory manager in a private company, one worked in the food industry and others were teaching at their home universities. These activities tended to be undertaken between the completion of their bachelor's degree and the start of their master's degree. Nine of them also engaged in volunteer work, which was also related to their professional interests.

The family backgrounds of the fellows are similar in terms of educational attainment. There has been significant progress in their generation's level of education compared to that of their parents and especially their grandparents (see Chapter 11 for similar findings in a sample of Bolivian women in STEM). The information provided by the postdocs shows a very low level of educational attainment for their grandparents: grandparents were illiterate, did not attend primary school and only in a few cases did they manage to complete it. The case of one grandmother who completed sufficient studies to become a teacher, stands out as unique.

The parents of the grantees and their siblings have higher levels of education when compared to grandparents, with the siblings being relatively more likely to have a baccalaureate or bachelor's degree. Even then, in all but two cases, the grantees are the most highly educated members of their families and hometowns. The grantees come from low-income families, with fathers who are small farmers, labourers, artisans, small traders and, in three cases, primary school teachers. Among the mothers, there were housewives, kitchen helpers, domestic workers and two primary school teachers.

Grantees also report receiving high levels of support from their nuclear families. This crucial support enabled almost all the grantees to complete their studies within the deadlines set for each level of education. Family support included financial, emotional, moral and motivational supports. This involved a demanding and time-consuming effort on the part of the grantees' parents. In addition to this support, there were siblings – usually the eldest – who also contributed financially to their sisters' studies and other close relatives who, in some cases, hosted the scholars in the city they were studying.

The motivations and pathways to STEM specialisation of the indigenous women supported by PEPMI are particularly relevant. Among other reasons, it allows identifying traits that differentiate them from women from other social backgrounds who also work in STEM fields. These are not young female scientists with only theoretical interests or oriented towards market-driven technological development. Their lines of research are oriented towards the production of socially useful knowledge, especially for disadvantaged groups. As members of disadvantaged groups themselves, grantees have important perspectives to offer. Growing up in or close to rural contexts and direct knowledge of the problems of the respective populations have permeated their research interests. The desire to learn more and to look for ways to improve the living conditions of their communities, and with wider social projections, was clear in their postdoctoral research projects. One fellow expressed this link in the following way:

> In the rural community, agriculture was one of the main activities carried out by both men and women, but many have abandoned this activity and opted to work in the nearest cities. I grew up in an agricultural environment, which sparked my interest in seeking development options that make appropriate use of the resources and capacities of rural farming communities.

Another fellow emphasised the significance of her status as an indigenous woman:

> As a woman from an indigenous community, I am acutely aware of the specific needs of rural communities. This has informed my decision to pursue studies in the field of sustainable rural development. To a greater or lesser extent, my research can contribute to the well-being of rural families. Furthermore, my status as an indigenous woman affords me a greater degree of empathy, which enables me to develop my research with greater motivation.

Another motivating factor that encouraged grantees to pursue a STEM specialisation was the influence of their family members, particularly their fathers, followed by their mothers, and in some cases, their grandparents and siblings. Grantees also pointed to the role of secondary and high school teachers in fostering their interest in mathematics and science as relevant. By the time they reached university and graduate school, their vocation was clearly defined. Nevertheless, the assistance provided by some of the professors in these academic settings was of particular importance. The professors' support facilitated the formation of networks and identification of potential opportunities. Additionally, they offered well-informed guidance on suitable pathways and academic institutions for studies and developing a scientific career.

PEPMI and its associated study represent a significant initial step in the national agenda to enhance the representation and participation of indigenous women in science in Mexico. The information summarised in this section documents the existence, profile, interests and scientific work of a subset of indigenous women about whom no prior information was available. Viewed from a wider perspective, their trajectories reflect on the access routes to scientific careers for the larger, albeit small, population group to which they belong. They are the tip of the iceberg of a larger but to date unknown universe of indigenous women with interest and capacity to contribute to the production of scientific knowledge in the country.

Reflections on the contributions, scope and limitations of PEPMI

Latin America is one of the two regions in the world in which gender parity has been achieved among researchers, with women representing approximately 45% of the total number of researchers (Bello & Estébanez, 2022). Although nowhere near the heights of countries such as Venezuela (60%), Argentina (53%) and Uruguay (50%), Mexico has experienced recent improvements towards gender parity: from 2000 to 2016 female participation in the total number of researchers increased from 28% to 33%. This increase in women's participation in research is the result of the various policies and programmes implemented at different levels this century. However, the lack of parity also speaks to the need for continued vigorous and sustained action to improve women's participation in STEM. One of the key arguments made in this chapter is that PEPMI has made contributions towards the achievement of this goal.

It would be inaccurate to suggest that a scholarship programme that supported 12 women and was in operation for five years had a significant impact on a large scale (see Chapter 10 for information about a set of programmes designed to benefit women in STEM across the Global South). However, PEPMI was not designed to achieve large numbers or to prompt immediate far-reaching transformations. Rather, its aim was to have a qualitative impact on two main levels: first, enhancing the careers of its grantees; and second, increasing the visibility of indigenous women scientists.

Regarding the first, the programme was successful in reinforcing the skills and knowledge necessary to put the postdocs in better positions to continue their aspirations and efforts to develop professionally as scientists. It allowed grantees to become known and to broaden their networks in their small and competitive fields of research. With one exception,[13] all fellows expressed a high degree of satisfaction at the end of their postdoctoral stay. One case exemplifies this:

> I am very happy with what I have achieved with this great opportunity. It was an enormous learning experience. Apart from working with my tutor, it has allowed me a lot of autonomy, to know how to move, how to carry out my own processes as a researcher, and it has also helped me to train myself a great deal.

Secondly, by focusing on indigenous women, the programme recognised, addressed and documented the existence of a subset of women that has largely been ignored in efforts to increase women's participation in STEM in Mexico or Latin America more broadly. PEPMI allowed for the understanding and subsequent addressing of challenges faced by indigenous women at the postdoctoral level. Indigenous women in STEM are faced with limited access compared to other women attempting to establish or establishing a presence in science. In addition to their gender and socio-economic status, stereotypes about their ethnicity reinforce the widespread questioning of their ability to become relevant actors in scientific production. One fellow, a PhD and specialist in polymeric materials, recalled the following about her initial postdoctoral period:

> When I arrived here, I did see that part of being indigenous, I did have that conflict, didn't I? That they expected someone different and they didn't believe that one had indigenous origins ... they didn't think that an indigenous person could have a postgraduate degree ... But I should clarify, not from the researchers, but from the students.

The PEPMI programme has been instrumental in addressing the pervasive stereotypes and prejudices that have historically been directed towards

---

13 The grantee who expressed some dissatisfaction attributed this mainly to the lack of support she received from her tutor. Conversely, she indicated high satisfaction with her CPI as a venue for conducting research and expanding her professional contacts and networks.

indigenous women in Mexico. In addition to its focus on indigenous women scientists in STEM, PEPMI moved beyond the conventional limitations of fellowship programmes – which are typically constrained to their operational implementation – by incorporating a component to ensure the visibility of the programme's existence and outcomes. A pivotal element of PEPMI's dissemination efforts was the availability of the information, analysis and reflections provided by the research study as the programme developed. An account of the programme's outcomes was published at its conclusion, accessible to a broad readership (Navarrete G. et al., 2023).

One of the aims of the programme was for the grantees to acquire or reinforce the attributes necessary to serve as role models, thus encouraging more indigenous women to pursue careers and participate in science (see Chapter 12 for discussion on considerations when using role models to address gender disparities in Africa). As the postdocs progressed through their respective stays, they exhibited an increase in both individual and group self-confidence. Some stated that, at various points in their personal, academic and professional lives prior to receiving the fellowship, they concealed their indigenous identity. During and following the fellowship, grantees felt they were able to openly display their indigenous identities in interviews and conferences. With the initiative and financial support of the programme, grantees established the country's inaugural indigenous in science network (REDMIC).

Figure 2: REDMIC logo

It is also noteworthy that the programme provided support to pioneering research in a range of fields, including biomedicine, plant physiology and nutrition, food chemistry, organic agriculture, the solidarity economy, ecology and climate change, and sustainable development. These studies were conducted by a cohort of young indigenous women scientists, guided by the desire to enhance the quality of life for their communities and regions, as well as for Mexican society as a whole.

This chapter illustrates the value of fellowship programmes such as PEPMI in promoting STEM career paths and supporting and making visible young indigenous women scientists. That said, PEPMI was not without limitations. The programme was implemented in a limited number of CPIs, and therefore the reported experiences do not extend to all CONACYT research centres. Even in the CPIs that participated in the programme, the presence of the fellows was largely confined to their assigned laboratories or academic departments, with low engagement in other areas.

Moreover, the implementation of measures to combat the spread of the SARS-CoV-2 virus in 2020 and 2021 resulted in the disruption of the integration process and the proximity of fellows to the academic community of the host CPIs. Consequently, the visibility that would have been afforded to them under normal circumstances was also reduced.

The time that has elapsed since the end of the programme allows us to observe the limited use that has been made of this experience at the institutional level. Until 2023, CONACYT maintained its provision of postdoctoral fellowships for indigenous women. In 2024, the call for applications was opened to both indigenous women and men. Contrary to PEPMI, the scholarships offered in 2023 did not include any additional support for research, capacity-building or community projects. This emphasises the significance of international collaboration in advancing intervention models that exceed the financial capabilities of national public institutions, or whose priorities undergo a transformation upon the conclusion of respective cooperation agreements.

Conclusion

It is of the utmost importance to direct attention towards the value and proven results of interventions with broad social benefits, such as PEPMI. This programme pioneered a novel and far-reaching approach to fostering the participation of young indigenous women scientists in STEM disciplines. The programme also outlined and documented specific strategies for the recruitment, selection and support of indigenous women postdoctoral indigenous fellows. These strategies, in conjunction with the insights gained from their implementation, represent a valuable resource for informing and refining the design and execution of future actions and programmes inspired by similar objectives. Alongside the valuable individual benefits for grantees, such programmes can facilitate pathways towards social inclusion and the democratisation of highly segmented scientific systems and societies, including Mexico and other Latin American countries.

Acknowledgements

PEPMI was funded by the International Development Research Centre (IDRC) and the Consejo Nacional de Ciencia y Tecnología (CONACYT). The programme was implemented by the Centro de Investigaciones y Estudios Superiores en Antropología Social (CIESAS). I acknowledge CONACYT for their support in providing postdoctoral fellowships, which included a monthly stipend for the fellows' expenses, a lump sum for relocation and installation costs, and access to medical services through the public health system. I also acknowledge the significant contribution of IDRC, which provided funding for research and dissemination activities, as well as a seed fund for community projects and initiatives. I would also like to thank Antonieta Gallart, PEPMI Coordinator, for her invitation and valuable support in conducting the evaluative research study.

About the Author

David Navarrete G. is a Professor and full-time tenured Researcher at the Centro de Investigaciones y Estudios Superiores en Antropología Social (Centre for Research and Advanced Studies in Social Anthropology, CIESAS) in Mexico.

References

Andrade Baena, G. (2023). *Informe sobre la brecha de género en STEM en la formación técnico profesional en México*. Movimiento STEM. https://movimientostem.org/wp-content/uploads/2024/07/OIT_UNICEF-_-Infografia-Brechas-genero-EFTP-STEM.pdf

ANUIES (Asociación Nacional de Universidades e Instituciones de Educación Superior). (2022). *Anuarios estadísticos de educación superior 2021–2022*. ANUIES. http://www.anuies.mx/informacion-y-servicios/informacion-estadistica-de-educacion-superior/anuario-estadistico-de-educacion-superior

Assorbi, D. (2023). *Reduciendo la brecha de género en STEM en América Latina: ¿Pasando a la acción?* UNESCO. https://unesdoc.unesco.org/ark:/48223/pf0000386465

Bello, A., & Estébanez, M. E. (2022). *An unbalanced equation: Increasing participation of women in STEM in LAC*. UNESCO. https://forocilac.org/wp-content/uploads/2022/02/PolicyPapers-CILAC-Gender-ENG-VFEB22.pdf

Carnoy, M., Santibañez, L., Maldonado, A., & Ordorika, I. (2002). Barreras de entrada a la educación superior y a oportunidades profesionales para la población indígena mexicana. *Revista Latinoamericana de Estudios Educativos, 32*(3), 9–43.

CDI (Comisión Nacional para el Desarrollo de los Pueblos Indígenas). (2015). *Indicadores socioeconómicos de los pueblos indígenas de México, 2015*. CDI.

CONEVAL (Consejo Nacional de Evaluación de la Política de Desarrollo Social). (2019). *La pobreza en la población indígena de México, 2008–2018*. CONEVAL. https://www.coneval.org.mx/Medicion/MP/Documents/Pobreza_Poblacion_indigena_2008-2018.pdf

Didou, S. (2011). La promoción de la equidad en educación superior en México: Declinaciones múltiples. *Reencuentros. Estudios Sobre Educación*, (61), 7–18. https://reencuentro.xoc.uam.mx/index.php/reencuentro/article/view/769

Gobierno de México. (2018). *Mujeres indígenas, datos estadísticos en el México actual*. Gobierno de México. https://www.gob.mx/inpi/articulos/mujeres-indigenas-datos-estadisticos-en-el-mexico-actual?idiom=es%20

González Girón, J. M., & Martínez García, A. (2022). El proceso de inclusión de los indígenas en la educación superior. *Revista de Ciencias de la Educación Academocus*, 1(20), 34–48.

INEGI (Instituto Nacional de Estadística y Geografía). (2022). *Estadísticas a propósito del día internacional de los pueblos indígenas*. INEGI. https://www.inegi.org.mx/contenidos/saladeprensa/aproposito/2022/EAP_PueblosInd22.pdf

IPADE (Instituto Panamericano de Alta Dirección de Empresa) & Movimiento STEM. (2020). *Mujeres eligiendo carreras STEM*. IPADE, Movimiento STEM. https://www.movimientostem.org/wp-content/uploads/2021/01/Mujeres-eligiendo-carreras-STEM-%E2%80%93-MovimientoSTEAM-%E2%80%93-CIMAD.pdf

Navarrete G., D. (2013). Becas de posgrado para indígenas: Un programa no convencional en México. *Cuadernos de Pesquisa*, 43(150), 968–985. https://doi.org/10.1590/S0100-15742013000300012

Navarrete G., D. (2017). Widening the participation of indigenous people in Mexican higher education: Results, challenges and perspectives. *Revista de Educación Superior Del Sur Global*, (4), 43–66. https://doi.org/10.25087/resur4a3

Navarrete G., D., & Gallart, A. (2018). ¿Mujeres indígenas con posgrado? Hallazgos y aprendizajes de quince años de trabajo en el Centro de Investigaciones y Estudios Superiores en Antropología Social-CIESAS, 2001–2016. In D. Mato (Ed.), *Educación superior y pueblos indígenas y afrodescendientes en América Latina. Políticas y experiencias de inclusión y colaboración intercultural* (pp. 395–410). EDUNTREF.

Navarrete G., D., & García Martínez, A. (2023). Investigación evaluativa de las experiencias académicas de las becarias del Programa de Estancias Posdoctorales para Mujeres indígenas en Ciencias, Tecnología, Ingeniería y Matemáticas. CIESAS. Unpublished report.

Navarrete G., D., García Martínez, A., & Fagoaga, R. (2023). *Mujeres científicas indígenas en México: Figuras y aportes estudio de las experiencias posdoctorales de las becarias del PEPMI (2018–2022)*. CIESAS.

ONU Mujeres. (2020). *Las mujeres en ciencias, tecnología, ingeniería y matemáticas en América Latina y el Caribe*. ONU Mujeres. https://lac.unwomen.org/sites/default/files/Field%20Office%20Americas/Documentos/Publicaciones/2020/09/Mujeres%20en%20STEM%20ONU%20Mujeres%20Unesco%20SP32922.pdf

Ramírez Hernández, M., Juvera Ávalos J., & Escudero-Nahón, A. (2022). Las vocaciones científicas STEM desde la perspectiva de género. In C. Vicario-Solórzano & A. Escudero-Nahón (Eds.), *Mexicanas del futuro: Desafíos y perspectivas para inspirar vocaciones sociotecnocientíficas en la era digital* (pp. 17–32). ANUIES.

Romero-López, R., & Anell-Parra, X. (2023). Análisis de los programas de posgrado en México con relación a las variables género, área de formación, entidad federativa, hablantes de lengua indígena y personas con discapacidad. *UVserva*, (16), 36–58. https://doi.org/10.25009/uvs.vi16.2986

CHAPTER 6

Fostering Open Data on Women in STEM across Latin America: The ELLAS Network

Cristiano Maciel, Indira R. Guzman, Karen da Silva Figueiredo Medeiros Ribeiro, Franci Suni-Lopez, Luciana B. Frigo, Luciana Salgado, Rita Cristina Galarraga Berardi, Sílvia Amélia Bim, Boris Branisa, Elizabeth Jimenez and Luana Bulgarelli Mendes

Introduction

In Latin America, investment in gender data across socio-economic indicators has lagged over the past five years (World Bank Group, 2024). The lack of open and reliable data on women in Science, Technology, Engineering and Mathematics (STEM) and their career trajectories poses a significant barrier to global efforts to close the gender gap in science (UNESCO, 2020; UNESCO, 2024). More data across intersectional lines is needed to track progress and address the challenges women and other underrepresented groups face in STEM fields.

Latin America faces a distinct mix of economic inequality, political instability and deep-rooted gender norms that affect women's participation in science and technology fields (García-Holgado & García-Peñalvo, 2022); without context-specific data, the development and implementation of effective, evidence-based policies that promote gender equality and leadership in STEM are hindered.

In response to this challenge, in 2022, a consortium of researchers from Bolivia, Brazil and Peru created the Equality in Leadership for Latin America STEM (ELLAS) research network to expand the field of studies in Latin America.

The ELLAS Network[1] is an interdisciplinary team that includes professionals from eight universities, spanning fields such as computer science, economics, psychology, social sciences and education. ELLAS launched the "Latin American Open Data for Gender Equality Policies Focusing on Leadership in STEM" initiative (Maciel et al., 2023) intending to gather and analyse data on women in STEM across Bolivia, Brazil and Peru, and create an open data platform (ODP) where this information could be shared and accessed by all.

An ODP is a digital infrastructure that provides public access to a wide range of datasets, offering tools for searching, filtering and visualising data (Keserű & Chan, 2015). By blending their diverse expertise, cultural perspectives and backgrounds, the ELLAS interdisciplinary team aims to offer context-specific insights into research and the ODP development processes.

This chapter highlights the process leading to the development of the ODP and the overview of the collection and structuring of datasets that feed it. Our contribution explores several key dimensions of the ELLAS Network research and its connection to open data. After a brief introduction, we provide a comprehensive overview of the practical aspects of open data, describing how the ELLAS research team collects and structures this information, while highlighting the central research questions it addresses. We then present the ELLAS platform, showcasing its functionalities and illustrating how the ODP serves as a valuable tool for a wide range of societal applications. Lastly, we offer recommendations based on our findings and outline potential directions for future work.

The open data approach for Latin America

The existing data about women in STEM in Latin America is often fragmented, dispersed across open government and non-governmental platforms, or embedded in unstructured formats such as academic papers, grey literature and social media posts. The ELLAS Network positions itself within this context. Our qualitative applied research (Babbie, 2020) proposes an open data approach for Latin America (starting with Bolivia, Brazil and Peru) with a dual focus: first, to explore, extract and structure pre-existing data on these countries about Latin American women in STEM careers as open data; and second, to generate, structure and make available *additional* open data, collected through a comprehensive survey targeted at the three countries' audiences, as detailed in Davila et al. (2024).

---

1 https://ellas.ufmt.br/

Gathering pre-existing data

Existing data was gathered and organised by the ELLAS research team from various primary and secondary data sources. In the context of ELLAS ODP, 'primary data' refers to unstructured data obtained from scientific literature texts, such as academic papers, grey literature such as official reports, textual content from social media pages and data from a survey created and applied in the three countries. 'Secondary data' refers to pre-existing structured data collected by someone else for a different purpose, usually available in spread-sheets on official websites (Berardi et al., 2024). In our research, secondary data were obtained from publicly accessible spreadsheets and datasets.

Figure 1 presents a flowchart outlining the process our research team has followed to obtain and integrate data for the ODP. The process began with the identification of factors affecting women in STEM in the Latin American context. Once each factor was identified, the next step was to search for exist-ing data related to these issues at national or regional levels within Latin America. If data were available, open and structured (i.e. secondary data), they were directly translated or converted into structured formats for the ODP. If data were available and open, but unstructured (i.e. primary data), they were analysed and then transformed into structured data for the ODP. In cases where data were available but not in open formats, our researchers actively engaged with data custodians to advocate for open access. When data were unavailable, relevant information was incorporated into our survey instrument (Davila et al., 2024). This survey was administered across the three countries to generate new data, which were subsequently analysed and formatted for inclusion in the ODP.

After the collection and organisation of all the data, a process of integra-tion and connection was executed to transform the data into linked open data in the format of the ELLAS ODP (further described in the next main section). Linked open data is based on a set of best practices for publishing and connect-ing data in knowledge graphs on the web. These best practices were introduced by Berners-Lee (2006) in his linked data architecture and became known as the Linked Data Principles, adopted by W3C as linked data publishing standards.

The flowchart in Figure 1 represents a systematic approach to handling gender data in STEM in Latin America. Ultimately, the ODP's goal is to make all data related to women in STEM in Latin America accessible, integrated and usable through the ELLAS platform.

With this in mind, data identification and gathering of pre-existing data began in 2022, when we defined the key concepts we would like to address

Figure 1: Process of systematic data collection and transformation for the ODP

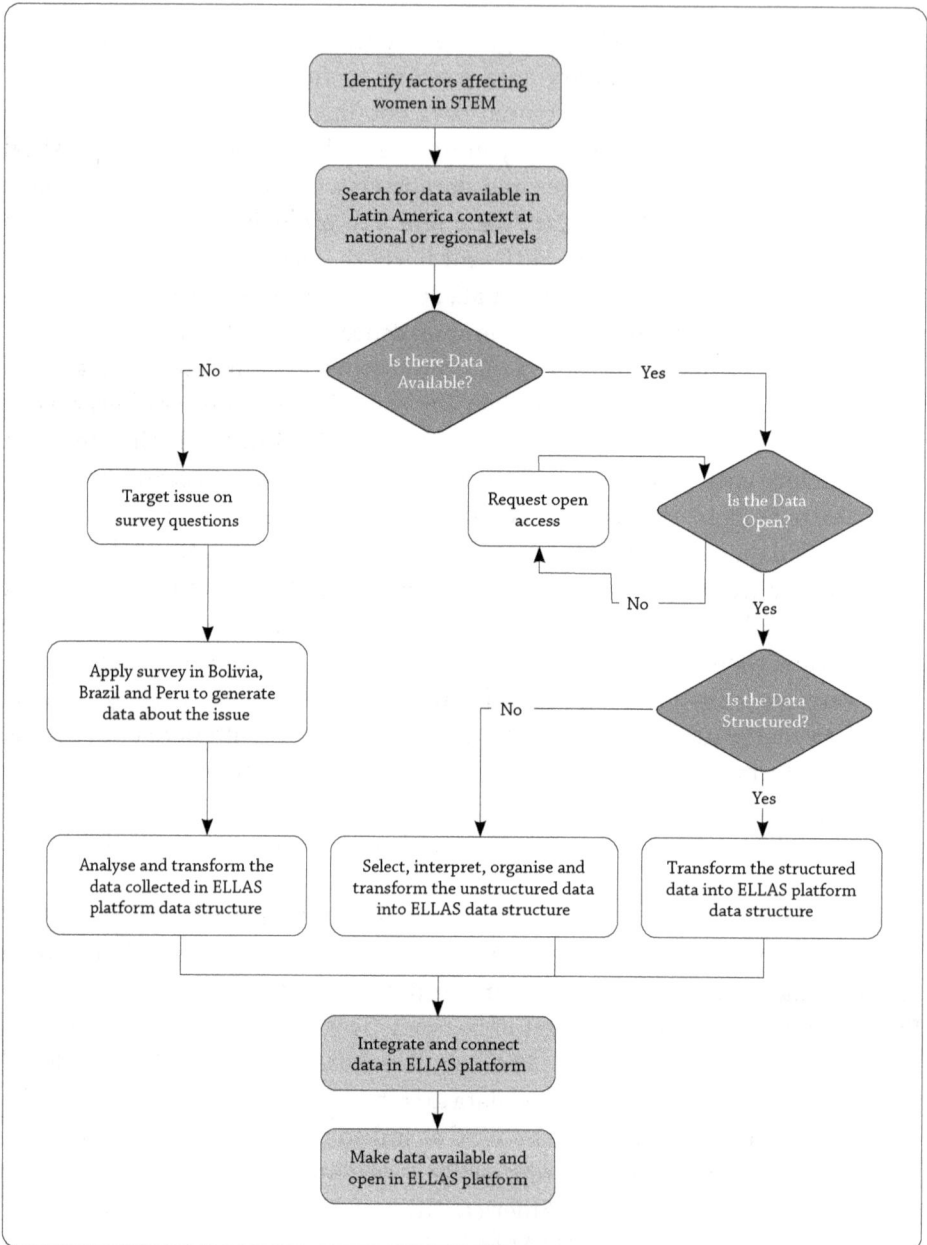

with the data: policies, initiatives, contextual factors and contextual indicators related to women's careers in STEM, directly or indirectly (see Figure 2 for definitions and examples). We believe that those concepts are crucial for revealing the structural and cultural barriers faced by women considering entering or already working in STEM, and as such, are necessary for identifying opportunities to promote gender equity. In addition, Latin America faces unique challenges related to social, economic and gender disparities, making it essential to analyse these variables to inform effective public policies and develop strategies that foster inclusion and female leadership in STEM fields.

Figure 2: Key concept definitions and data samples by country

	Policies	Initiatives	Contextual factors	Contextual indicators
Definition	Official guidelines, regulations, and frameworks established by governments, organisations or institutions to promote gender equality directly or indirectly	Targeted actions or programmes designed to promote gender equality at all levels	Specific social conditions that shape the environments and may act as barriers and enablers to gender equality	Measurable variables that provide insight into the contextual conditions impacting gender equality directly or indirectly
Examples				
BOLIVIA	National Plan for Equal Opportunities "Women building the New Bolivia to Live Well"	Mujeres TICs BO facebook.com/ MujeresTICsBO	Lack of role models (Rosales Rodríguez, 2020)	Women represented 30% of those employed in senior and middle management in 2022 (World Bank Group, 2024)
BRAZIL	CNPq / MCTI / MMulheres Call No. 31/2023, Girls in Exact Sciences, Engineering and Computing	Programa Meninas Digitais https://meninas.sbc. org.br/	Gender pay gap (Lucena et al., 2024)	11.6% of professionals are Black women in the ICT sector in Brazil (Brasscom, 2022)
PERU	Supreme Decree No. 008-2019-MIMP, National Gender Equality Policy (PNIG)	Peruvians in STEM linkedin.com/ company/ peruvians-in-stem/	Participation in gender equity initiatives (Tull et al., 2018)	47% of STEM graduates are female (UNDP, 2024)

Policies refer to the formal guidelines, regulations and frameworks established at different levels by governments, organisations or institutions to promote gender equality. In the context of our study, these policies may include laws, strategic plans, specific funding, affirmative action programmes and calls for gender quotas aimed at reducing gender disparities related to STEM or women's leadership. In the countries investigated, national-level policies are still limited, but organisational and institutional policies have emerged (Guzman et al., 2023a; Guzman et al., 2024).

Initiatives include targeted, organised actions, projects or programmes designed to promote gender equality in STEM at different levels. These initiatives can include mentorship programmes, scholarships, training workshops or networks that aim to empower women, enhance their skills or increase their visibility and participation in STEM careers. They are mostly connected to professional networks and academic institutions rather than government bodies.

Contextual factors refer to the specific social, cultural, economic and institutional conditions that shape the environment in which women live and pursue careers and may act as barriers or enablers to gender equality in STEM. These factors include societal attitudes towards gender roles, the availability and quality of education and professional development opportunities, economic disparities and workplace behaviour. In Latin America, these factors vary widely between countries and regions because of the cultural differences that influence women's opportunities and challenges in their lives and STEM careers. A study for Bolivia, for instance, found that traditional gender roles, family influence and discrimination in the labour market discourage women from pursuing STEM careers, even when cognitive ability is not seen as a limitation (Branisa et al., 2020). Understanding the level of influence of these contextual factors is crucial for developing effective strategies and policies to support women in STEM, as they provide insight into the underlying barriers and enablers of gender equity in these professions. In our research, we categorised the contextual factors we identified in our literature search into individual, interpersonal, academic, work-related, family-related, socio-economic, social and historical domains (Davila et al., 2024; Drummond et al., 2023).

Context indicators are measurable variables that provide quantitative insight into the conditions impacting gender equality in those countries. These indicators could be directly or indirectly related to STEM, women's careers or leadership, such as data on gender gaps in STEM education enrolment, employment rates, wage disparities or representation in leadership roles. Context indicators help quantify the influence of various contextual factors and track progress towards gender equality in STEM.

To collect data related to these concepts, we conducted several systematic reviews of academic literature, grey literature and social media to search the web and gather the available data, such as the Figure 2 examples (Arndt et al, 2023; Drummond et al., 2023; Frigo et al., 2024; Guzman et al., 2023b; Guzman et al. 2024; Ribeiro et al., 2024; Rondon-Pereira, et al., 2024). The data found in these systematic reviews were structured to compose the ELLAS platform's dataset.

Collection of additional data

In addition to utilising pre-existing data sources, a survey was designed to collect primary data from the populations of these countries; the survey design approach is explained by Davila et al. (2024). The primary goal of this survey was to collect quantitative data on the factors that influence STEM career choices and motivation to lead in STEM in the three countries using the previously conducted systematic literature reviews as a foundation. The survey data offer comparable open data across the three countries, providing essential support to researchers, policymakers and other decision-makers dedicated to closing the gender gap in STEM in Latin America. Moreover, this survey can be replicated by researchers in other regions within and beyond Latin America to identify the contextual factors that hinder or empower women in STEM careers. We made the survey instruments open and accessible via the ELLAS website (ELLAS, n.d.).

The survey instrument was made available in three languages – Spanish, Portuguese and English. We obtained more than 10 000 responses from participants in Bolivia, Brazil and Peru. The primary data collected provide valuable insights into the motivations, challenges and factors that influence women's career decisions and aspirations in STEM (Davila et al., 2024). The responses were meticulously analysed, and in parallel, selected data underwent curation to transform survey data into open data, making it accessible on the ELLAS platform, as shown in Figure 3.

Challenges with data

The ELLAS team used various strategies, incorporating different methods, techniques, procedures and technological tools, to develop the ODP and conduct research to generate data for the ODP. This section outlines the methodological steps and how we overcame challenges to achieve our objectives.

The process of gathering pre-existing data led to several challenges, including inconsistencies in data availability across different countries due to varying levels of transparency and openness in national data policies. For instance, while Brazil's Access to Information Law facilitates public access to government data, Bolivia lacks similar legislation, posing significant barriers to data access (Hildebrand et al., 2024). Additionally, identifying relevant data sources, determining which courses qualify as STEM and ensuring the data were gender-disaggregated required careful consideration and adaptation of best practices.

In response to these challenges, the ELLAS Network adopted innovative methods, such as incorporating data from social media platforms like Instagram (de Arruda Nunes et al., 2024; Gonçalves et al., 2023), which proved particularly effective in identifying grassroots initiatives that support women in STEM. Traditional data collection methods, such as English-language academic searches, often failed to capture locally relevant information, highlighting the importance of considering local languages and alternative data sources. In the context of Brazil, where only a small percentage of the population has some knowledge of English, leveraging local platforms and languages not only improved data collection but also ensured that the research findings were more relevant and accessible to local stakeholders (Carvalho et al., 2023).

The data organisation of the ELLAS platform involves combining data from different sources that use various vocabularies, different levels of detail and possibly different interpretations. This diversity adds complexity to the integration process, which involves more than just putting the data in one place. We developed methods to organise the data through connections to centralise the data and make interactions with the platform clear and manageable. These connections standardise the data and ensure consistent interpretation by defining the terms used.

In other words, these connections are designed to address ambiguities. For example, suppose we collect data from different sources about initiatives and policies where there are two initiatives with a "Target Audience" label, while there is one policy with an "Audience" label. Although both terms refer to the same concept, they are used differently regarding initiatives versus policies. This makes it hard to integrate the data. In the ELLAS platform, organising and standardising the data ensures that both initiatives and policies are understood as having a "Target Audience" relationship. This approach helps centralise and simplify data interpretation.

We also connect data across the three languages used on the platform. Our methods handle three languages, so even if the target audience refers to "Undergraduate students", "Estudiantes de pregrado" (in Spanish) or "Estudantes de Graduação" (in Portuguese), the connections we established in our data model recognise them as synonyms. Without proper connections, it might seem like different target audiences; however, it is conceptually the same.

This adaptive approach to data gathering demonstrates the value of using contextually appropriate methods to collect and structure comprehensive and actionable data. By prioritising local context and leveraging diverse data sources, the ELLAS Network's open data approach addresses current gaps and sets a foundation for more inclusive and informed decision-making. This work can not only support public policymakers in addressing gender disparities in STEM but also contribute to the global call for increased investment in gender-disaggregated data, thereby fostering environments that support women's leadership and career advancement in STEM fields across Latin America.

The process depicted in Figure 3 illustrates the structured methodology adopted by the ELLAS research team to systematically gather, integrate and transform diverse data sources into a unified ODP. This systematic approach reinforces the project's commitment to addressing the gender data gap and advocating for open data practices, ultimately facilitating more informed research, policymaking and strategic actions to promote gender equity in STEM fields. The open data available in the ELLAS platform is presented in the form of graphs and text-based results, which means it can compile data at regional and country geographic levels, it has configurable data filters and people can download the results in open formats.

Figure 3: ELLAS open data approach for Latin America

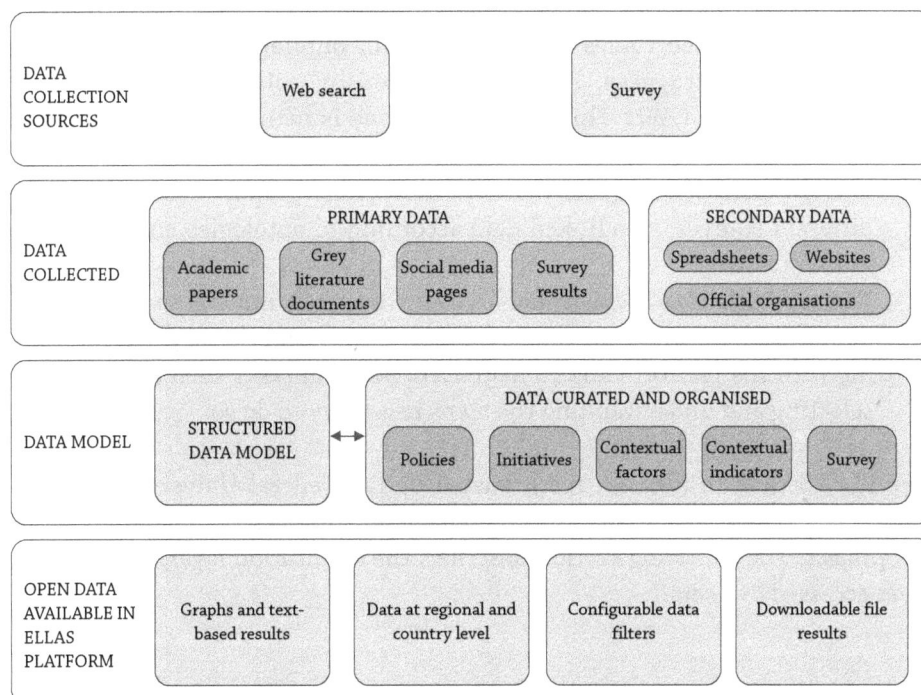

The ELLAS linked open data platform

The platform architecture

We start this section by briefly explaining the open data ELLAS platform architecture, which represents the fundamental structure of our software system and is designed to allow the system to grow, providing a better user experience without performance loss. The open data ELLAS platform architecture can be viewed in more technical detail in Maciel et al. (2024). The designed architecture allows for the curation of different data sources, from raw data to linked data, to be consumed by individual users such as researchers, policymakers and decision-makers working on STEM and gender issues. The ELLAS platform has a layered architecture using cloud services throughout all processes, as we can see in Figure 4. This comprises:

- The *data layer* which organises two types of data sources defined in the context of the ELLAS platform as "primary" and "secondary" data, as previously explained. Multidisciplinary and multicultural teams collaborated to curate and prepare the data for integration into the next layer.
- The *processing layer* which collects structured files (with specific comma-separated values – CSV format) for ontology modelling in three languages (Portuguese, English and Spanish), using technologies such as Protégé and OWL. This complex pipeline is managed by Pentaho and Python technologies, involving platform and ontology developers. Finally, it is possible to integrate data via knowledge graphs, scattered across different sources, into linked data according to ontologies created by the ELLAS team.
- The *application layer* which enables users to search, understand and utilise data. It is being designed to ensure a good user experience when interacting with the platform and to help users perform tasks such as searching, selecting and understanding the steps necessary to do so.

The ELLAS website (ELLAS, n.d.), hosted by the Federal University of Mato Grosso (UFMT), provides access to the ODP and additional information about the project. The following section describes the application layer, which is the layer accessed by users.

Figure 4: Open data ELLAS platform architecture

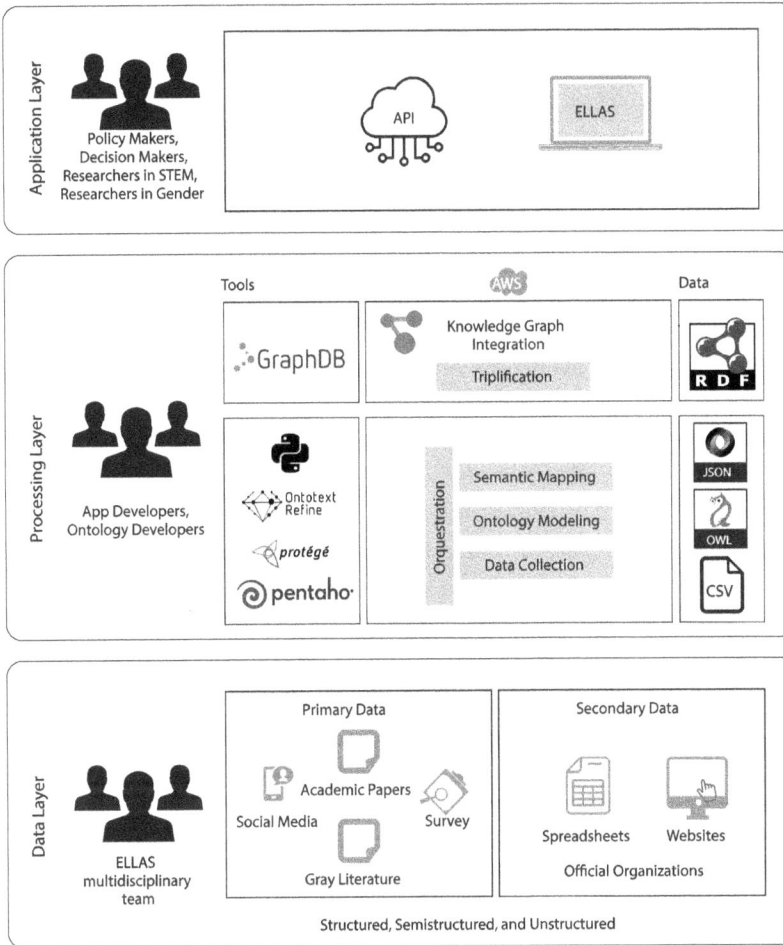

Source: Maciel et al. (2024)

The application layer: Intended use of the ELLAS platform

The ongoing project follows a gender-sensitive design based on feminist human-computer interaction (HCI) (Bardzell, 2010; Bardzell & Bardzell, 2011; Bellini et al., 2022; Drummond et al., 2024), highlighting the importance of including gender considerations from the initial conception of the platform to promote diversity on the social web. Figure 5 shows the interaction design (ID) methodology (Oliveira et al., 2024).

By creating and making available a data platform that can be consulted at no cost, and initially available in three languages (Portuguese, Spanish and English), we believe that we are offering a model of how to develop accessible gender databases and platforms. Additionally, by providing access to data in Portuguese and Spanish, we are minimising language barriers and hopefully increasing opportunities for Brazilian and Latin American women scientists to contribute to research in this field.

We also believe that by interacting with the data available on the platform, people could better understand gender inequalities in leadership positions in technology and engineering contexts. Consequently, with knowledge and better comprehension of inequalities, ELLAS ODP users could promote positive change for women in their professional environments.

Finally, the platform can facilitate collective learning and foster collaborative research environments for anyone with fluency in the available interface languages, digital literacy and internet connectivity. For example, in the area of initiatives, we collected data about each initiative's social media information and the gender of its coordinators. Users can ask: *What is the initiative's social network(s)?* to gain access to the social media information for the initiative. Users can also search for the following: *What is the social gender of the people responsible for the initiatives?*, to find information about the gender of those coordinating the initiatives if it was available in the initiative's public media. This feature allows the platform to identify and highlight women leaders in STEM and to facilitate the creation of new women's networks. However, it is important to clarify that the platform does not provide individuals' direct contact details but offers general information about initiatives. The focus on ethical and privacy considerations ensures that the shared data represent demographic overviews rather than personal details.

We collected sex – and gender – as disaggregated data at the country level, allowing for users to make searches by country. For example, by selecting the question *What types of gender policies were implemented in countries in a given year?*, the user can select which country(ies) they want to search.

We also collected data that indicate the educational levels of all initiatives. Consequently, from selecting the question: *What initiatives are being developed at a given school level?*, the user can choose which school level they would like to investigate.

The platform offers the possibility for a user to provide feedback regarding their satisfaction with the data presentation and if they find any technical issues or errors.

Figure 5 shows a storyboard with an example of an interaction scenario. We expect that with these functionalities, the platform can foster a culture of accountability and collaboration with the contribution of the public interacting with it and sharing their data with regular updates.

Throughout the platform's design process, we aimed to ensure that photos, symbols and illustrations represent Latin American women in technology and engineering, mainly women from the countries directly involved in the project: Bolivia, Brazil and Peru. We believe that by doing this, we can recognise and address implicit biases from the evaluation of the platform prototype, thereby contributing to reducing gender stereotypes and promoting inclusion, diversity and equity. For example, the Bolivian team answered that they did not feel represented by the photos used in the first prototype. So, with the help of a Bolivian female student, we searched for other photos that could be more inclusive and then included a photo of a Cholita, representing indigenous women in Bolivia.

By accessing and using the ELLAS ODP, users can explore data related to initiatives, contextual factors, context indicators, policies and survey data from Bolivia, Brazil and Peru. The ELLAS ODP offers users access to curated datasets that can be downloaded for further exploration and analysis. This organised data can serve as a valuable starting point for further exploration and informed discussion. We hope this resource will be especially useful to decision-makers, researchers and policymakers in the following ways:

- **Data on initiatives could help in the identification of best practices, resource allocation and programme design:** Data on various initiatives from these countries could assist in identifying which programmes and approaches are encouraging women's participation and leadership in STEM. By navigating the data, insights from existing initiatives could guide decision-makers on where to allocate resources to maximise impact. Furthermore, a greater understanding of past initiatives already established in these countries could aid in designing new programmes.
- **Data on contextual factors could help to better understand barriers in order to tailor solutions and measure progress:** Contextual data helps in identifying cultural, social and economic barriers that women face in STEM fields. By understanding the specific context of each country, policies and initiatives could be tailored to address unique local challenges. Also, context indicators such as gender equality indices, education levels and employment data are available on the platform to download and could be used to understand their impact.

Figure 5: Storyboard illustrating an interaction with the ELLAS platform

Interaction scenario example

Patrícia Ribeiro is a student at a university in Latin America who is active in the feminist and student movements. This semester, she is taking an elective course on Public Policy. One of her course assignments involves searching the internet for data on the gender gap in STEM. Patrícia needs to research the gender indices of Latin American countries and universities, the types of gender policies already implemented by countries or universities, and what gender aspects these policies address.

Patrícia recently learned that a data platform made by the ELLAS Network is available, so she decided to explore the data from this source. She searched for policies, refining the search by country and time interval (in years). The results were presented in different formats, such as a map, tables and graphs. Patrícia was very pleased with the results. She downloaded the results to include them in her class presentation. The debate with the class, based on the data collected by Patrícia on the ELLAS platform, was very rich and informative.

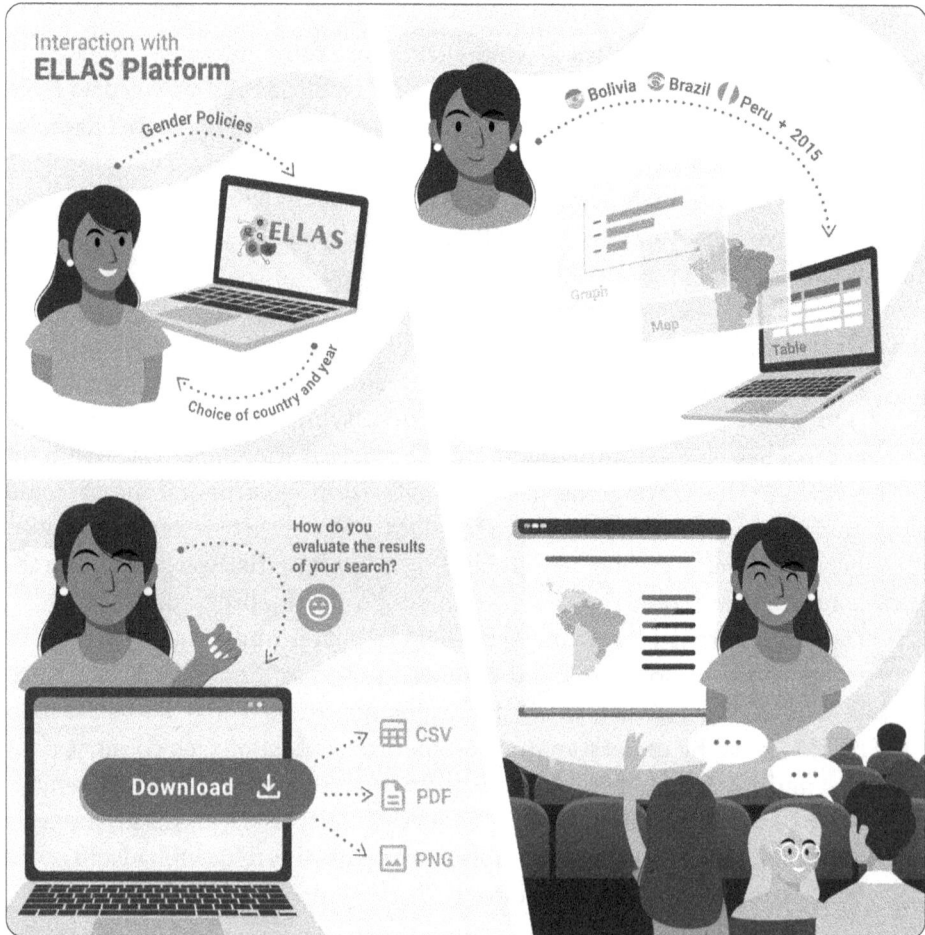

- **Data on policies could help policy development, evaluation, advocacy and lobbying:** The ELLAS ODP presents data about STEM-related policies identified across these countries, which could help in evaluating the effectiveness of different policy approaches. Learning from existing policies could aid in the development of new, more effective policies. Additionally, analysing the data on existing policies, alongside survey data on individual perceptions of these policies, could be used as evidence for advocating for changes at both national and regional levels.
- **Data from the survey can help in analysing the impact of the different factors and make comparisons among the three countries:** The survey data could help decision-makers understand the primary factors that encourage or discourage women from pursuing STEM careers in Bolivia, Brazil and Peru. By knowing what drives or hinders career choices, policies and programmes can be developed to address specific barriers and enhance motivations. The comparable data across the three countries can allow policymakers to identify common trends and country-specific challenges, facilitating tailored and more effective interventions. The shared data can foster collaboration between Bolivia, Brazil and Peru, allowing for the exchange of best practices and the development of joint strategies to promote women in STEM. The data may help in crafting contextually appropriate solutions, ensuring that policies and programmes resonate with the unique experiences and challenges faced by women in each country. Additionally, the open nature of the survey instrument allows for replication in other regions, enabling policymakers to extend their understanding of the factors influencing women in STEM beyond these three countries and apply successful strategies in diverse contexts.

The overall benefits of the use of the ELLAS platform by decision-makers and policymakers are the evidence-based decision-making process to craft effective policies, the regional collaboration that comes with understanding the different approaches and outcomes to promote women in STEM in neighbouring countries, and the cultural features of the platform data to ensure that policies are culturally sensitive and more likely to succeed in their specific contexts. By leveraging the ELLAS platform data, decision-makers and policymakers could create more effective, gender-equitable and sustainable strategies to enhance women's participation and leadership in STEM across Bolivia, Brazil, Peru and other Latin American countries with data on the platform. The platform and available data can be accessed on the ELLAS website (ELLAS, n.d.).

Conclusion

In this chapter, we shared the outcomes of our efforts to promote open data for gender equality in STEM fields in Latin America (for additional work on gender equality in Latin America, see chapters 2, 5 and 11). We presented the core concepts driving the ELLAS project – including policies, initiatives, contextual factors and indicators – demonstrating how these frameworks guided the retrieval of existing data from the web and the collection of new data through a survey on women in STEM in Bolivia, Brazil and Peru. We also described how we created a model to structure this data as open data and made it accessible through a platform that we designed and developed called ELLAS ODP.

The ELLAS ODP empowers people to access valuable data on women in STEM in Latin America, enabling research, analysis and evidence-based policy and decision-making to enhance the representation of women in these fields. Furthermore, the structural model created is designed to be connectable, flexible and scalable, allowing others to contribute new data to the platform to expand its coverage across other countries. We recognise the scarcity of data on this topic and its impact on the visibility and career advancement of women in STEM across the region. This is why we believe that advocating for open data is crucial in addressing this issue and that our work is a meaningful step towards supporting gender equality in STEM in Latin America.

By increasing data availability and centralising it in one accessible and contextually sensitive designated place, the ELLAS platform becomes a practical tool that people can rely on and use for various purposes, like research, curiosity, inspiration or in their careers. We hope to spark curiosity, inspire action and encourage more people to explore and utilise these data, contributing to a future where gender equality in STEM is not just an aspiration but a reality.

The ELLAS platform provides a structured and accessible way to collect and report open gender data (Guzman et al., 2020) at various levels, directly contributing to monitoring and promoting transparency and gender equality across Latin America.

As the ELLAS Network, we focus on advancing gender equality in STEM through informed, strategic and actionable measures. We advocate for promoting transparency by making data about women in STEM, particularly in leadership roles, openly available. This transparency is crucial for fostering accountability and driving progress. Additionally, we emphasise the importance of creating a culture where open gender data is utilised for evidence-based policy and decision-making, particularly at local and regional levels where context-specific solutions are often needed. To facilitate this, we recommend developing user-friendly and culturally sensitive open data and open science platforms and tools that make gender data accessible and actionable. Lastly, we stress the need to support and integrate open data platforms, such as the ELLAS platform, to ensure long-term sustainability and effectiveness. By implementing these recommendations, we aim to create a robust infrastructure that enhances data availability and drives meaningful and sustained improvements in gender equality within STEM fields.

Looking ahead, our future work will focus on broadening the impact and utility of the ELLAS platform. We plan to socialise the use of the open gender data platform with diverse audiences, ensuring that a wide range of stakeholders can leverage its resources. To enhance the reliability and applicability of our data collection efforts, we aim to validate the survey data via statistical analysis to formalise it as a replicable tool for gathering gender data on women's leadership in STEM. We will also develop comprehensive documentation and protocols to guide users in utilising the ELLAS platform and its data for evidence-based policy and decision-making via use cases. Additionally, we are committed to ensuring the scalability of the ELLAS data warehouse, expanding its capacity to include new primary and secondary datasets from other Latin American and Caribbean countries, as well as from other countries in the Global South. To secure the platform's long-term viability, we will build pathways towards sustainability by integrating data translation processes and aligning with established national and international open data standards. Through these efforts, we strive to enhance the platform's impact and contribute to the ongoing advancement of gender equality in STEM across the region.

Previous publications are available for those interested in learning more about the ELLAS Network; these publications provide details about the methods, techniques and tools used in different stages of the research process and development of the platform. For example, Maciel et al. (2024), Berardi et al. (2024) and Lima et al. (2023) elaborate on the platform architecture. The conceptual models used to build the survey are available in Drummond et al. (2023) and Guzman et al. (2023a), while the survey itself can be found in Davila et al. (2024), and the information they collected for the platform in other studies is described by Ribeiro et al. (2024), Rondon Pereira et al. (2024), Guzman et al. (2024) and Frigo et al. (2024).

Acknowledgements

We appreciate the financial support of the International Development Research Centre (IDRC) of Canada and the administrative support of the Fundação de Apoio e Desenvolvimento da Universidade Federal de Mato Grosso (UNISELVA). We would also like to thank all individuals who have contributed to the ELLAS project and research network.

About the Authors

Cristiano Maciel is a Professor at the Institute of Computing, Federal University of Mato Grosso (UFMT), Brazil – ELLAS Project General Coordinator.

Indira R. Guzman is a Professor of Computer Information Systems and Director of the Mitchell Hill Center for Digital Innovation, California State Polytechnic University, Pomona, USA – ELLAS Research Consultant.

Karen da Silva Figueiredo Medeiros Ribeiro is a Professor at the Institute of Computing, Federal University of Mato Grosso (UFMT), Brazil – ELLAS Research Consultant at UFMT.

Franci Suni-Lopez is a Professor at the Laboratorio de Inteligencia Artificial, Universidad de Lima, Perú – ELLAS Research Consultant at ULima.

Luciana B. Frigo is a Professor at the Knowledge Engineer Department, Federal University of Santa Catarina (UFSC), Brazil – ELLAS Local Manager at UFSC.

Luciana Salgado is a Professor at the Institute of Computing, Fluminense Federal University (UFF), Brazil – ELLAS Local Manager at UFF.

Rita Cristina Galarraga Berardi is a Professor at Federal University of Technology – Paraná (UTFPR), Brazil – ELLAS Local Manager at UTFPR.

Sílvia Amélia Bim is a Professor at the Academic Department of Informatics, Federal University of Technology – Paraná (UTFPR), Brazil – ELLAS Local Leader at UTFPR.

Boris Branisa is a Professor at the School of Production and Competitiveness (ePC), Universidad Católica Boliviana (UCB) "San Pablo", Bolivia – ELLAS Local Manager at UCB.

Elizabeth Jimenez is a Professor at the Centre for Multidisciplinary Development Studies (CIDES), Universidad Mayor de San Andres (UMSA), Bolivia – ELLAS Local Manager at UMSA.

Luana Bulgarelli Mendes is the ELLAS Project Manager, Foundation for Support and Development of the Federal University of Mato Grosso (UNISELVA), Brazil.

References

Arndt, G. J., Gonçalves, M. B., Miguel, R. D. B. P., & Frigo, L. B. (2023). Mulheres em STEM: Produções acadêmicas no contexto brasileiro. *Interfases*, (018), 133–148. https://revistas.ulima.edu.pe/index.php/Interfases/article/view/6615

Babbie, E. R. (2020). *The practice of social research* (15th ed.). Cengage. https://books.google.co.za/books?hl=en&lr=&id=lFvjDwAAQBAJ&oi=fnd&pg=PP1&ots=I4yT4z2UOb&sig=-s0uh_z0KSefdHyjky-VOmXeKonU&redir_esc=y#v=onepage&q&f=false

Bardzell, S. (2010). Feminist HCI: Taking stock and outlining an agenda for design. In *CHI '10: Proceedings of the SIGCHI conference on human factors in computing systems* (pp. 1301–1310). Association for Computing Machinery. https://doi.org/10.1145/1753326.1753521

Bardzell, S., & Bardzell, J. (2011). Towards a feminist HCI methodology: Social science, feminism, and HCI. In *CHI '11: Proceedings of the SIGCHI conference on human factors in computing systems* (pp. 675–684). Association of Computer Machinery. https://doi.org/10.1145/1978942.1979041

Bellini, R., Meissner, J., Mitchell Finnigan, S., & Strohmayer, A. (2022). Feminist human-computer interaction: Struggles for past, contemporary and futuristic feminist theories in digital innovation. *Feminist Theory*, 23(2), 143–149. https://doi.org/10.1177/14647001221082291

Berardi, R. C. G., Auceli, P. H. S., Maciel, C., Davila, G., Guzman, I. R., & Mendes, L. (2024). ELLAS architecture and process: Collecting and curating data on women's presence in STEM. *Journal on Interactive Systems*, 15(1), 530–540. https://journals-sol.sbc.org.br/index.php/jis/article/view/3853

Berners-Lee, T. (2006, July 27). Linked data [Blog post]. *W3C*. https://www.w3.org/DesignIssues/LinkedData.html

Branisa, B., Cabero, P., & Guzmán, I. (2020). *¿Por qué tan pocas mujeres en Bolivia optan por carreras universitarias relacionadas con STEM (Ciencia, Tecnología, Ingeniería y Matemáticas) y qué podemos hacer para cambiar esta situación?* SDSN Bolivia. https://www.sdsnbolivia.org/wp-content/uploads/2020/10/10-Estudio-Transversal-Por-que-tan-pocas-mujeres-optan-por-carreras-universitarias-relacionadas-con-STEM-en-Bolivia-y-que-podemos-hacer-para-cambiar-esta-situacion.pdf

Brasscom. (2022). Relatório de Diversidade no Setor TIC. https://brasscom.org.br/wp-content/uploads/2024/03/BRI2-2023-013-Diversidade-v18-1.pdf

Carvalho, L. P., Bim, S. A., Santoro, F. M., & Oliveira, J. (2023). A critical analysis on Brazilian computational scientific events linguistic aspects. In *IHC '23: Proceedings of the XXII Brazilian symposium on human factors in computing systems* (pp. 1–11). Association of Computing Machinery. https://doi.org/10.1145/3638067.3638125

Davila, G. A., Guzman, I. R., Rodriguez, N., Frigo, L., Bim, S. A., & Maciel, C. (2024, June). *Development of a survey instrument for assessing the gender gap in STEM* [Paper presentation]. Paper presented at the 19th Iberian Conference on Information Systems and Technologies (CISTI), University of Salamanca, Salamanca, Spain.

de Arruda Nunes, A. C., Moro, F. F., Frigo, L. B., Miguel, R. d. B., & Bim, S. A., (2024). Mapeamento de iniciativas Brasileiras em STEM no Instagram: Uma discussão metodológica. In *XVI Congress of Latin American women in computing 2024 (LAWCC/CLEI)* (pp. 75–86). https://ceur-ws.org/Vol-3872/paper7.pdf

Drummond, B. M., Cardoso de Castro Salgado, L., &Viterbo Filho, J. (2024). From barriers to inclusion: A female-inclusive assessment framework for interface evaluation. In *Anais do XV Workshop sobre aspectos da interação humano-computador na web social* (pp. 37–44). Sociedade Brasileira de Computação. https://sol.sbc.org.br/index.php/waihcws/article/view/32172

Drummond, B., Salgado, L., Avelino, M., Viterbo Filho, J., Ribeiro, K., Cigüeñas, M., Dávila, G., & Branisa, B. (2023). Mapping contextual aspects that influence women in computing in Latin America. *Interfases*, (018), 19–30. https://revistas.ulima.edu.pe/index.php/Interfases/article/view/6610/6663

ELLAS. (n.d.). *Equality in Leadership for Latin America STEM* [Website]. ELLAS. https://ellas.ufmt.br/

Frigo, L. B., Ferreira dos Santos, A., Rodriguez-Rodriguez, N., de Barros Pinto Miguel, R., Bim, S. A., Maciel, C., & Guzman, I. R. (2024). Mapping women STEM initiatives in Latin American Countries: Bolivia, Brazil and Peru. In Á. Rocha, C. Ferrás, J. Hochstetter Diez & M. Diéguez Rebolledo (Eds.), *Information technology and systems. ICITS 2024*, *933*(1), 401–409. Springer.

García-Holgado, A., & García-Peñalvo, F. J. (2022). A model for bridging the gender gap in STEM in higher education institutions. In *Women in STEM in higher education: Good practices of attraction, access and retainment in higher education* (pp. 1–19). Springer.

Gonçalves, M. B., Arndt, G. J., Miguel, R. de B. P., & Frigo, L. B. (2023). "El lugar de una mujer está en la tecnología": Un análisis de perfiles eños de Instagram sobre mujeres en tecnología. *Interfases*, (018), 159–167. https://revistas.ulima.edu.pe/index.php/Interfases/article/view/6617

Guzman, I., Berardi, R., Maciel, C., Cabero Tapia, P., Marin-Raventos, G., Rodriguez, N., & Rodriguez, M. (2020). Gender gap in IT in Latin America. *AMCIS 2020 Proceedings*. 4. https://aisel.aisnet.org/amcis2020/panels/panels/4

Guzman, I. R., Sánchez, A., Gonzales Lopez, R. (2023a). Motivation to lead of IT professionals: The role of IT occupational culture, commitment, and gender equality policies in Latin America. *AMCIS 2023 Proceedings*. 2. https://aisel.aisnet.org/amcis2023/lacais/lacais/2

Guzman, I. R., Viterbo, J., dos Santos Nunes, E. P., Suni-Lopez, F., Jimenez, E., & Casagrande, A. L. (2023b). Gender equality policies in STEM in Latin America – The use of gray and systematic literature searches. *SIGMIS-CPR '23: Proceedings of the 2023 computers and people research conference* (Article 21, pp. 1–2). Association for Computing Machinery. https://doi.org/10.1145/3579168.3632631

Guzman, I. R., Viterbo, J., dos Santos Nunes, E. P., Suni-Lopez, F., Jimenez, E., Casagrande, A. L., & Maciel, C. (2024). Gender equality policies in STEM in Latin America – A systematic literature review. In Á. Rocha, C. Ferrás, J. Hochstetter Diez & M. Diéguez Rebolledo (Eds.), *Information technology and systems. ICITS 2024, 933*(1), 410–419. Springer. https://doi.org/10.1007/978-3-031-54256-5_39

Hildebrand, N. D., Amador, B. O., Maciel, C., & Berardi, R. C. G. (2024, July). A escassez de dados abertos estruturados em Países Latino-Americanos com enfoque de gênero na educação superior. In *Women in information technology* (pp. 161–172). Sociedade Brasileira de Computação (SBC). https://sol.sbc.org.br/index.php/wit/article/view/29561/29364

Keserű, J., & Chan, J. K-S. (2015). *The social impact of open data*. Paper presented at the 3rd International Open Data Conference 2015 (IODC), 28–29 May, Ottawa. https://www.researchgate.net/publication/298646716_The_Social_Impact_of_Open_Data

Lima, P. R. S., Salgado, L. C. de C., & Bim, S. A. (2023). Primer paso en el proyecto para la interacción de una plataforma de datos abiertos con la lente feminista interseccional. *Interfases*, (018), 65–74. https://revistas.ulima.edu.pe/index.php/Interfases/article/view/6605/6667

Lucena, L., Santos, M., Gonçalves, S., & Coutinho, J. (2024). Gênero, parentalidade e remuneração em cargos de desenvolvimento na indústria de software. In *Anais do XVIII Women in information technology* (pp. 24–34). Sociedade Brasileira de Computação (SBC).

Maciel, C., Guzman, I., Berardi, R., Caballero, B. B., Rodriguez, N., Frigo, L., Salgado, L., Rodriguez-Rodriguez, N., Bim, S. A., & Tapia, P. C. (2023). Open data platform to promote gender equality policies in STEM. In *Proceedings of the Western Decision Sciences Institute (WDSI)*. https://ellas.ufmt.br/open-data-platform-to-promote-gender-equality-policies-in-stem/

Maciel, C., Guzman, I. R., Berardi, R. C. G., Rodriguez-Rodriguez, N., Salgado, L., Frigo, L. B., Branisa, B., & Jimenez, E. (2024). An open data platform to advance gender equality in STEM in Latin America. *Communications of the ACM, 67*(8), 90–92. https://doi.org/10.1145/3653294

Oliveira, R., Salgado, L., Bim, S. A. (2024). Desenvolvimento de uma plataforma de dados abertos a partir do design sensível ao gênero. In *Anais do XV workshop sobre aspectos da interação humano-computador para a web social (WAIHCWS)* (pp. 29–36). Sociedade Brasileira de Computação. https://sol.sbc.org.br/index.php/waihcws/article/view/32171

Ribeiro, K., Gomes, J. M., & Aguiar, B. R. (2024). Abertura e disponibilidade de dados de gênero sobre liderança de mulheres Brasileiras em TI. In *AMCIS 2024 Proceedings*. 2. https://aisel.aisnet.org/amcis2024/span_lacais/span_lacais/2/

Rondon Pereira, L. R., Ferreira de Lima, S. D., Maciel, C., & Guzman, I. R. (2024). Equity in focus: A qualitative study of female representation in the context of academic administration and STEM of federal universities in Brazil. *SIGMIS-CPR 2024: Proceedings of ACM computer people research* (pp. 1–8). Association of Computing Machinery. https://doi.org/10.1145/3632634.3655858

Rosales Rodríguez, M. A. (2020). Relación entre la inclusión y el abandono de mujeres jóvenes en carreras y áreas STEM y TIC. *Fides et Ratio-Revista de Difusión Cultural y Científica de la Universidad La Salle en Bolivia, 20*(20), 141–166.

Tull, R., Jangha, S., Medina, Y., Bell, T., & Parker, R. (2018). Sharing peace engineering with US-based minority students, through the UN's Sustainable Development Goals, in Peru. In *2018 World Engineering Education Forum – Global Engineering Deans Council (WEEF-GEDC)* (pp. 1–6). IEEE. https://doi.org/10.1109/WEEF-GEDC.2018.8629764

UNDP (United Nations Development Programme). (2024, May 7). Coded bias: The underrepresentation of women in STEM in Latin America and the Caribbean [Blog post]. *United Nations Development Programme.* https://www.undp.org/latin-america/blog/coded-bias-underrepresentation-women-stem-latin-america-and-caribbean

UNESCO (United Nations Educational, Scientific and Cultural Organization). (2020). *Closing the gender gap in STEM: Drawing more girls and women into Science, Technology, Engineering, and Mathematics* [Programme and meeting document]. UNESCO. https://unesdoc.unesco.org/ark:/48223/pf0000245717?posInSet=1&queryId=ead18c73-9f22-45aa-a7dc-d908b865ebc4

UNESCO. (2024). *UNESCO Call to action: Closing the gender gap in science* [Programme and meeting document]. UNESCO. https://unesdoc.unesco.org/ark:/48223/pf0000388641

World Bank Group. (2024). *Gender Data Portal: Gender data availability*. https://genderdata.worldbank.org/en/data-availability

Gender-Lensed Supervision and Mentorship Framework for STEM Postgraduate Training in East Africa: Processes, Experiences and Lessons Learned

Florah Karimi, Leah Mwangi and Hesborn Wao

Introduction

The sub-Saharan Africa (SSA) region continues to lag behind other regions in its efforts to meet global development goals. Of great concern is the low percentage of research outputs (1%) coming from SSA (World Bank Group, 2014) and the small number of research scientists (1.1%) (Okeke et al., 2017) from the region compared to other parts of the world, despite the region accounting for approximately 15% of the global population (Marincola & Kariuki, 2020). Furthermore, the percentage of women research scientists in the region remains low, at 30% (Huyer, 2015) and of these women, few hold leadership positions. In fact, women academics in Science, Technology, Engineering and Mathematics (STEM) account for only 31% of all leadership positions (Kimani-Murage, 2022) in SSA, and only 2.5% of universities in the SSA region are led by female vice-chancellors (Lirri, 2019). These statistics elicit concern and highlight the need to investigate whether the voices and perspectives of women are adequately being captured at decision-making tables in SSA.

To ensure gender equality in representation, particularly in leadership roles, and to promote effective and inclusive participation in socio-economic development, decision-making and policy direction in SSA, strengthening the capacity of African researchers and development practitioners, including women, is critical (Mpoke-Bigg, 2019; Poltera, 2019). The underrepresentation of women in these spaces limits the diversity of perspectives that inform research and policymaking in Africa, often resulting in development agendas that do not fully reflect the needs and experiences of all populations. Understanding the structural, cultural and institutional factors that contribute to this under-representation is therefore essential, as is examining how women's voices are captured and interpreted in research and decision-making processes. By increasing both the quantity and quality of women's participation, particularly through targeted support for their academic and professional development, countries can benefit from more inclusive, contextually relevant and sustainable solutions. Investment in high-quality and equitable postgraduate training is one way to build capacity, as it equips women with the skills, credentials and networks needed to contribute meaningfully to research and leadership. In particular, supporting women's participation in STEM postgraduate programmes is vital, given the growing importance of STEM in addressing development challenges. Such investments not only help close gender gaps in critical sectors but also strengthen the overall research ecosystem, enabling SSA to make progress towards achieving the Sustainable Development Goals (SDGs) (De Jongh et al., 2023; Dugbazah et al., 2022; Igumbor et al., 2020; Maier, 2007; McCowan, 2016).

Initiatives on women in STEM postgraduate training in SSA: The APHRC's efforts

The African Population and Health Research Center (APHRC)[1] is a premier research-to-policy institution that generates evidence, strengthens research and related capacity in the African research and development (R&D) ecosystem, and engages policy to inform action on health and development. The Center seeks to drive change by developing strong African research leadership and promoting evidence-informed decision-making across SSA. Consequently, APHRC engages with policymakers to influence policy decisions and tackle development challenges in SSA. Its profile has significantly grown over the past 20 years, and its reputation has become synonymous with research rigour,

---

1 https://aphrc.org/

leadership, influence and capacity strengthening of individuals, institutions and the research and development (R&D) ecosystems in SSA.

APHRC has led and implemented several initiatives that seek to strengthen the capacity of postgraduate training for women in STEM in SSA. The Consortium for Advanced Research Training in Africa (CARTA),[2] one of APHRC's flagship programmes, includes a gender position that addresses gender-related barriers for early-career researchers pursuing doctoral degree training. The CARTA Gender Position[3] highlights the importance of gender equality for development, taking cognisance of the distinct differences in the exposure and experiences of men and women within the African context. Tracking of CARTA sex-disaggregated data illustrated that within the programme, women made up 56% of its 245 early-career researchers as of 2024. APHRC is well positioned to provide insight on gender perspectives that relate to postgraduate training, research and leadership in SSA.

In 2020, APHRC, in collaboration with the Inter-University Council of East Africa (IUCEA),[4] embarked on a study to examine the participation and experiences of women in postgraduate training in STEM programmes in universities in East Africa. The two institutions have previously led joint initiatives with universities in the region that resulted in the development of *Standards and guidelines for postgraduate studies in East Africa* (IUCEA, 2018) with the aim of standardising and improving the quality of doctoral supervision across the East African region. A review of these standards revealed the lack of a gender lens and inadequate focus on supervision and mentorship in the document. This necessitated the establishment of gender-related parameters that would further strengthen postgraduate training in East Africa. Consequently, a three-year study was conducted to examine the participation and experiences of women in postgraduate training in STEM programmes in universities in East Africa. The study also emphasised supervision and mentorship parameters that contributed to women's participation in STEM postgraduate training with the aim of developing related strategies and a framework that would optimise their experience within the region.

Highlights of the study

In the collaborative study between APHRC and IUCEA, we employed a descriptive approach to examine the participation and experiences of women in

---

2 https://cartafrica.org/
3 https://cartafrica.org/carta-gender-position/
4 https://www.iucea.org/

postgraduate training in STEM programmes in universities in East Africa. Participants were drawn from five East African countries – Burundi, Kenya, Rwanda, Tanzania and Uganda. Data were drawn from:

- An online survey administered to 711 respondents, including students, faculty members and research leaders across the five East African countries;
- Five targeted in-person focus group discussions, each with an average of 11 women discussants (senior lecturers and research leaders and postgraduate supervisors, mentors and students) drawn from each of the five East African countries respectively;
- Semi-structured interviews with 66 participants, including senior researchers, research leaders and postgraduate students.

Our analysis, according to the *Supervision and mentorship of women in science, technology, engineering and mathematics' postgraduate programmes in sub-Saharan Africa: Final technical report of 2025* (APHRC, 2025), revealed the existence of significant gender disparities in the enrolment and graduation of women in STEM master's and doctoral degree programmes in favour of men across the various East African countries during the period 2011 to 2020. Although the number of women represented in postgraduate training increased yearly during this period, women accounted for a significantly smaller proportion of postgraduate students than men in both STEM enrolment and graduation phases. This shows that the underrepresentation of women in STEM postgraduate training, coupled with its effect on women's contributions to research, leadership and decision-making, continues to remain a concern in the African region (Christoplos et al., 2015).

Several individual, institutional and systemic factors were reported to have contributed to gender equality in STEM postgraduate programmes in East Africa. Of interest was the critical role that supervision and mentorship played in promoting quality postgraduate training for women in STEM in East Africa, taking cognisance of similar perspectives held globally (Igumbor et al., 2020; Lindahl et al., 2021; Okeke-Uzodike, 2021; Somefun & Adebayo, 2020; Wu et al., 2024). The report illustrated the need for greater intentionality in strengthening the capacity of supervision and mentorship to guide women towards quality postgraduate experiences in their postgraduate training and leadership and into the future.

According to the report, efforts had been made within the East African region to address gender diversity, equity and inclusivity in identified policy documents. However, the policies and related practices lacked a focus on strengthening supervision and mentorship in universities in East Africa (see Chapter 3 for a broader discussion of gender policies in universities across Africa). Only 6% of postgraduate policy documents obtained from the various universities in East Africa mentioned the provision of technical support to complement the supervisory experience, while only 17% of them recognised the need for formal training of mentors and supervisors as best practice, thus demonstrating the dire need for greater emphasis on supervision and mentorship in both policy and practice.

Similar to other reports (Saleem & Mahmood, 2023), this report emphasised the critical role played by effective supervision and mentorship in enhancing women's experiences and participation in postgraduate training and their academic and professional development. However, supervision and mentorship continued to remain a challenge in postgraduate training.

According to the report, having a supervisor who was well aligned with one's research area and sensitive to socio-economic, cultural and gender challenges provided students with a highly supportive environment. Supervisors who were proactive and offered scientific guidance, emotional support and accommodation were also seen as particularly beneficial. For example, women appreciated supervisors who were understanding during pregnancy. Such empathetic support fostered strong relationships and was instrumental in enabling women to navigate challenges and succeed in their research work and postgraduate training, despite the challenges of motherhood. Additionally, effective policies and leadership were considered helpful in ensuring that the students were accountable and that they met set deadlines.

Despite the positive gains associated with effective supervision, some women reported negative experiences. Sexual harassment, a lack of alignment between the supervisee and the supervisor, and intermittent or delayed feedback and guidance were among the factors that most negatively affected women's experiences. Further, supervisors who failed to be sensitive to gender differences contributed to unsupportive and discriminatory academic environments, adversely affecting the supervision process, progress and well-being of women. Similar perspectives have been documented by previous researchers who have identified power dynamics and related gender and intersectionality aspects as barriers to effective supervision and research (Wisker & Fossland, 2023).

The report further highlighted several positive aspects of mentorship that significantly contributed to women's success. Strong interpersonal connections, supportive relationships, regular feedback, counselling and motivation were found to be great contributors to positive mentorship experiences for women.

Moreover, strong mentorship that focused on personal and professional development (including skills development) was critical to women's progress in postgraduate training.

Additionally, the report illustrated that effective mentors were those who fostered trust and collaboration, providing both professional guidance and personal encouragement. Constructive feedback and iterative improvements facilitated by mentors contributed to the mentee's academic proficiency and publication quality. Moreover, the benefits of effective mentorship extend beyond academic success. Mentors who motivated and guided their mentees significantly influenced their career trajectories, helping them progress from junior to senior academic positions. This continued support and inspiration highlighted the long-term impact of mentorship. These views aligned with those in other studies that highlight the role of mentorship in strengthening mentees' academic performance, intrapersonal and interpersonal skills, and professionalism (Deb et al., 2022). In general, mentors who actively promoted STEM education, especially for women, and provided personalised encouragement played a crucial role in fostering diversity and inclusion in these postgraduate training programmes. Mentors who emphasised values such as responsibility, integrity, compassion and excellence were also found to significantly contribute to the mentee's professional and personal growth. Accordingly, mentors who engaged in activities such as monthly group meetings (especially for underrepresented groups), addressed specific issues (including gender disparities) and provided valuable resources for their support were most helpful. This form of mentorship supported career development and fostered a community of practice among early-career professionals. These observations are consistent with existing literature (Deb et al., 2022; Hill et al., 2022) that emphasises the benefits of mentorship in providing personal and emotional support, alongside networking opportunities.

There were also some negative mentorship experiences that were highlighted in the report. They included misalignment between the mentors' and mentees' expectations, lack of sufficient engagement, commitment and support and inadequate time investment from the mentors, all of which can lead to missed opportunities for professional growth among mentees. More comprehensive details of the study can be found in the report.

Towards developing the gender-lensed SMF

In this chapter, we seek to highlight the journey towards the development of the gender-lensed Supervision and Mentorship Framework (SMF) for STEM

- Researchers based in regional African research organisations with a focus on STEM;
- Managers, administrators and coordinators of postgraduate training programmes;
- National commissions for higher education and research agency officials.

The purpose of the study was to examine the participation and experiences of women in STEM postgraduate training programmes and careers in East African countries, and to specifically provide evidence on the status of gender equality in STEM-related postgraduate training and careers in East Africa; and the factors that contribute to participation of women in STEM-related post-graduate training and careers in East Africa.

The study was descriptive in nature and utilised a mixed-methods design that included document analysis, scoping review, and qualitative and quantitative analyses based on information received from online surveys, key informant interviews (KIIs) and focus group discussions (FGDs)

Stakeholder engagements

We engaged in-country and regional stakeholders throughout the project, particularly between 2021 and 2024. The purpose of stakeholder engagements was to create awareness of the project, seek greater buy-in and commitment to the project and co-create various strategies for the project (see Chapter 11 for an alternative stakeholder engagement approach). More specifically, we held a total of nine stakeholder engagements that comprised: two regional inception meetings; five in-country validation workshops; one regional co-creation workshop in 2024; and one regional dissemination workshop in 2024.

Regional inception meetings

We held two virtual regional inception meetings in 2021 – one in February and the other in June. A total of 62 (68% women) key stakeholders drawn from East Africa participated in the meetings. They included vice-chancellors, deputy vice-chancellors, registrars, directors and deans of research and postgraduate studies, research scientists, doctoral and post-doctoral students, quality assurance directors, senior researchers, staff and faculty members (all drawn from universities associated with IUCEA) and relevant government ministry and agency officials. The aim of the inception meetings was twofold – to create awareness on the project and its related implementation plan; and to brainstorm and co-create the project study questions on the participation and quality of experiences of women in STEM postgraduate training programmes and careers in East Africa. The agenda of the regional inception virtual meetings included:

- An overview of the project;
- Discussions, in breakout sessions, on the participation and quality of women's experiences in STEM postgraduate training programmes and careers in East Africa;
- Brainstorming and validation of the objectives and research questions – in breakout sessions;
- Presentation of the implementation plan and way forward for the project.

In-country validation workshops

It is worth noting that the results of the study were validated through in-country stakeholder workshops within each of the five countries and a regional co-creation workshop in East Africa. These processes ensured ownership by the various stakeholders to foster further deliberations and capture additional insights for supervision and mentorship of women in STEM postgraduate training in East Africa. Upon completion of the project study on examining the participation and experiences of women in postgraduate training in STEM programmes in universities in East Africa, we held face-to-face validation workshops in each of the five countries (see Table 2).

Table 2: Description of validation workshop participants per country

Country	Participants
Rwanda	33 (68% women) key stakeholders including faculty members, registrars, researchers, postgraduate students, ministry officials and representatives from APHRC and IUCEA
Burundi	33 (61% women) key stakeholders including the Permanent Executive Secretary of the National Commission of Science, Technology and Innovation, faculty from various universities, researchers and representatives from APHRC and IUCEA
Uganda	31 (52% women) key stakeholders including officials from the Ministry of Education and Ministry of Agriculture and Innovation, faculty members from various universities and representatives from APHRC and IUCEA
Tanzania	34 (59% women) key stakeholders including a representative of the Commission for Science and Technology, university members and representatives from APHRC and IUCEA
Kenya	37 (65% women) key stakeholders including faculty members from universities in Kenya, researchers, postgraduate students, ministry officials and representatives from APHRC and IUCEA

The aim of the workshops was to validate the data collected from the respective countries, increase their ownership, and jointly brainstorm and co-design supervision and mentorship strategies applicable to each country, based on the study results. The validation workshops entailed: the presentation of preliminary in-country findings from the study; discussions on the key study findings and formulation of relevant recommendations; and discussions on possible strategies towards optimising supervision and mentorship within East Africa.

Regional co-creation engagement

We convened a regional collaborative co-creation workshop in Kenya in August 2024 to co-create a comprehensive framework for gender-responsive supervision and mentorship in STEM postgraduate training for East Africa, based on the findings of the project study and recommendations from the in-country validation workshops. The workshop consisted of 60 (52% women) key stakeholders drawn from the East African region, including directors and vice-chancellors of institutions offering STEM postgraduate training programmes, government representatives in higher education and research, faculty leaders, STEM postgraduate students and representatives of research regulatory bodies across East Africa. Through the two-day co-creation workshop, we provided the basis for adoption of the SMF at the regional level, and specifically:

- Validated the supervision and mentorship strategies that were co-designed at the country levels;
- Co-created the regional gender-lensed SMF for optimum postgraduate training in East Africa;
- Sought greater buy-in, commitment and assurance to strengthen supervision and mentorship in the region.

We provided the participants with an overview of the project and presented them with the project milestones and results and feedback from the in-country validation meetings, including areas of commonality and divergence. The participants further co-created the SMF template, in randomly designated groups, and identified the key elements of the framework, feeding into each group's templates and enriching them. In addition, country teams discussed the co-created elements of the SMF, seeking to define country-specific actionable steps, including roadmaps and related roles and responsibilities.

Dissemination workshop

Following the approval of the SMF by the East African Community (EAC), through the IUCEA, we convened a virtual regional dissemination workshop in November 2024. The virtual workshop comprised 150 key stakeholders from the East African region. They included directors and vice-chancellors of institutions offering STEM postgraduate training programmes, government representatives in higher education and research, faculty leaders, STEM postgraduate students and representatives from research regulatory bodies across East Africa. The purpose of the dissemination workshop was mainly to create awareness of the approved SMF, for greater buy-in and adaptation in postgraduate training in the East African region and at the regional, national and institutional levels. During the virtual workshop, we gave the participants an overview of the entire project, engaged them in the various components of the approved SMF and led them in discussions on the next steps towards its implementation, including its piloting.

Overall, the gains of the stakeholder engagements were threefold:

- Create awareness of the status and experiences of women in STEM postgraduate training in East Africa;
- Solicit buy-in and commitment to the process of promoting gender-lensed supervision and mentorship within the region;
- Co-create the gender-lensed strategies and framework for the promotion of supervision and mentorship in postgraduate training in East Africa, based on the obtained data.

Extensive consultations were carried out with the key stakeholders to determine the supervision- and mentorship-related strategies that would promote the participation of women in postgraduate training to co-create a comprehensive gender-lensed framework tailored to address the unique needs of STEM postgraduate students in this region. This collaborative approach ensured active engagement with the stakeholders, and that the framework was well-rounded, inclusive and aligned with the needs and perspectives of various stakeholders involved in higher education and research in the region (Rădulescu et al., 2023; Vargas et al., 2022). Moreover, the stakeholders considered themselves part and parcel of the process, thus facilitating greater buy-in, ownership and commitment towards the implementation of the framework, in addition to the sustainability of the initiative beyond the project's life (Avila-Garzon & Bacca-Acosta, 2024)

Approval of the regional gender-lensed SMF

Subsequent to the co-creation process, the SMF was refined by a team drawn from APHRC and IUCEA; reviewed and validated by participants in the regional co-creation workshop; officially submitted to the IUCEA management team by the APHRC team; presented by the IUCEA management for approval; and reviewed and approved by the IUCEA Committees in charge of higher education and the EAC in meetings held in Uganda in August 2024. This process was necessary to increase the regional rating and credibility of the SMF as a tool to enhance optimal postgraduate training in East Africa, thus validating its incorporation into the *Standards and guidelines for postgraduate studies in East Africa* (IUCEA, 2018). The approved gender-lensed SMF for postgraduate training in East Africa (IUCEA, 2024) was disseminated to the various stakeholders and uploaded onto the IUCEA website. The final process, which was ongoing at the time of this write-up, was the piloting of the SMF, before its full implementation in the East African region.

Gender-lensed supervision and mentorship strategies and framework

Effective supervision and mentorship are crucial components of STEM postgraduate training (Gangrade et al., 2024; Lindahl et al., 2021; Wu et al., 2024). In East Africa, where the demand for high-quality education and research continues to grow, understanding and implementing desirable supervision and mentorship strategies were considered essential to enhance women's performance in postgraduate training and their future trajectories as researchers and leaders in the region.

Key stakeholders, during the country-specific validation and co-creation workshops, recommended the integration of mentorship with supervision into existing policies, standards and guidelines at the postgraduate level, resulting in the formulation of gender-lensed strategies. They also recommended the establishment of supportive structures and the breaking of gender stereotypes to create a more inclusive and supportive environment for the supervision and mentorship of women in STEM postgraduate training in East Africa. Figure 2 highlights the areas that were identified by stakeholders as critical to both supervision and mentorship in postgraduate training in East Africa.

The stakeholders highlighted the need to ensure that the supervisors and mentors have appropriate attributes for supervision and mentorship, respectively, and to have their respective capacities built, as shown in Figure 2.

Figure 2: Desirable strategies for supervision and mentorship in postgraduate training in East Africa

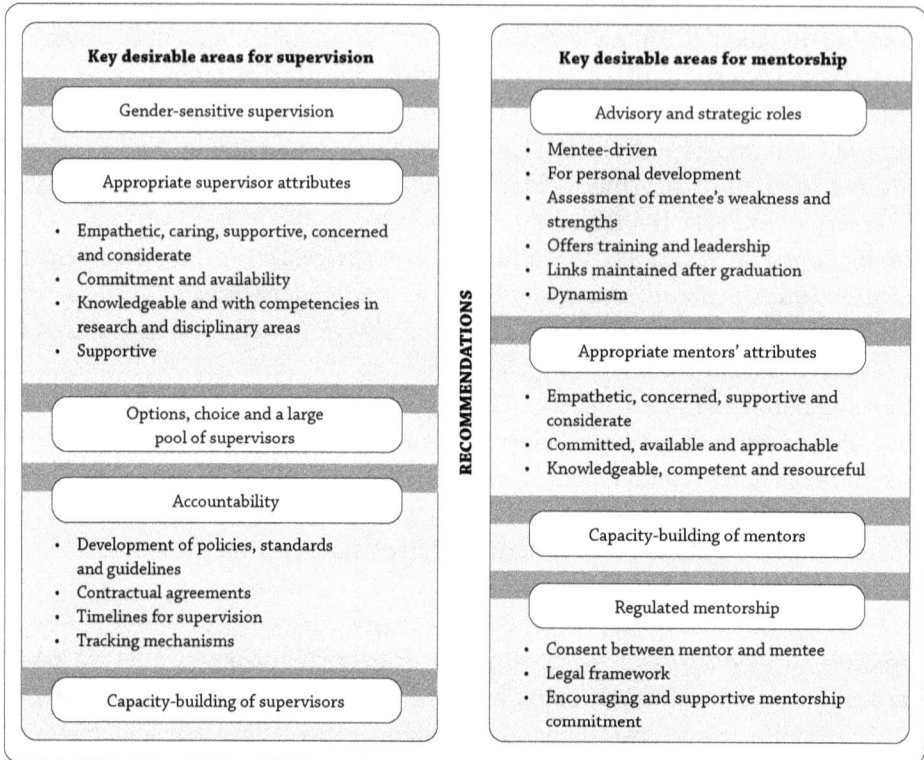

More specifically, the stakeholders considered the following supervision- and mentorship-related strategies as essential in optimising women's participation in STEM postgraduate training in East Africa.

Effective supervision strategies

Supervisors need to be aware of gender differences, issues and inequalities, and to consider them during supervision, recognising how gender roles and responsibilities affect individual students and their academic trajectories, as well as how to address these parities appropriately.

Effective supervision relies on supervisor attributes. These attributes included commitment, availability, empathy, knowledge, competence in research and disciplinary areas, support, care, concern and consideration, as well as the ability to provide constructive feedback. Supervisors who demonstrated a genuine interest in their students' development and created a supportive environment had the potential to significantly impact their academic and professional trajectories. In this respect, supervisors should strengthen their technical expertise and enhance their ability to understand and address the unique challenges faced by supervisees, particularly women.

Considering the *opinion of students* during the allocation of supervisors allows them to have supervisors whose styles of leadership and supervision align with their specific needs and preferences. The freedom to be part of the decision-making process for the selection of their supervisors empowers the supervisees and fosters a sense of autonomy in their educational journey. It also increases the likelihood of the supervisees finding appropriate supervisors who would offer personalised guidance and support, tailored to their individual circumstances.

Facilitation and formalisation of effective supervision relationships through clear *contractual agreements* are necessary. These agreements should be aligned with the expectations, responsibilities and commitments of both the supervisor and supervisee. Such formalised structures would ensure accountability and clarity, preventing misunderstanding and promoting a professional relationship. This facilitation should include the provision of resources and support systems that enable the supervisees to engage in meaningful interactions with their supervisors, including through regular meetings, workshops and access to professional development opportunities.

Accountability mechanisms, including peer reviews, feedback surveys and performance assessments, are vital to maintaining the integrity and effectiveness of the supervision process. Consequently, regular evaluation and feedback loops should be made available at the various institutional levels to ensure that supervisors and supervisees uphold high standards of conduct and respond to the needs of the latter.

Comprehensive *training programmes for supervisors* should be availed. Such training programmes would equip supervisors with the skills and knowledge required to support students effectively, including understanding gender dynamics, fostering inclusive environments and employing effective communication strategies. The training programmes would also ensure that supervisors are well-prepared to address the diverse needs of their supervisees.

Robust policies that lead to the institutionalisation of gender-sensitive supervision should be developed and implemented at various institutional levels to support postgraduate training in East Africa. These policies should address parameters that promote equal access to opportunities, anti-harassment measures and work–life balance, among other aspects. *Tracking mechanisms*, such as progress monitoring and data collection on supervision outcomes, should also be instituted to evaluate the effectiveness of these policies. These mechanisms would provide insight into the impact of supervision and highlight areas for improvement, ensuring continuous enhancement of practices.

Timeliness in supervision is a critical factor in effective supervision. Supervisors should be available and responsive, providing timely feedback and support to their supervisees. This responsiveness would enable students to stay on track with their academic and professional goals, addressing challenges as they arise and maintaining momentum in their development. Institutions needed to emphasise the importance of timely supervision and provide structures that facilitate regular and consistent supervisor–supervisee interactions.

Effective mentorship strategies

With respect to mentorship, the stakeholders considered the mentor's role as a *strategic advisory* one that needed to be *mentee-driven* and that would enhance the mentee's personal development. According to Figure 2, mentors needed to exhibit the following *attributes* that were considered appropriate for an effective mentorship process – *empathetic, supportive, considerate, committed, available, approachable, knowledgeable, competent and resourceful*.

Several other effective mentorship strategies were identified, including the *provision of a supportive and gender-sensitive mentorship environment; mentors making practical adjustments to accommodate personal responsibilities; and encouragement of women to mentor other women*, while recognising that effective mentorship can be influenced by either gender. Other effective mentorship strategies included *advisory and strategic support from mentors* and *aligning guidance with the mentee's goals and needs*. Consequently, the mentors needed to have *relevant experience and a willingness to adapt their approach to the mentee's evolving requirements*.

The stakeholders emphasised the *value of mentors who guide their mentees towards leadership roles and provide access to resources*. This support involved not only aiding academic progress but also facilitating networking opportunities and leadership development. *Maintaining a strong, approachable relationship* also emerged as an essential strategy in mentorship (Hill et al., 2022). Ensuring *mentorship extended beyond academic training* to include long-term career guidance and support was also crucial for the sustained success of the mentee. Another strategy that was recommended was the *regulation of mentorship in postgraduate training* in East Africa, as depicted in Figure 2. This would entail the provision of a legal mentorship framework that would enhance the commitment of both the mentor and the mentee to the mentorship process.

Co-creation of the gender-lensed SMF

Based on the identified strategies, the stakeholders co-created a framework for the optimal implementation of the gender-lensed supervision and mentorship strategies for strengthening women's participation in STEM postgraduate training in East Africa. The stakeholders underscored the importance of four key components to ensure the effectiveness and inclusivity of the gender-lensed SMF for postgraduate training in East Africa, which is accessible on the IUCEA website. The four key components of the framework are summarised below and include (1) execution and management; (2) stakeholder engagement; (3) capacity strengthening initiatives and governance control; and (4) assurance and enhancement. All of which were applied to the institutional, national and regional levels to ensure comprehensive and tailored implementation across different contexts. Together, these efforts would create a supportive and equitable framework for gender-lensed supervision and mentorship in STEM postgraduate training in East Africa.

Execution and management

Comprehensive planning, which includes setting strategic goals, conducting needs assessments and integrating gender equity into institutional policies, is necessary in the execution and management of the supervision and mentorship framework. Moreover, the planning process needs to be aligned with institutional, national and regional strategic objectives. There is a need for adequate resourcing, which includes equitable allocation of funding, equipment and opportunities, alongside recruitment and strengthening the capacity of staff members who are committed to gender-sensitive practices. This would maintain operational effectiveness in the execution and management of the gender-lensed framework.

Developing and maintaining efficient systems and organisational structures, alongside cultivating a culture of excellence and instilling core values, is necessary to reinforce positive behaviours and ethical standards. An appropriate culture and values that foster inclusive academic environments, diversity and gender equity need to be cultivated at institutional, national and regional levels. In addition, leaders need to model these values for the greater effective execution of the framework. It is also necessary that the various levels of institutions implement robust motivation and performance management systems to drive excellence and achieve high levels of staff engagement and productivity while executing the gender-lensed supervision and mentorship framework. This includes setting achievable goals, recognising achievements and providing incentives for engagement.

Stakeholder engagement

There is a need for thorough stakeholder mapping and engagement to identify and involve key players, ensuring diverse perspectives are included in supervision and mentorship decision-making processes. Effective communication is needed to build trust and facilitate collaboration. Moreover, participation from a broad range of stakeholders is crucial for robust outcomes to be achieved in supervision and mentorship in STEM postgraduate training in East Africa.

Capacity strengthening initiatives

Capacity strengthening for effective supervision and mentorship is crucial to maintaining high standards and encouraging innovation (Igumbor et al., 2020). Moreover, institutions need to enhance the mentorship and supervision capacities of their staff members and researchers by offering regular training opportunities. Equally important are peer learning initiatives that foster knowledge-sharing and collaborative growth, allowing individuals to learn from one another's experiences and expertise. These efforts not only enhance individual competencies but also facilitate the building of a more cohesive and capable institutional workforce, while promoting gender equity and cultivating quality research. Training and peer learning also prepare the institutions to address complex challenges and achieve their strategic goals for supervision and mentorship.

Governance control, assurance and enhancement

There is a need for effective governance controls at the institutional, national and regional levels to maintain high standards in research and institutional operations with respect to gender-lensed supervision and mentorship. Comprehensive gender-lensed policies that provide clear guidelines and expectations for effective and inclusive supervision and mentorship need to be developed, and aligned with regional, national and institutional visions, missions, goals and regulatory requirements. Continuous monitoring and evaluation need to be prioritised, tracking progress, ensuring compliance and identifying areas for improvement in the gender-lensed SMF. Moreover, mechanisms need to be instituted to effectively monitor and evaluate performance using clear and fair criteria and provide regular feedback to the various stakeholders on gender-related disparities. Robust gender-lensed supervision and mentorship risk assessment and management strategies also need to be employed at the various institutional levels to identify potential threats and develop proactive measures to mitigate them, safeguarding diversity, equity and inclusivity parameters, institutional interests and operational continuity.

Lessons learned

The development of the gender-lensed SMF (IUCEA, 2024) for STEM postgraduate training in East Africa was a success and culminated in its regional adoption. We highlight the lessons learned in its development in this section.

Despite having the backing of IUCEA, we still experienced university and national-level bureaucratic hurdles during the data collection, specifically in obtaining relevant approvals at the two levels. This affected our survey distribution and delayed the collection of data in specific universities and countries. We therefore underscore the importance of proactive planning, robust communication channels and building strong local partnerships to mitigate delays during the data collection phases of such multi-country and multi-institutional projects. By anticipating such potential challenges and establishing clear communication pathways, project teams can align themselves accordingly and prepare to promptly address related concerns. This approach not only enhances efficiency but also reduces the risk of setbacks that could impede progress.

Project teams should be agile, flexible and adaptable to methodological changes that are geared towards addressing unexpected obstacles during the phases. The ability to adjust plans and methodologies in response to unforeseen challenges allows project teams to navigate challenges effectively and maintain the integrity of their work. Project teams should therefore be adaptable to approaches that seek to accommodate varying national regulatory frameworks and operational constraints across different countries, enhance proactive planning for contingencies and embrace robust communication channels when necessary. By embracing flexibility, teams can mitigate delays in project development and implementation, uphold ethical standards and optimise effective resource utilisation.

Leveraging our existing regional partnership with IUCEA and in-country collaborations facilitated connections with other institutions, enabling the project to progress, amidst COVID-19 pandemic restrictions. The in-country collaborators also facilitated team set-up, data collection and research approvals, thereby enhancing the validity and applicability of research findings in diverse contexts. We recommend that future project teams foster collaborative relationships and leverage local expertise to enhance the validity and applicability of project outcomes from diverse contexts. Further, we recommend that project teams seek to establish and leverage strong local and strategic networks, equitable partnerships and collaboration with regional and national authorities and conveners, such as IUCEA, to facilitate access to member universities. These networks and partnerships would also provide support, local expertise and shared resources, knowledge and good practices, thereby facilitating more efficient and effective project processes and sustainability of initiatives (Horan, 2022). Enhanced collaboration also promotes the dissemination, validation and adoption of project results and supports the development of innovative solutions.

Our engagements with the in-country collaborators provided invaluable perspectives on the nuances of implementing multi-country studies amidst the backdrop of the pandemic, and on diverse research system dynamics and contextual factors influencing research practices and outcomes. Project teams should seek to establish strong partnerships with in-country entities that can provide invaluable support and expertise, and who can facilitate the successful implementation of multi-country projects. Local in-country expertise and support are particularly critical during challenging circumstances, as they provide essential advice, insights and coordination of all required resources. Based on our partnership and collaboration interactions at regional and country-specific levels, we further underscore the significance of a future comparative study to identify similarities, differences and best practices across different research environments.

The in-country validation and regional co-creation workshops provided critical inputs for developing a comprehensive gender-lensed framework for supervision and mentorship in postgraduate STEM programmes. This collaborative approach ensured that the results were grounded in the real-world experiences and needs of stakeholders, supporting the development of actionable strategies to enhance gender equality in STEM. The stakeholder engagements fostered a collaborative environment where expectations were clearly defined, and everyone was committed to the research objectives. This alignment was crucial for the smooth execution of project activities, follow-up and the successful dissemination of results. Project teams should employ strategies that promote clear communication and regular meetings with relevant stakeholders to ensure buy-in, commitment and alignment in working methodologies.

The SMF for postgraduate training in East Africa has been adopted at the regional level and needs to be cascaded to national and institutional levels in the region. The process of piloting the framework at a small scale would further validate the SMF, giving way to its full-scale adaptation within the East African region. We present the framework and recommend that other African regions adopt and adapt it to strengthen supervision and mentorship, and ultimately, the participation of women in STEM postgraduate training in SSA. We further recommend that similar projects be carried out in other African regions to provide a more comprehensive picture of STEM postgraduate training in the region, leveraging approaches, experiences and lessons learned in the East African scenario. Moreover, we recommend that regional teams carrying out similar projects establish and nurture strong partnerships and collaborations with local stakeholders, including universities and the strategic regional government in charge of postgraduate training and research in their specific regions. Such collaborations not only enhance resilience but also leverage local expertise and resources to optimise project outcomes. By fostering such partnerships and collaborations, project teams can navigate bureaucratic hurdles more effectively and ensure the validity and applicability of interventions in diverse contexts.

Conclusion

Supervision and mentorship play a critical role in advancing the participation of women in STEM postgraduate training programmes in East Africa, and by extension, SSA. Women experience challenges that hamper their advancement in postgraduate training, research and consequently leadership in the region. Key stakeholders drawn from countries within the region identified gender-lensed strategies that were necessary to strengthen supervision and mentorship in STEM postgraduate training and research in East Africa. This led to the co-creation and approval of a gender-lensed SMF to strengthen support for STEM postgraduate training in East Africa.

The success in the development of the gender-lensed framework is greatly attributed to various processes that were put in place to mitigate against the advanced effects of the challenges and to optimise the outputs of the project. The processes employed included leveraging existing strategic partnerships with the IUCEA, which had regional convening powers for universities in East

Africa, identifying key country-specific collaborators, and regularly engaging with key regional and national stakeholders at all stages of the project.

The approved regional gender-lensed SMF for postgraduate training in East Africa will need to be implemented at the regional level and cascaded to the national and institutional levels, as well as evaluated at each level. That said, given the achievements of this project thus far, we suggest it is worth establishing similar frameworks to promote women in STEM postgraduate training, research and leadership in the other SSA regions. Relevant researchers and policy actors in postgraduate training should consider how to scale up the initiatives described in this chapter in the other SSA regions, leveraging the methodological gains, challenges and lessons learned.

Acknowledgements

The authors express sincere gratitude to the International Development Research Centre (IDRC), Ottawa, Canada, for funding the project on Supervision and Mentorship of Women in Science, Technology, Engineering and Mathematics (STEM) Postgraduate Programmes in Sub-Saharan Africa, through grant number 109144-001, and to the IDRC team – Katie Bryant, Hannah Whitehead and Matilda Catherine Dipieri – for their technical guidance and support. We also thank IUCEA, and more specifically the lead, Michael Mawa, and the country collaborators from Uganda, Rwanda, Tanzania and Burundi for their vital roles in implementing the initiative. Appreciation is also extended to all key stakeholders and the APHRC research team, and more specifically, Hiram Kariuki, who coordinated the data collection, for their active participation, research efforts and contributions to developing the Supervision and Mentorship Framework.

About the Authors

The authors are all affiliated with the African Population and Health Research Center (APHRC), Kenya, and include:

Florah Karimi, Head of Research Capacity Strengthening, Project Principal Investigator (PI) and correspondent author.

Leah Mwangi, Project Coordinator.

Hesborn Wao, Head of Individual Capacity Strengthening and Co-Principal Investigator (Co-PI).

References

APHRC (African Population and Health Research Center). (2025). *Supervision and mentorship of women in science, technology, engineering and mathematics' postgraduate programmes in sub-Saharan Africa: Final technical report*. APHRC. https://knowhub.aphrc.org/handle/123456789/2532

Avila-Garzon, C., & Bacca-Acosta, J. (2024). Thirty years of research and methodologies in value co-creation and co-design. *Sustainability (Switzerland)*, *16*(6). https://doi.org/10.3390/su16062360

Christoplos, I., Zwi, A., & Lindegaard, L. S. (2015). *Evaluation of the Consortium for Advanced Research Training in Africa (CARTA)*. Sida. https://www.sida.se/en/about-sida/publications-archive/evaluation-of-the-consortium-for-advanced-research-training-in-africa-carta-final-report

De Jongh, J.-C., Titus, S., Roman, N., & Frantz, J. (2023). The role of research units at higher education institutions: Intention or reality? *Journal of Research Administration*, *55*(3), 126–224.

Deb, L., Desai, S., McGinley, K., Paul, E., Habib, T., Ali, A., & Stawicki, S. (2022). Mentorship in postgraduate medical education. In *Contemporary Topics in Graduate Medical Education* (Volume 2). https://doi.org/10.5772/intechopen.98612

Dugbazah, J., Glover, B., Mbuli, B., Kungade, C., & Shikwambane, N. (2022). Heightening the participation of African women in science, technology, engineering and mathematics career paths [Blog post]. *NEPAD*. https://www.nepad.org/blog/heightening-participation-of-african-women-science-technology-engineering-and-mathematics#_FTNREF2

Gangrade, N., Samuels, C., Attar, H., Schultz, A., Nana, N., Ye, E., & Lambert, W. M. (2024). Mentorship interventions in postgraduate medical and STEM settings: A scoping review. *CBE Life Sciences Education*, *23*(3), ar33.

Hill, S. E. M., Ward, W. L., Seay, A., & Buzenski, J. (2022). The nature and evolution of the mentoring relationship in academic health centers. *Journal of Clinical Psychology in Medical Settings*, *29*(3), 557–569. https://doi.org/10.1007/s10880-022-09893-6

Horan, D. (2022). A framework to harness effective partnerships for the sustainable development goals. *Sustainability Science*, *17*(4), 1573–1587. https://doi.org/10.1007/s11625-021-01070-2

Hulme, P. E. (2014). Bridging the knowing-doing gap: Know-who, know-what, know-why, know-how and know-when. *Journal of Applied Ecology*, *51*(5), 1131–1136. https://doi.org/10.1111/1365-2664.12321

Huyer, S. (2015). Is the gender gap narrowing in science & engineering? In *UNESCO Science Report: Towards 2030* (pp. 85–103). UNESCO. https://unesdoc.unesco.org/ark:/48223/pf0000235447

Igumbor, J. O., Bosire, E. N., Karimi, F., Katahoire, A., Allison, J., Muula, A. S., Peixoto, A., Otwombe, K., Gitau, E., Bondjers, G., Fonn, S., & Ajuwon, A. (2020). Effective supervision of doctoral students in public and population health in Africa: CARTA supervisors' experiences, challenges and perceived opportunities. *Global Public Health*, *17*(4), 496–511. https://doi.org/10.1080/17441692.2020.1864752

IUCEA (Inter-University Council for East Africa). (2018). *Standards and guidelines for postgraduate studies*. IUCEA. https://www.iucea.org/mdocs-posts/standards-and-guidelines-for-postgraduate-studies/

IUCEA. (2024). *Supervision and mentorship framework*. IUCEA. https://www.iucea.org/mdocs-posts/supervision-and-mentorship-framework-2024/

Kimani-Murage, E. (2022). Female scientists in Africa are changing the face of their continent. *Nature*, *602*(7898), 547–548. https://doi.org/10.1038/d41586-022-00492-x

Lindahl, J., Colliander, C., & Danell, R. (2021). The importance of collaboration and supervisor behaviour for gender differences in doctoral student performance and early career development. *Studies in Higher Education*, *46*(12), 2808–2831. https://doi.org/10.1080/03075079.2020.1861596

Lirri, E. (2019, October 31). Women supporting women. *University World News – Africa Edition*. https://www.universityworldnews.com/post.php?story=20191029090031380

Maier, C. S. (2007). A nation among nations: America's place in world history. *Journal of American History*, *94*(1), 232–233. https://doi.org/10.2307/25094797

Marincola, E., & Kariuki, T. (2020). Quality research in Africa and why it is important. *ACS Omega, 5*(38), 24155–24157. https://doi.org/10.1021/acsomega.0c04327

McCowan, T. (2016). Universities and the post-2015 development agenda: An analytical framework. *Higher Education, 72*(4), 505–523. https://doi.org/10.1007/s10734-016-0035-7

Mpoke-Bigg, A. (2019). *Leadership, voice, and visibility*. Malmo University. https://www.diva-portal.org/smash/get/diva2:1481882/FULLTEXT01.pdf

Okeke-Uzodike, O. E. (2021). Postgraduate supervision in a South African transforming academic environment: A reflexivity approach. *Issues in Educational Research, 31*(4), 1175–1194.

Okeke, I. N., Babalola, C. P., Byarugaba, D. K., Djimde, A., & Osoniyi, O. R. (2017). Broadening participation in the sciences within and from Africa: Purpose, challenges and prospects. *CBE Life Sciences Education, 16*(2), 1–9. https://doi.org/10.1187/cbe.15-12-0265

Poltera, J. (2019). Exploring examples of women's leadership in African contexts. *Agenda, 33*(1), 3–8. https://doi.org/10.1080/10130950.2019.1602977

Rădulescu, M. A., Leendertse, W., & Arts, J. (2023). How can co-creation support capacity building for adaptive spatial planning? Exploring evidence from a co-creative planning process in The Netherlands. *Planning Theory and Practice, 24*(5), 639–662. https://doi.org/10.1080/14649357.2023.2288203

Saleem, T., & Mahmood, N. (2023). Profiling the supervision experiences of postgraduate research students with different personal and institutional factors in open and distance learning environment. *Bulletin of Education and Research, 45*(3), 83–110. https://files.eric.ed.gov/fulltext/EJ1422190.pdf

Somefun, O. D., & Adebayo, K. O. (2020). The role of mentoring in research ecosystems in sub-Saharan Africa: Some experiences through the CARTA opportunity. *Global Public Health, 16*(1), 36–47. https://doi.org/10.1080/17441692.2020.1776365

UN-DESA PD (United Nations Department of Economic and Social Affairs, Population Division). (2022). *World population prospects 2022: Summary of results*. UN DESA/POP/2021/TR/NO.3. United Nations. https://www.un.org/development/desa/pd/sites/www.un.org.development.desa.pd/files/wpp2022_summary_of_results.pdf

Vargas, C., Whelan, J., Brimblecombe, J., & Allender, S. (2022). Co-creation, co-design and co-production for public health: A perspective on definitions and distinctions. *Public Health Research and Practice, 32*(2), 1–7. https://doi.org/10.17061/phrp3222211

Vetter, T. R. (2017). Descriptive statistics: Reporting the answers to the 5 basic questions of who, what, why, when, where, and a sixth, so what? *Anesthesia and Analgesia, 125*(5), 1797–1802. https://doi.org/10.1213/ANE.0000000000002471

Wisker, G., & Fossland, T. (2023). Tackling gender inequality in doctoral supervision: An intersectional toolkit involving hearts, minds, policies, and practices. *Journal for New Generation Sciences, 21*(1), 99–115. https://doi.org/10.47588/jngs.2023.21.01.a8

World Bank Group. (2014). *A decade of development in sub-Saharan African science, technology, engineering and mathematics research*. World Bank Group & Elsevier. https://documents1.worldbank.org/curated/en/237371468204551128/pdf/910160WP0P126900disclose09026020140.pdf

Wu, S., Oubibi, M., & Bao, K. (2024). How supervisors affect students' academic gains and research ability: An investigation through a qualitative study. *Heliyon, 10*(10), e31079.

CHAPTER 8

Advancing Women in STEM Leadership: Policy Analysis with Insights from Water-related Sectors in Ghana and Kenya

Adelina Maria Mensah, Faith Njoki Karanja, Cynthia Addoquaye Tagoe,
Adwoa Owusuaa Bobie, Charlotte Wrigley-Asante, Rita Boateng, Caroline Kabaria,
Blessing Mberu, Ivy Chumo, Leunita Sumba, Simon Thuo and Betsy Makena Mugo

Introduction

In sub-Saharan Africa (SSA), efforts to promote gender equality in workplaces have made progress, but significant gaps remain. The *Global gender gap report* (World Economic Forum, 2023) reveals persistent disparities, particularly in leadership in Science, Technology, Engineering and Science (STEM) fields. Women hold under 30% of middle and senior positions (Hanna et al., 2024) and are even less represented in high-level STEM leadership, with only 17.8% acting as Vice Presidents and 12.4% as Chief Officers (Hanna et al., 2024).

Many countries have ratified international and regional human rights instruments; however, a gap persists between these commitments and their actual implementation at the national level (UNDP & AUC, 2023). This is primarily due to slow implementation and a lack of supportive legislation and policy environments, which hinder the domestication and enforcement of these human rights instruments. Societal expectations, stereotypes and systemic biases further impede women's advancement to leadership roles (Mousa et al., 2021), particularly in patriarchal communities where traditional gender roles conflict with professional aspirations. Consequently, women's contributions remain underutilised, adversely affecting economic and social development (Nhamo et al., 2018). While many studies have focused on the barriers to women's career progression, there is limited research on effective strategies to elevate women to leadership positions. Furthermore, there is a lack of systematic data to fully understand the interlinkages between education and career (Mousa et al., 2021), highlighting the need for targeted research to develop more effective policies and practices, especially in low- and middle-income contexts.

The importance of promoting women in leadership is especially evident in the WASH (water, sanitation and hygiene) sector. A World Bank (2019) report shows that out of 64 water and sanitation service providers in 28 global economies, women constitute just 18% of workers, 32% of these service providers have no female engineers and 12% have no female managers. Research indicates that involving women in water management significantly enhances project effectiveness and sustainability, with success rates increasing six to seven times compared to projects without female involvement (Jenniskens, 2022). Additionally, companies with more women in decision-making roles perform better, delivering social, environmental and economic benefits (Jenniskens, 2022).

Ghana and Kenya serve as compelling case studies for examining these challenges and opportunities, particularly within the water sector where women face numerous career bottlenecks (World Bank, 2019). One challenge is the gender imbalance in STEM training within higher education, which results in fewer women entering the workforce in these fields (Hammond et al., 2020). For example, at the University of Nairobi, between 2021 and 2023, only 42% of engineering students were female, with an even smaller percentage (22%) successfully graduating.[1] Similarly, in the Faculty of Science and Technology, while 51% of students who enrol are female, only 30% complete their studies. This gender disparity in engineering studies extends to and is exacerbated in the workforce, where only 7% of registered engineers in Kenya are women (Engineers Board of Kenya, 2023). Additionally, women scientists are more likely to work in academic and government institutions, while their male counterparts tend to be employed in the private sector, which generally offers better pay and career opportunities (The AAS, 2020). Similarly, at the University of Ghana, about 59.7% of graduates from the College of Basic and Applied Sciences in 2022 were male, compared to 40.3% female graduates.[2] Both Kenya and Ghana illustrate the systemic challenges that women face, including a lack of training, networking and mentorship opportunities, as well as pervasive socio-cultural

---

1 University of Nairobi student enrolment reports (Personal communication, 2022, 2023).
2 Based on published reports for 2022 from the University of Ghana, Institutional Research and Planning Office (IRPO) (see https://irpo.ug.edu.gh/facts-figures).

norms and gender stereotypes that limit their advancement (Boateng & Gaulee, 2019). This research aims to uncover policy gaps and identify opportunities to enhance diversity and equity by first providing an overview of policies related to women in STEM in both countries. It will then focus specifically on the experiences of women in the water sector.

We investigate whether current policy guidelines and practices in Ghana and Kenya are adequate not only to attract and retain women in STEM roles but also to facilitate their advancement into leadership positions. The main aim is to assess how national policies, legal frameworks and operational guidelines in Ghana and Kenya effectively support women's career progression and reduce attrition rates along the way. Drawing from the experiences of women and men within selected institutions, the study interrogates how these policies enable women's advancement in STEM careers and identifies barriers and opportunities that may cause women to leave these career paths or enable them to attain leadership positions.

The research is guided by three central questions regarding water sector-related institutions in both countries:

1. How have current national and institutional policies addressed the interlinkages between gender, STEM and leadership?
2. What institutional policies or changes have either limited or supported equal opportunities and career advancement for women in water-related fields?
3. What specific opportunities can these policies provide to advance women into leadership positions in water sector-related institutions?

Methods

Research design

This qualitative study used a combination of secondary and primary data to assess the barriers and opportunities for women's advancement in STEM fields, particularly within water-related sectors in Ghana and Kenya. Secondary data analysis focused on policies and guidelines related to STEM, gender and the water sector, while primary data were gathered through in-depth interviews and key informant interviews. Secondary data, mainly in the form of reports, were sourced from official e-repositories and websites of national government ministries (such as water, sanitation, irrigation, health, education, social services, labour and social security), county websites and national council websites.

The inclusion criteria targeted public and private water sector institutions engaged in research and industry. Policies included in the analysis covered international and regional documents on STEM and gender, along with national policies and strategic frameworks on STEM, gender, education and the water sector. This approach aimed to evaluate how gender is mainstreamed into STEM and water sector activities, and vice versa.

Ethics approval for the project was obtained from the University of Ghana Ethics Committee (ECBAS 075/21-22) and Amref Health Africa's Ethics and Scientific Review Committee in Kenya (REF no: P1180 – 2022), in addition to a research permit by Kenya's National Commission for Science, Technology and Innovation (NACOSTI).

Study sites

In Ghana, data were collected from four case institutions within the water sector in Accra (i.e. academia, research, government and a coalition of non-governmental organisations). Additional data were collected from various government ministries and agencies. In Kenya, the study included faculty members from research and university institutions within STEM fields, professional bodies, academia and research institutions, government and parastatal agencies and industry, including water sector institutions and private sector institutions.

Data extraction methods

For research question one, content analysis (Hsieh & Shannon, 2005) was used to examine policies, development-related documents and strategic plans at the global, regional and national levels. A total of 27 documents (from Ghana) and 23 documents (from Kenya) were reviewed (see Table 1).

Table 1: Global, regional and national policies reviewed – Ghana and Kenya

Level of policy/document	Ghana	Kenya
Global	5 (13%)	5 (14%)
Regional	6 (16%)	6 (18%)
National	27 (71%)	23 (68%)
Total	38	34

For the second and third research questions, semi-structured in-depth interviews (IDIs) were conducted in Ghana with senior management (i.e. high-ranking staff and board members involved in institutional decision-making) and with female and male leaders heading national, regional or departmental units of the four case study institutions (Table 2a). In addition, key informant interviews (KIIs) were conducted with six females and two males from four governmental ministries, identified through referrals when inquiries were made about appropriate contacts for the project's objectives. In Kenya, IDIs were conducted with four members of senior management and with nine female and six male leaders from the surveyed institutions (Table 2b). KIIs were also conducted with 88 female and 30 male participants holding various levels of responsibility across these institutions.

Table 2(a): Ghana – Leadership participants from surveyed institutions

Category	Academia	Research	Government	NGO
Senior management	3	3	5	2
Female leaders	7	4	5	1
Male leaders	2	5	3	3
Total	12	12	13	6

Table 2(b): Kenya – Leadership participants from surveyed institutions

Category	Water sector institutions	Professional body	National government and parastatals	Private sector
Senior management	1	1	1	1
Female leaders	4	0	2	3
Male leaders	2	0	2	2
Total	7	1	5	6

Data analysis

The SAGA Policy Matrix (UNESCO, 2017) framework was used to evaluate the extent to which various policies implemented by institutions promote gender equality in science, technology and innovation (STI), including policies and policy instruments that have a differential impact on gender equality. While the SAGA Policy Matrix uses the term STI, this is often used interchangeably with STEM in many contexts. For consistency within this chapter and the broader collection, we refer to STEM where appropriate. The analysis considered several factors, including the nature of the policy, the implementing body, the type of policy, STEM objectives to which the policy contributes, target beneficiaries, implementation period, geographical coverage and target Sustainable Development Goals (SDGs).

For qualitative data, framework analysis (Gale et al., 2013) was employed using NVivo 12 (QSR International, Australia) and QDA Miner (Provalis Research, Canada) for coding and analysis. Researchers familiarised themselves with the data by listening to recordings and reviewing transcripts. To ensure reliability, two researchers independently developed a coding framework, followed by a consensus meeting to finalise the themes. The data were then coded, charted, mapped and interpreted based on the developed framework. The analysis framework was structured on the following two levels:

1. First-level analysis variables:
   - Document title, type and level (global, regional or national).
   - Policy analysis variables: "Evidence" (presence of STEM or gender equality), "Context" (historical or structural objectives), "Engagement" (main stakeholders).
   - Gaps: Identified STEM and gender gaps.
2. Second-level analysis variables:
   - Document jurisdiction (global, regional, national).
   - Focus areas: STEM only, gender only, STEM and gender, STEM, gender and leadership.

Results

This section responds to the three central questions that aim to assess policy gaps and opportunities for enhancing diversity and equity in STEM leadership based on literature and the experiences of participants from water-related sectors in Ghana and Kenya.

National and institutional policies and interlinkages with gender, STEM and leadership

National gender policies in both Ghana and Kenya have shaped institutional mechanisms aimed at promoting gender equality and supporting women's empowerment. In both countries, the establishment of Gender Desks (or gender focal points) across various ministries has played an important role in increasing the representation of women and providing support for their educational and professional development. These units or designated contact points focus on promoting gender equality and mainstreaming gender considerations into their organisational policies and practices (see Chapter 3 for an in-depth discussion of gender mainstreaming). In Ghana, since the establishment of the Ministry of Gender, Children and Social Protection and the promotion of Gender Desks in various ministries, there has been a noticeable increase in the number of women directors and enhanced support for women's empowerment, including educational sponsorship –within two years of implementing the Gender Desk, the numbers increased from four to 10 out of the current 36 directors.

Similarly, in Kenya, the Ministry of Gender, Culture, Arts and Heritage, through the State Department for Gender and Affirmative Action, has worked towards creating a society free from gender discrimination and violence. Gender Desks have been established in various institutions, including the University of Nairobi, which became the first institution of higher learning to launch a Gender Desk in 2022. This initiative addresses the prevalence of unreported cases of gender-based violence and aligns with international efforts, such as UNESCO's O3 Plus initiative, which aims to create awareness and provide support to young people in universities and tertiary institutions (UNESCO, 2024).

Despite these positive steps, there is a substantial *lack of integrative policies* that effectively combine gender, STEM and leadership, and significantly limit the advancement of women into leadership roles. First, most STEM-related policies and strategic developmental documents *are not fully gender-main-streamed*. These documents often emphasise access to and use of technologies and equipment but lack gender mainstreaming, in that they fail to consider the specific needs and challenges faced by women and other vulnerable groups, such as persons with disabilities. Without explicit gender mainstreaming, these policies overlook the broader societal and cultural contexts that influence women's participation and progression. For example, policies that merely aim to increase technological access without addressing the systemic biases and barriers women face are unlikely to be effective.

Second, social development documents, including national programmes and strategic plans, often treat technology and STEM-related initiatives *as secondary or supportive components* rather than as central elements for achiev-ing broader developmental goals. This approach minimises the critical role of STEM education and careers in supporting social and economic development. Policies that view STEM only as an 'accessory' fail to recognise its potential to drive social change and economic empowerment, particularly for women who remain underrepresented.

Finally, there is a *disconnect between government STEM educational policies and national employment policies* concerning female STEM employees. In both Ghana and Kenya, there are gender-mainstreamed educational policies designed to encourage girls and women to pursue STEM education. However, these policies are not sufficiently linked to employment strategies that would ensure women's retention and progression. For instance, in Ghana, although some policy documents mention the goal of increasing the number of female STEM students from primary through tertiary education, there is a lack of specific policies that ensure the transition of female graduates into STEM-related job fields and leadership roles. Policies such as the National Vision for Girls Education in Ghana and the National Science, Technology and Innovation Policy lack mechanisms to support the absorption of women into the STEM workforce and their advancement into leadership positions. Similarly, while Kenya's Education Act of 2013 has been successful in promoting gender equity in education, there is insufficient alignment with employment policies to support women's career progression. This disconnect and lack of coherence between education and employment policies result in a significant drop-off or 'leakage' of women from the STEM pipeline, as they exit STEM career paths due to lack of opportunities and support for career advancement.

Policy structures supporting and limiting career advancement for women in STEM

In both countries, *positive* institutional policies and structures include the establishment of gender advocacy centres and unions, gender-sensitive recruitment policies, implementation of inclusive workplace environments, family-friendly policies, in-house support programmes to help women advance their careers, as well as mentorship and capacity-building programmes.

Gender advocacy centres within institutions in both countries have been crucial in promoting gender equality and addressing gender-related issues. The Centre for Gender Studies and Advocacy (CEGENSA) at the University of Ghana is dedicated to policy development, advocacy and creating a supportive environment for both men and women. CEGENSA has been instrumental in drafting and ensuring the implementation of the Sexual Harassment and Misconduct Policy and the Gender Policy, ensuring that gender issues are mainstreamed across the university. Similarly, women's unions, as found in the Ghana Water Company Ltd. (GWCL) and Women in WASH (WIWASH) in both countries, serve as powerful advocacy groups. They also engage in community outreach to educate and inspire young girls about opportunities in STEM fields, address important issues such as hygiene and advocate for the advancement of women within their institutions. As highlighted by a female leader in Ghana's public water sector:

We're pulling the engineers, those with the science background, to propa-
gate STEM education. We do a lot of programmes to whip up interest in
the WASH sector like this Menstrual Hygiene Day which is in May. We do
hygiene education, ... and educate them on courses, that they can pick up
in the sciences that will enable them to pursue a career in the water sector
... We also train women to pick up leadership roles to ensure that we're not
just in the WASH sector, but our voices can be heard.

In Kenya, several water sector institutions have implemented gender-sensitive recruitment policies to increase the representation of women in technical
and leadership roles. These policies set specific gender targets or quotas to
promote gender parity in hiring practices. For instance, the Water Services
Regulatory Board (WASREB) and Kenya Water Institute (KEWI) have made
deliberate efforts to ensure gender parity in their hiring practices, leading to
a more balanced workforce and providing women with greater opportunities
to progress.

Efforts to create inclusive workplace environments that actively challenge
gender stereotypes and promote diversity are evident. Some water sector institutions have established gender committees or task forces that regularly review
and recommend changes to organisational policies and practices. Six participants reported the presence of gender committees in their institutions.

Additionally, family-friendly policies have been adopted by some institutions
to enable women to balance their professional and personal responsibilities,
thereby reducing the likelihood of career interruptions. For example, ten
participants from the water sector in Ghana reported that their organisations
had implemented flexible working hours, remote work options and job-sharing. The initiative not only supports work–life balance but also encourages
the retention of women in the workforce, especially those who may otherwise
leave their careers due to family obligations. A female leader in the public water
sector explained,

... what we have is that when you resume from your maternity leave, you
close two hours earlier than the normal time. And the policy is such that if
you stay at home, like I did for six months, I have one year from the day I
resume to close two hours before time. Yes. So that is there ... at this point
in life, it makes work-life better ... .

Institutional leaders sometimes go beyond statutory requirements to offer
additional benefits that support women's career progression and work–life

balance by implementing in-house supportive policies through their personal leadership strategies and creating an inclusive work environment. For example, at three institutions in Ghana, internal policies extend beyond national statutory provisions to offer additional benefits like nursery facilities and 'nanny allowances' for work-related travel. These in-house measures have been instrumental in enabling women to sustain their career progression, particularly in the water sector, where field experience is essential for advancement. As noted by a female NGO leader in Ghana:

> We can do two weeks at a place and ... well they have this nanny support where if you are a nursing mother, for the first six months after delivery, upon resumption [of work], when you have to go to the field ... [the institution] will bear half the cost of the nanny's PDM [per diem] and accommodation.

This commitment to supporting women's professional growth is also reflected in leadership attitudes within these institutions. As one male public senior manager in Ghana noted:

> So, that is how this present MD [managing director] has distinguished himself. You see, most of them [women] are not engineers. And in this company, it is all about engineering. So, ideally, the top should be occupied by engineers. But this present MD, said no. So now, when you even look at some of our policies, we are saying that ideally, for a position to be vacant, if a woman is qualified, the woman should be considered first.

The introduction of mentorship and capacity-building programmes is a supportive measure. Organisations like the Rural Water Supply Network (RWSN) and Kenya Water and Sanitation Civil Society Network (KEWASNET) have established mentorship initiatives that pair young female professionals with experienced leaders in the sector (see Chapter 7 for a discussion of a regional mentorship and supervision framework). These programmes offer guidance, knowledge sharing and networking opportunities, which are crucial for women seeking to advance in traditionally male-dominated fields.

Despite these supportive measures, some critical gaps and challenges persist at the institutional level, which hinder the career advancement of women in their fields. These include the lack of awareness of policies and guidelines, the lack of or ineffective implementation of policies, the lack of clarity in policies and guidelines, and the inadequacy of policies to address issues specific to women.

Many study participants reported insufficient knowledge or inadequate awareness of gender-related policies in their institutions, which impedes effective implementation and reduces potential impact. The effectiveness of STEM policies and guidelines is often dependent on successful awareness creation. As a female key informant from one of Ghana's ministries noted: *"You know Ghana, we have all the laws. But we don't read them and we don't know. We have signed conventions [that] we are not aware of ... I think it is an eye-opener to know our policies."* Similarly, in Kenya, the need for sustained awareness efforts was emphasised by a senior female key informant: *"One-time awareness campaigns may not be sufficient to foster lasting understanding and support for STEM policies ... requiring ongoing efforts of key messages."*

Even where well-intentioned policies exist, their lack of effective implementation to ensure compliance often extends gender disparities rather than reducing them, resulting in gaps between policy intentions and actual outcomes. A Kenyan senior female key informant noted that: *"Low implementation of existing policy guidelines to support women in STEM has been the order of operations in many institutions. Not only in our place but in many other institutions where my colleagues work."*

Without clear and enforceable guidelines to ensure compliance, many organisations do not prioritise the necessary changes that are needed for an equitable work environment. A male participant from Kenya highlighted that: *"In the water sector, I have seen the importance of robust enforcement of policies supporting women in STEM. Without it, even strong policies can fail, as organisations may not prioritise gender equity. Effective enforcement and regular assessments are essential."*

This challenge is compounded by funding constraints, as noted by a female key informant from one of Ghana's ministries: *"It all boils down to funding. But when we [don't] have the resources, at times we just fall on our donors to sponsor, and they do."*

In addition, the lack of clarity in policy guidelines presents a significant challenge. Many participants indicated that ambiguous language in policy documents makes it difficult to interpret and translate policies into actionable steps. The importance of both clarity and enforcement was underscored by a female Kenyan participant: *"Language of policy is important in the implementation. Sometimes we do not even understand the language used in the policy and there is no way we will educate others on what we do not know much about."*

Finally, study participants emphasised that the current policies and guidelines addressing women in STEM are inadequate, as they often fail to account for the unique challenges faced by women with multiple marginalised identities, such as those based on race, socio-economic status, disability or geographical location. For example, a policy designed to support women in STEM may provide general measures for gender equity but might not consider the additional barriers faced by women from rural areas who may lack access to quality education and mentorship opportunities. Similarly, policies in engineering fields frequently do not consider the specific needs of women who are unable to perform strenuous manual tasks, such as lifting heavy machinery or climbing high buildings, due to physical limitations or health concerns.

By failing to consider these specific needs, policies inadvertently reinforce a one-size-fits-all approach that does not account for the varied capabilities and contributions of women in the water sector and other STEM fields. In Kenya, a female participant underscored this issue, stating: *"Policies on women in STEM often miss the mark by not addressing the unique challenges faced by those with multiple marginalised identities. To truly promote inclusivity, we must recognise and address these intersectional factors."*

Institutional policies supporting women's advancement into leadership roles

The research highlights policies that support women's advancement into leadership positions in the water sector. These focus on structured mentorship, professional development, gender diversity targets, advancing inclusive organisational cultures and enhancing research and data collection.

Advancing women to take up leadership roles in the Ghanaian and Kenyan water sectors requires targeted policies and initiatives, particularly in mentorship programmes. Participants reported how women often faced challenges in breaking into senior roles due to a lack of networks and guidance. As such, they emphasised the need for structured mentorship initiatives that provide aspiring women leaders with valuable career advice, networking opportunities and visibility within the industry, as a female sector leader in Kenya underscored: *"Mentorship has been a game-changer for many women in our sector. It not only provides guidance but also opens doors to networks and opportunities that are crucial for career advancement and are challenges faced by women in STEM."*

Similarly, participants in Ghana reiterated the importance of mentorship, noting how such support could help women avoid common pitfalls and accelerate their career growth. As one female leader mentioned: *"I would have wanted to be mentored in this place if there was a senior female leader because once you get the mentorship, you'll skip some mistakes … ."*

Beyond mentorship, there is a clear need for policies focused on professional development and leadership training opportunities. Participants highlighted the necessity for women to access specialised training to prepare them for leadership roles, including skills development in management, strategic thinking and decision-making. These programmes should be designed to build confidence and competence, equipping women with the tools necessary to excel and remain in leadership positions. Female participants in Kenya emphasised how prioritising such development opportunities, could better equip women with the skills needed to lead effectively:

> To prepare women for leadership roles, we must invest in specialised training that enhances their skills in management, strategic thinking and decision-making. The training ought to build the confidence necessary for women to step into and thrive in leadership positions.

Moreover, initiatives such as the DANIDA Project in Ghana, which specifically targets women for knowledge transfer and coaching at the ministries, demonstrate the positive impact of tailored professional development programmes. A female key informant from one of the ministries described their approach:

> The DANIDA Project targets only women …, they are coming to transfer the knowledge. They are coming to coach the younger generation so they can also take up after us. When we came, we also organised a session to share our experiences … .

The findings also illustrate the need for policies supporting gender diversity targets and quotas, which can drive systemic change. In Kenya, a female participant described how establishing clear targets for women's representation in leadership roles ensured accountability and provided a structured approach to increasing diversity and balanced representation in leadership positions: "Setting clear targets for women's representation in leadership roles creates accountability and fosters a more inclusive environment. It helps to address the systemic biases that have traditionally hindered women's advancement in the water sector."

Similarly, in Ghana, there have been efforts to increase women's representation at the science and research levels. As a male senior manager in research explained:

> Yeah, there's some improvement in inclusivity. For some time, the ratio of women to men, let's say, was very, very low. But in recent times, there's

been an effort to increase the number of women at the science and research level. So usually when you have two people [competing] at a level, it's likely the woman will get it ...

Participants also described the need to develop an *inclusive organisational culture*, reiterating the need to adopt and implement policies that promote a culture of respect and equity, where women contribute to ideas and lead projects and programmes. According to the participants, this included adopting and implementing anti-harassment measures, ensuring fair evaluation processes and supporting women in negotiating for fair compensation and promotions. As described by a female leader in Kenya: *"An inclusive culture where women feel valued and supported is crucial for their success. This means implementing strong anti-harassment policies, ensuring fair evaluations and supporting women in negotiating for promotions and fair compensation."*

Additionally, creating opportunities for women to lead is vital, as a Ghanaian female leader in academia recommended:

So, I would suggest that women should be given the opportunities to lead. And I believe it will help very well. Because women pay particular attention to issues ... if they get them involved, the output will certainly be great.

Finally, participants emphasised the importance of collecting gender-disaggregated data during recruitment exercises and other data-collection processes to inform decision-making. Such data is crucial for analysing women's participation and progression to STEM leadership positions and enhancing policy guidelines that support their advancement. The need for dedicated funding for research on the barriers faced by women in STEM was supported by participants from both countries. In Kenya, a female leader suggested: *"Mandate the collection of gender-disaggregated data on STEM employment, leadership positions and pay. Allocate dedicated funding for research on the barriers faced by women in STEM and the development of evidence-based policies."*

Policy recommendations

To advance gender equality and support women's progression to leadership positions in water-related sectors in both countries, we propose five key policy recommendations to enhance gender equity by promoting a more inclusive environment (Table 4).

Table 4: Policy focus areas with proposed actions, expected outcomes and considerations necessary for effective implementation

Policy focus	Proposed actions	Expected outcomes	Implementation considerations		Stakeholders (see Annex. 1)
			Challenges	Solutions	
Enhance policy awareness and participation in policy processes	Restructure promotion processes. Gender-based violence prevention and response measures. Robust monitoring and evaluation frameworks. Work–life balance policies. Inclusive policy participation.	Increased awareness and understanding of policies. Enhanced representation in policymaking processes. Improved gender equity through better monitoring, evaluation and accountability measures. Greater retention and career progression of women in STEM fields.	Potential resistance from existing institutional structures. Limited access to training and resources for women to engage effectively.	Provide training workshops on policy engagement for women. Allocate resources for sustained advocacy and awareness campaigns.	Collaborate to implement initiatives: Government ministries (e.g., ministries of education and gender), Parliamentary Committees on Gender, National Gender and Equality Commissions.
Develop and implement formalised mentorship programmes	Celebrate women's achievements. Implement formal mentorship programmes.	Increased retention and advancement of women in STEM. Strengthened professional networks and reduced feelings of isolation. Creation of a supportive community that encourages career progression and leadership development.	Establishing a sustainable mentorship framework. Ensuring sufficient participation from senior professionals.	Incentivise participation through recognition programmes and career development opportunities for mentors. Engage private sector and professional bodies in mentorship initiatives.	Lead development and implementation of programmes: Private sector organisations, Water sector institutions, Professional bodies and networks.

Policy focus	Proposed actions	Expected outcomes	Implementation considerations		
			Challenges	Solutions	Stakeholders (see Annex. 1)
Provide capacity-building and training opportunities	Provide scholarships and training. Implement comprehensive training programmes. Support re-integration for new mothers. Inclusive training for all genders.	Improved skills and competencies among women in STEM, enhancing their readiness for leadership roles. Increased visibility and participation of women in leadership positions within the water sector. Greater workplace inclusivity and more supportive policies.	Financial constraints in funding extensive training programmes. Cultural resistance to women in leadership.	Partner with international organisations and NGOs for funding. Create awareness campaigns highlighting the benefits of gender diversity in leadership.	Collaborate to provide training and opportunities: STEM educational institutions, Government ministries, Professional bodies and networks.
Promote flexible work arrangements	Introduce flexible work policies. Support for new mothers.	Improved retention rates of women in the water sector. Enhanced work–life balance for women, leading to increased participation in leadership roles.	Potential pushback from traditional management structures. Difficulty in managing remote or flexible teams.	Provide training for managers on leading flexible teams. Use technology to facilitate remote work and collaboration.	Adopt and promote flexible arrangements: Private water sector institutions, Government ministries, Private sector organisations.
Data collection and monitoring for gender equity	Develop a comprehensive data collection and monitoring system. Facilitate collaboration and transparency in data sharing and policy evaluation.	Comprehensive data collection clearly shows gender disparities within STEM. Intersectional analysis will enable more precise and effective interventions. Regular monitoring and evaluation frameworks will create accountability. Collaboration and data sharing among stakeholders will encourage a unified approach.	Data privacy and security concerns, standardisation challenges, resistance to data collection efforts and potential lack of capacity for analysis. Difficulty in coordinating data sharing and collaboration among diverse stakeholders.	Ensure compliance with laws and ethical guidelines. Develop standardised data-collection protocols. Provide training and resources. Establish clear communication, define roles and responsibilities.	Develop and enforce collection protocols and share best practices: Government ministries, STEM educational institutions and private sector organisations, Professional bodies/ networks/women's groups/platforms.

Policy awareness and participation in policy processes

Awareness of policy and participation in the policy process allow us to directly confront the challenge of deeply rooted socio-cultural norms by promoting a culture of shared responsibility and advocacy. Roles for women in policy awareness programmes and their participation in policy processes are crucial for achieving gender equality and promoting inclusive governance. By actively participating in policy processes such as those outlined below, women can ensure that their unique perspectives and experiences are considered in the formulation and implementation of policies.

- Restructuring promotion processes and providing sufficient resources for research to guarantee women have equal opportunities for advancement.
- Coordination and enforcement of gender-based violence prevention and response.
- Robust monitoring and evaluation frameworks to track progress and ensure accountability in gender equity initiatives.
- Policies on working hours and childcare support.
- Policy participation processes for both men and women that promote a culture of shared responsibility and advocacy.

Formalised mentorship programmes in institutions to support women's career progression

The research showed that informal mentorship played a critical role in encouraging many women, with guidance, support and role models. Formalised mentorship can therefore facilitate career progression, build professional networks and overcome feelings of isolation often experienced by women in male-dominated fields. This can be achieved through policies that:

- Highlight and celebrate the achievements of women who have broken through barriers in STEM fields. These success stories serve as powerful inspirations and provide tangible examples of what is possible, encouraging other women to pursue similar paths.
- Develop and implement formal mentorship programmes aimed at supporting women in water-related sectors. These programmes can leverage the positive experiences and outcomes observed from informal mentorship practices in both Ghana and Kenya, providing a structured approach to mentorship that ensures consistency and widespread access.

Capacity-building and training opportunities

Capacity-building and training opportunities are essential for ensuring that women can compete on an equal footing with their male counterparts. As the job market rapidly evolves, there is a need to address the disparities between men and women in accessing enhanced learning and technical knowledge. Women need to be equipped with the necessary tools to succeed in leadership roles. This can be achieved through policies that:

- Provide scholarships, networking opportunities and targeted training, to enhance women's capacity and visibility.
- Implement training programmes that cover a range of essential skills, including negotiation, leadership roles, understanding institutional environments, cultural norms and influences, and work–life balance. These programmes are crucial for equipping women with the tools they need to succeed and advance in their careers.
- Provide re-integration programmes for returning new mothers to ensure a smooth transition back into the workforce. These programmes should offer training and resources to help new mothers balance their professional and personal responsibilities effectively.
- Encourage both men and women to participate in programmes that promote understanding of the departmental climate and collegiality relative to gender differences. Such inclusive training promotes a supportive work environment that helps to break down gender barriers and promotes a workplace environment where all employees feel valued and supported, regardless of gender.

Promote flexible work arrangements

Flexible work arrangements are essential for retaining women in the workforce, especially those with caregiving responsibilities. Such policies help women remain engaged and progress in their careers without compromising their work–life balance. This can be achieved through policies that:

- Offer flexible work hours, remote work options and job-sharing to help women balance professional and personal responsibilities.
- Establish re-integration programmes for new mothers to support their smooth transition back into the workforce.

Data collection and gender equity in STEM monitoring for policy and tracking progress

Without accurate, gender-disaggregated data, career progression and leadership attainment, policies aimed at promoting gender equality cannot be effectively formulated, implemented or evaluated. This policy focus addresses the need for comprehensive data collection systems that provide a clear understanding of the current state of gender equity, as well as the effectiveness of ongoing interventions. It is, therefore, crucial to implement the following actions:

- Establish standardised protocols for collecting gender-disaggregated data at all levels of the workforce, including recruitment, retention, promotion rates and pay equity. Incorporate monitoring of gender diversity targets and quotas into regular data-collection efforts to assess progress and identify areas needing improvement.
- Strengthen collaboration and transparency in data sharing among institutions and stakeholders to better identify gaps, measure progress and share best practices towards achieving gender equity in STEM fields.

Conclusion

This chapter highlights key insights regarding the linkages between gender, STEM and leadership in Ghana and Kenya. While national and institutional policies have made strides towards promoting gender equality, such as establishing Gender Desks and implementing gender-sensitive recruitment practices, significant gaps remain. These policies often lack comprehensive integration of gender, STEM and leadership components, with limited connections between educational initiatives and employment strategies. This limits efforts to support women's advancement in STEM fields and into leadership roles.

Supportive institutional policies, such as mentorship programmes, professional development and leadership training, flexible work arrangements and gender diversity targets, have shown positive impacts. However, challenges persist due to poor policy implementation, inadequate awareness, ambiguous guidelines and insufficient consideration of the unique barriers faced by women from marginalised backgrounds. Many of these recommendations can be applied to other contexts, although their successful adaptation will require careful consideration of local socio-cultural norms, economic conditions and institutional capacities. For example, flexible work arrangements or mentorship programmes may need to be tailored to account for resource constraints, organisational structures or the specific challenges faced by women in different industries, such as healthcare or education.

Finally, for these recommendations to be effective, robust mechanisms must be established to ensure policy implementation, monitoring and evaluation. Regular assessments, stakeholder engagement and collaboration between government, the private sector and community organisations are essential to adapting and scaling these strategies across diverse contexts. These offer a pathway for promoting a more inclusive environment that supports women's leadership in STEM and leadership globally.

Acknowledgements

This research was funded by the International Development Research Centre (IDRC) in Canada. We would like to acknowledge the contributions of participants from the four institutions in Ghana and from universities and institutions in Kenya, including the Lake Victoria North Water Works Development Agency, which agreed to serve as pilot case studies in co-developing and testing innovative strategies of advancing women in STEM leadership.

About the Authors

Adelina Maria Mensah is a Senior Research Fellow at the Institute for Environment and Sanitation Studies at the University of Ghana, Ghana.

Faith Njoki Karanja is an Associate Professor in the Department of Geospatial and Space Technology at the University of Nairobi, Kenya.

Cynthia Addoquaye Tagoe is a Senior Research Fellow at the Institute of Statistical, Social and Economic Research at the University of Ghana, Ghana.

Adwoa Owusuaa Bobie is a Research Fellow at the Centre for Cultural and African Studies at Kwame Nkrumah University of Science and Technology, Ghana.

Charlotte Wrigley-Asante is affiliated with the Department of Geography & Resource Development at the University of Ghana, Ghana.

Rita Boateng is a Lecturer at the Academic City University and a part-time Lecturer at the University of Ghana Business School, Ghana.

Caroline Kabaria is an Associate Research Scientist at the African Population and Health Research Center, Kenya.

Blessing Mberu is a Senior Research Scientist and Head of Urbanisation and Wellbeing at the African Population and Health Research Center, Kenya.

Ivy Chumo is a Researcher at the African Population and Health Research Center, Kenya.

Leunita Sumba is a Researcher at the Women in Water and Sanitation Association, Kenya.

Eng. Simon Thuo is affiliated with the Women in Water and Sanitation Association, Kenya.

Betsy Makena Mugo is a Tutorial Fellow at the Department of Geospatial and Space Technology at the University of Nairobi, Kenya.

References

Boateng, F., & Gaulee, U. (2019). From studentship to academia: The academic female STEM trajectory in Ghana. *Journal of Underrepresented and Minority Progress*, 3(1), 67–86. https://doi.org/10.32674/jump.v3i1.1077

Engineers Board of Kenya (2023). Speech for the Registrar/CEO Engineers Board of Kenya, Eng. Margaret Ogai, CE during International Women's Day Dinner awards recognition. https://ebk.go.ke/lib.php?f=speech-for-the-registrar-ceo-engineers-board-of-kenya-eng-margaret-ogai-ce-during-international-womens-day-dinner-awards-recognition

Gale, N. K., Heath, G., Cameron, E., Rashid, S., & Redwood, S. (2013). Using the framework method for the analysis of qualitative data in multi-disciplinary health research. *BMC Medical Research Methodology*, 13, 117. https://doi.org/10.1186/1471-2288-13-117

Hammond, A., Rubiano Matulevich, E., Beegle, K., & Kumaraswamy, S. K. (2020). *The equality equation: Advancing the participation of women and girls in STEM*. World Bank Group. https://www.worldbank.org/en/topic/gender/publication/the-equality-equation-advancing-the-participation-of-women-and-girls-in-stem

Hanna, T., Meisel, C., Moyer, J., Azcona, G., Bhatt, A., & Duerto Valero, S. (2024). *Forecasting women in leadership positions* [Technical brief]. UN Women. https://www.unwomen.org/sites/default/files/2023-11/forecasting-women-in-leadership-positions.pdf

Hsieh, H.-F., & Shannon, S. E. (2005). Three approaches to qualitative content analysis. *Qualitative Health Research*, 15(9), 1277–1288. https://doi.org/10.1177/1049732305276687

Jenniskens, A. (2022). *With women better results in water management*. Women for Water Partnership (WfWP). https://siwi.org/wp-content/uploads/2022/07/women-for-water-partnership-2.pdf

Mousa, M., Boyle, J., Skouteris, H., Mullins, A. K., Currie, G., Riach, K., & Teede, H. J. (2021). Advancing women in healthcare leadership: A systematic review and meta-synthesis of multi-sector evidence on organisational interventions. *eClinicalMedicine*, 39, 101084. https://doi.org/10.1016/j.eclinm.2021.101084

Nhamo, G., Muchuru, S., & Nhamo, S. (2018). Women's needs in new global sustainable development policy agendas. *Sustainable Development, 26*(6), 544–552. https://doi.org/10.1002/sd.1717

The AAS (The African Academy of Sciences). (2020). Mukhwana, A. M., Abuya, T., Matanda, D., Omumbi, J., & Mabuka, J. *Factors which contribute to or inhibit women in science, technology, engineering, and mathematics in Africa.* The AAS. https://portal.aasciences.app/storage/publications/01112022071736Women%20 in%20STEM%20Report_Final.pdf

UNDP & AUC (United Nations Development Programme & African Union Commission). (2023). *Gender equality and international law in Africa: The role of regional economic communities.* Equality Now, SOAWR, UNDP and AUC. https://equalitynow.org/resource/reports/ gender-equality-and-international-law-in-africa-the-role-of-regional-economic-communities/

UNESCO (United Nations Educational, Scientific and Cultural Organization). (2017). *Measuring gender equality in science and engineering: The SAGA Toolkit.* SAGA Working Paper 2. UNESCO. https://unesdoc. unesco.org/ark:/48223/pf0000266146

UNESCO (2024). *O3: Our rights, our lives, our future.* UNESCO. https://www.unesco.org/en/health-education/ o3-programme

World Bank. (2019). *Women in water utilities: Breaking barriers.* World Bank Group. https://openknowledge. worldbank.org/handle/10986/32319

World Economic Forum. (2023). *Global gender gap report 2023.* WEF. https://www3.weforum.org/docs/WEF_ GGGR_2023.pdf

Annexure 1: Key stakeholders and targeted institutions

Stakeholder institution	Role	Examples of institutions
STEM educational institutions	Incorporate findings into policies to support women in STEM.	Technical colleges, universities (e.g. University of Nairobi, Kenya Institute of Science and Technology)
Parliamentary Select Committee on Gender	Monitor and mainstream gender equality at national and parliamentary levels.	Parliamentary committees on gender and equality in national assemblies
National Gender and Equality Commission	Advise on and ensure equality and discrimination principles in policies and regulations.	National Gender and Equality Commission of Kenya
Government ministries	Inform educational and professional policy-making to support women in STEM fields.	Ministry of Education, Ministry of Gender, Children and Social Protection
Private sector organisations	Implement mentorship, flexible work policies and gender-responsive recruitment for women in STEM.	Technology providers like Jenga and Safi Organics and investment funds and development organisations such as Water.org
Water sector institutions	Enhance water services and promote women in STEM leadership.	Ministry of Water and Sanitation, NGOs, public utilities
Professional bodies/ networks/women's groups	Advocate for gender provisions in STEM policies through awareness and platforms.	Kenya Water and Sanitation Civil Society Network, Women in Water and Sanitation Association
Water sector institutions (public/private)	Recommend and promote women in STEM leadership.	Private companies such as Rural Water Focus, Runda Water and bottled water firms like Dasani Water

Pedagogical Efforts to Address Gender Disparities in STEM Higher Education in Sub-Saharan Africa: A Scoping Review

Esther Matemba, Baatseba Ramushu, Zach Simpson, Helen M. Inglis and Lucy A. Wakiaga

Introduction

"We African girls and women deserve to study science. Science needs us." Armanda Kouassi (2016)

Education in Science, Technology, Engineering and Mathematics (STEM) is seen by many countries as a national priority for economic development (Melak & Singh, 2021). Globally, fewer women than men enrol for STEM degrees, and retention and graduation rates are frequently unequally distributed between men and women. Gender inclusivity in STEM is influenced by gender stereotypes, mentoring and pedagogy (UNESCO, 2024a). These play out differently across cultural and political contexts, meaning that the reasons women may feel inhibited from participating in STEM in Southeast Asia would be different from those in North America, for example. This chapter contributes to the corpus of literature on women in STEM by focusing on sub-Saharan Africa (SSA), as limited research has been conducted to determine factors affecting women's STEM participation within this context. We present a scoping review identifying the research which has been conducted in SSA investigating the interactions between gender, pedagogy and STEM within undergraduate higher education. The research question addressed in this chapter is as follows:

What is the current state of evidence on the intersection of gender with pedagogy and policies in undergraduate STEM-focused disciplines in SSA higher education institutions?

To provide an in-depth investigation into this question, we overview the following areas as they pertain to this corpus of literature: the contextual landscapes around STEM education, the factors related to female success in STEM, interventions affecting female success in STEM, and policy and practice recommendations provided within these studies. This scoping review provides an overview of the current evidence on gender-responsive pedagogies in SSA, highlights opportunities for policy intervention, and informs policy and research recommendations. The goal of our review is to inform a collaborative research agenda regarding how pedagogical practices can address issues of gendered exclusion in STEM disciplines in SSA's higher education institutions (HEIs).

The underrepresentation of women in STEM stifles countries' capacities to solve their complex development problems: "women's experiences – along with men's experiences – should inform and guide the direction of engineering and technical innovation" (Hill et al., 2010, p. 92). Globally, an average of 35% of STEM graduates are women, a finding which is consistent across most world regions (UNESCO, 2024b). In addition, fewer women than men progress from one educational level to the next, that is, from bachelor's to master's to doctoral levels (Almukhambetova et al., 2023), and women complete advanced degrees at a lower rate than men (Fisher et al., 2020).

Although SSA has the same average female participation rate in STEM as the global average, there is variation between countries (UNESCO, 2024b). For example, in Tanzania more women than men graduate with STEM degrees, while in Niger, Chad and Ghana fewer than 20% of STEM graduates are female (UNESCO, 2024b). This disparity between countries underlines the importance of considering how women's participation in STEM studies interacts with cultural and political contexts.

To increase the participation and retention of women in STEM in higher education, it is first necessary to acknowledge that women face significant challenges while pursuing their studies. Women may be discouraged from participating in higher education by family and community expectations around marriage, child-rearing and domestic responsibilities (Tukahabwa, 2018). Female students in STEM HEIs in SSA are alienated by the teaching approaches used and by the attitudes of both their educators and their male classmates, who routinely underestimate their achievements and abilities (Chapin et al., 2020).

Socio-cultural perceptions that have traditionally constructed STEM as a masculine domain (Namatende-Sakwa, 2018; Onyeocha et al., 2023), and that males are 'better' at mathematics and science, inhibits the participation of women in these fields. Kouassi (2016), speaking from her experience, notes that girls in primary and secondary education with interest in STEM have been labelled as "half-men", and discouraged from taking scientific track subjects. Should they continue and attend university, women face isolation, hostility and a lack of female role models. Female engineering students report being intimidated by some male lecturers which leads them to participate only in 'soft' tasks during practical lessons, thus impeding their exploratory abilities (Omari & Kouevi, 2023). In group projects, female students are often relegated to administrative roles (Simpson & Bester, 2015).

The gender divide in STEM education is perpetuated by patriarchal education structures as well as by educators' beliefs and pedagogical practices (Chikunda & Chikunda, 2016). This is being addressed by national and regional policies which have instigated efforts to infuse a gendered approach into the teaching and learning process in general, and in STEM in particular. Underpinned by the work done by the Forum of African Women Educationalists (FAWE), the International Network for Advancing Science and Policy (INASP) in collaboration with partners in East Africa has developed a gender-responsive pedagogic framework for HEIs (Chapin et al., 2020). The Association of African Universities (AAU) (2006) similarly produced a toolkit on mainstreaming gender in higher education some years ago. The Partnership for Pedagogical Leadership in Africa (PedaL) is a collaboration between eight African HEIs to embed and catalyse systemic change in teaching and learning in African universities (PASGAR, 2023).

It is important to understand how, and to what extent, gender-inclusive policies and frameworks are enacted within the individual institutions and classrooms in the SSA higher education space. This chapter contributes to addressing this question via a scoping review of the literature. The purpose of the scoping review is to determine the extent and range of literature on this topic – using the publications as contextualised examples – and to identify gaps for future study. This is particularly necessary given that literature from SSA is limited and difficult to isolate within the large body of global literature on gender-inclusive pedagogy.

Methods

A scoping review is used here for two reasons: first, to examine the extent, range and nature of research activity around pedagogies of inclusion in gender; and second, to identify research gaps in the existing literature (Arksey & O'Malley, 2005). Arksey and O'Malley's (2005, pp. 21–22) methodological framework outlines five required stages for conducting a scoping review:

- Stage 1: Specify the research question
- Stage 2: Identify relevant literature
- Stage 3: Select studies
- Stage 4: Extract, map and chart the data
- Stage 5: Collate, summarise and report the results

In our approach, we have made pragmatic decisions to be sufficiently comprehensive while having the required work remain feasible. We have worked iteratively and interactively to refine the research question, the search strategy, the data extraction framework, and to extract and summarise the data. This is in line with Levac et al.'s (2010) recommendations.

Stage 1 – Specify the research question

The research question which guides the search strategy asks: "What is the current state of evidence on the intersection of gender, diversity, inclusion and pedagogy in STEM-focused disciplines in SSA HEIs?"

This research question is broader than the research question answered by the chapter, since in ongoing work we are also examining broader aspects of diversity and inclusion.

Stage 2 – Identify relevant studies

In Stage 2 of the scoping review framework, we identify relevant literature to answer the research question. We developed a search strategy based on the five key concepts in the research question, namely:

- SSA;
- Undergraduate higher education;
- STEM;
- Gender, diversity and inclusion; and
- Pedagogy.

Each concept was expanded using related terms, resulting in the search strings shown in Table 1. There is no standard definition for which fields should be considered as STEM disciplines. Since female participation rates in health sciences are considerably higher than in the natural sciences, engineering and technology (European Commission: Directorate-General for Research and Innovation, 2019), we have excluded health sciences from our definition of STEM. We have included agriculture, which is prominent in SSA research (see Chapter 4 for a detailed case study on agriculture as a STEM field).

Through initial searches, and in consultation with librarians at Curtin University and the University of Johannesburg, we developed a list of possible databases. We selected six databases: Web of Science, Scopus, ProQuest Central, ProQuest Dissertations and Thesis, ERIC and EBSCOHost. We searched using the search string shown in Table 1, including the title, abstract and summary fields as search fields. This resulted in 13 995 results.

Table 1: Search terms

Concept	Search terms (in title or abstract)
Sub-Saharan Africa	Africa* OR Algeria OR Angola OR Benin OR Botswana OR "Burkina Faso" OR Burundi OR "Cabo Verde" OR Cameroon OR Chad OR Comoros OR Congo OR "Côte d'Ivoire" OR "Equatorial Guinea" OR Eritrea OR Eswatini OR Ethiopia OR Gabon OR Gambia OR Ghana OR Guinea OR Kenya OR Lesotho OR Liberia OR Madagascar OR Malawi OR Mali OR Mauritania OR Mauritius OR Mozambique OR Namibia OR Niger OR Nigeria OR Rwanda OR "Sao Tome and Principe" OR Senegal OR Seychelles OR "Sierra Leone" OR Somalia OR "South Africa" OR "South Sudan" OR Sudan OR Swaziland OR Togo OR Uganda OR Tanzania OR Zambia OR Zimbabwe
Higher education	"higher education" OR universit* OR college* OR "tertiary education" OR "tertiary institute*" OR "higher learning" OR TVET OR "technical and vocational education and training"
STEM	STEM OR science* OR technolog* OR engineering OR maths OR mathematics OR astronomy OR astrophysics OR chemistry OR physics OR geoscience* OR biolog* OR biochem* OR biophysics OR microbiolog* OR zoology OR physiology OR agriculture OR computer OR programming
Gender and inclusion	gender* OR female OR diversity OR inclusi* OR women OR blind OR "vision impaired" OR disab* OR accessibility
Pedagogy	pedagog* OR teaching OR "teaching strategies" OR "student experiences" OR "social impact" OR factors OR support OR curricul* OR success OR intervention* OR learning OR "foundation programme*" OR "innovative teaching"

Note. Search terms included in the able are Boolean search terms. * represents that the search term could have any possible ending, for example "Africa*" would be inclusive of terms "Africa" and "African" and "universit*" would include "university" and "universities".

Stage 3 – Select studies

In the study selection process, items are screened to select sources of evidence to answer the research question. The 13 995 items found from the databases were first extracted to Zotero, where duplicates were removed. The remaining items were extracted to a spreadsheet for screening against the inclusion criteria, which are described in Table 2.

Table 2: Inclusion criteria to determine relevant papers

Inclusion criteria	Details
The study is located in SSA.	SSA is the focus of the review.
The study investigates undergraduate higher education.	This review considers only undergraduate tertiary education, including both university and vocational education. Primary and secondary education, postgraduate studies and work after graduation are excluded.
The study focuses on STEM courses.	Multiple definitions exist for STEM. As discussed above, we have excluded health sciences and have included agriculture.
The study explicitly investigates gender, diversity or inclusion.	Gender is the primary focus of the review. Other dimensions of diversity are also included as they may add insight.
The study reports on pedagogical interventions or success factors.	Pedagogical interventions are the primary focus of the review. Studies which investigate success factors are included to add context.
The study is written in English.	Due to limited resources for translation, we excluded papers not written in English.
The full study is available.	A small number of studies were excluded because we were not able to access the full text.

Due to the large number of items which were found, the screening was done in stages. The items were first screened based on title only and then screened based on the abstract. The full texts for the remaining items were downloaded for full text review. The process was consultative and done iteratively as required by the researchers. The results of the screening process are summarised in Table 3.

The inclusion/exclusion criteria ensure that only search results that pertain to undergraduate STEM higher education in SSA are included. The included results were categorised to identify literature that pertains to *pedagogy* (defined here as the methods and practices of teaching and learning as enacted through classroom, curricular and assessment practices) as opposed to enrolment, graduation rates and other *factors* that speak to female students' experiences in higher education, but do not specifically relate to pedagogy. The results were also classified to identify those which focused on *gender* as opposed to those which investigated other dimensions of *inclusion*.

The primary category of included articles was SSA studies in STEM higher education that integrated *"Pedagogy and gender"*. These studies report on or discuss pedagogical interventions in STEM in higher education in SSA through the lens of gender. This includes interventions aimed specifically at women, or those in which gender was a key variable studied. These studies are at the core of the scoping review analysis.

The second category of included articles was SSA studies in STEM higher education that integrate *"Factors and gender"*. These studies investigate STEM in higher education in SSA, but do not specifically involve pedagogy; instead, they report on empirical work that aims to understand the 'factors' that impact women's success, persistence, or enrolment in STEM programmes. These studies are included in the scoping review, but only insofar as they offer implications for STEM pedagogy in higher education.

Table 3: Items included at each stage of the search

Stage	Details	Exclusion
Initial search 13 995 items	**Sources:** EBSCOHOST (4 127), ERIC (605), Proquest Central (3 828), Proquest Dissertations and Thesis (768), Scopus (2 305), Web of Science (2 362)	Removed duplicates (5 602)
Title review 8 393 items		Not SSA, Not STEM, Not higher education, Not relevant, Not in English
Abstract review 1 640 items		Not SSA, Not STEM, Not higher education, Postgraduate / Workplace, No factors or pedagogy, No gender or inclusion, Infrastructure, Too broad, Not relevant, No abstract, Duplicate
Full text review 149 items	**Key themes:** Pedagogy and gender (29), Factors and gender (119), Gender (1)	No specific focus on gender, No specific focus on STEM, Not in higher education, Not in English, Not available
Final inclusions 25 items	**Key themes:** Pedagogy and gender (11), Factors and gender (14)	

Stage 4 – Extract the data

We began data extraction by reading 10 primary articles from those that had been selected for full text review. Based on these initial articles, three of the researchers (EM, BR and HI) developed a preliminary data extraction framework. Two of the researchers (EM and BR) then piloted the data extraction framework independently using a further subset of papers. This strategy allowed for discussion of the emerging findings and iterative editing of the framework. The finalised data extraction framework included:

- Author(s);
- Year of publication;
- Title of publication;
- Type of publication as well as publisher;
- Inclusion category;
- Study location (country the study is conducted in);
- Contextual landscape around STEM;
- Type of STEM;
- Topic;
- Study aim and/or research questions;
- Methodology;
- Data collection;
- Study populations and participants;
- Factors investigated;
- Intervention type;
- Outcome of intervention;
- Results and key findings; and
- Practice/policy recommendations.

The extracted data will be discussed in the Results section of this chapter.

Stage 5 – Collating, summarising and reporting the results

The researchers worked collaboratively to extract information from the papers into the data framework, discussing uncertainties and resolving conflicts. After full text screening, 25 papers were included for analysis, of which 11 were in the category of *"pedagogy and gender"* and 14 were in the category of *"factors and gender"*. The results from these papers are reported in detail in the next section. Note that, in contrast to a systematic review, according to Arksey and O'Malley (2005, p. 27), in a scoping review

> there is no attempt made to present a view regarding the 'weight' of evidence in relation to particular interventions or policies. This is because the scoping study does not seek to assess quality of evidence and consequently cannot determine whether particular studies provide robust or generalisable findings.

Results

Overview of the publications

The 25 papers which form the focus of this study include 18 journal articles, 3 conference papers, 3 dissertations and 1 book chapter. The journal articles were published in STEM education journals (n=5), education and higher education journals (n=7) and interdisciplinary and social sciences journals (n=6). The papers use a range of methodologies, including qualitative (n=12), quantitative (n=5) and mixed methodologies (n=8).

The search timeline was not restricted. The studies analysed in this chapter were published between 2001 and 2023, with the majority (n=18) published in the last 10 years, and only a few (n=7) published in the prior 15 years (see Figure 1). The papers represent studies conducted in 12 SSA countries, with the largest number of sources from Ethiopia (n=7); the distribution by country is illustrated in Figure 2.

The studies that were included focused on five main areas (note that some studies fall into two areas).

1. Gender disparity in STEM higher education (n=9), which includes participation of female students, gender gap, underrepresentation of women, enrolment and graduation issues, as well as access and retention.
2. Student success or performance in STEM higher education (n=8) including female students' persistence, academic performance and/or achievement, conceptual understanding, engagement and confidence.
3. Gender-sensitive/responsive pedagogy (n=2).
4. Female students' attitudes towards learning in STEM (n=4) including attitudes towards mathematics, computer sciences and programming, as well as reluctance to use mobile phones for learning.
5. Gender biases and discrimination (n=3) including sexual and gender-based violence and other challenges in learning STEM-based studies.

These areas are broadly representative of studies of gender in STEM higher education. The volume of literature in each category is limited compared to what has been produced globally, hence the importance of identifying literature from SSA contexts.

In the remainder of this section, we summarise the results of the included literature. Since we have not assessed the quality of the literature, we do not make general claims but limit ourselves to identifying themes and reporting on

Figure 1: Publication distribution by year

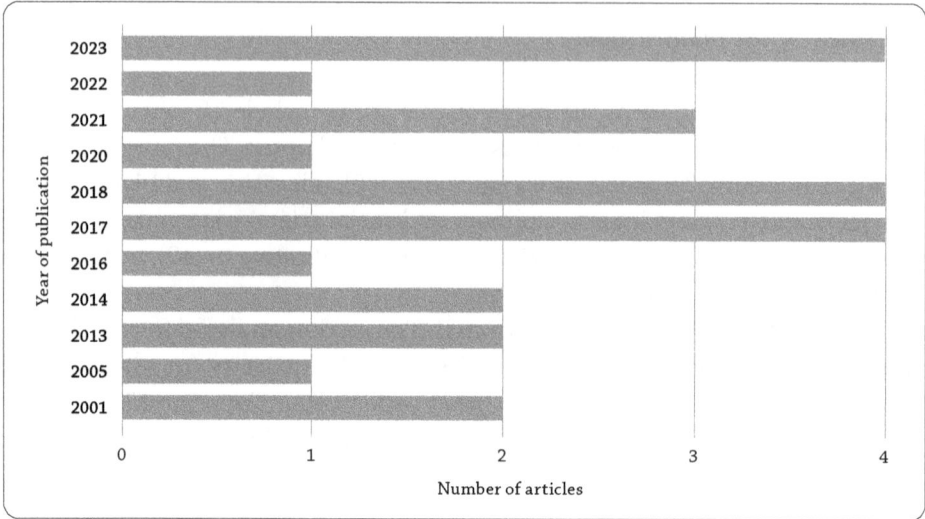

Figure 2: Publication distribution by country

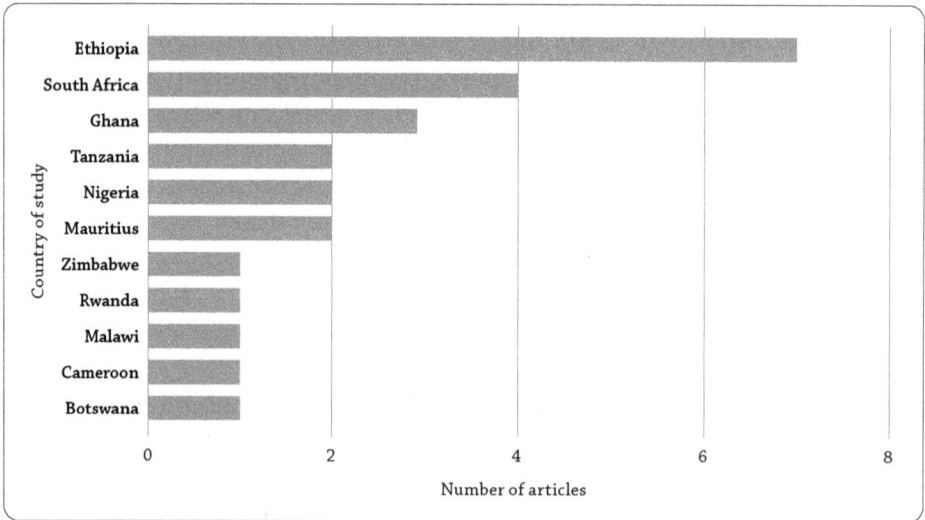

study results. First, we describe details of the national contexts in which STEM education takes place. Next, we discuss studies which have investigated the factors that influence female success in STEM higher education. Subsequently, we focus on pedagogical interventions which aim to improve success. Finally, we report on policy and practice recommendations arising from the surveyed literature and highlight policy–practice gaps.

Contextual landscape around STEM education

It is crucial to consider the contextual landscape around gender and higher education in the included literature as sub-Saharan Africa is a diverse region and contextual factors, such as higher education frameworks and policies, and the positioning of women in society have a marked effect on the participation of women in STEM. Below, we summarise some of the contextual factors raised in the included literature.

Most of the studies agree that despite there being many efforts in improving the gender disparity, participation of female students in STEM disciplines in higher education remains low (Baguant, 2021; Kahamba et al., 2017; Kassie, 2018; Sanga et al., 2013) although improving in some contexts such as Ghana (Appiah-Castel et al., 2020).

Several studies discuss a national focus on female enrolment in STEM education through a range of governmental policies. Ethiopia has invested significantly in higher education, which is supported by 43% of the total education budget (Hailu, 2018) with the aim of increasing STEM graduates. The government requires that 70% of overall university enrolment is in a science field, with the remaining 30% in the social sciences and business economics (Melak & Singh, 2021). Ethiopia also prioritises increasing the number of women studying STEM in higher education (Wuhib, 2017). This is achieved in public institutions by government placement of students in institutions and programmes of study, rather than students applying directly for their choice (Wuhib, 2017). Mbano and Nolan (2017) report that at the time of their study, STEM was the area of focus in Malawi and there was a policy to increase enrolment of females in non-traditional areas by the Malawian government. In Rwanda, a strategic plan pledged to ensure gender equality at all levels of education (Tukahabwa, 2018). In Zimbabwe, the government established a National Gender Policy with a section on the education and training sector. According to Chikunda (2014, p. 9), the policy section includes a number of strategic goals, including to "incorporate gender issues in all curricula at all levels of education" to "eliminate ... discrimination against boys and girls in education and skills training"; to "encourage girls to take on science, mathematics and technology at all levels of education"; and to "introduce gender awareness programmes to pre- and post-training teacher courses".

There are other contextual issues affecting the participation and performance of female students in STEM, including socio-cultural circumstances. For example, Rwanda's socio-political economic landscape bears the scars of the 1994 genocide. The post-genocide government has adopted a policy to recruit women in positions of power, which has played a role in motivating young women (Tukahabwa, 2018). In Ethiopia, Sadati (2018, p. 364) reports that "SGBV [sexual and gender-based violence] is one of the major problems faced by female students in post-secondary institutions". In Sierra Leone, the 2014 Ebola crisis, following on from the civil war which ended in 2002, reversed economic gains. This has increased women's economic vulnerability, reduced their access to education and exposed them to "multiple forms of sexual and gender-based violence" (Wignall et al., 2023, p. 130).

Factors which impact female success in STEM

Factors which the papers in the study identify as affecting women's success in STEM at university can be grouped into (1) factors which affect enrolment in STEM courses; (2) factors which affect persistence and achievement in higher education; and (3) women's experiences of studying STEM.

The enrolment of women in STEM higher education is impacted by their experience of STEM in secondary education. Baguant (2021) emphasises that the image of STEM contributes to women's choices, as does access to information on STEM fields. Baryeh et al. (2001) highlight the impact of counselling in secondary schools. Women's enrolment in STEM is also affected by encouragement from parents and teachers (Tandrayen-Ragoobur & Gokulsing, 2022). In many countries, there are strong socio-cultural influences that affect women's choice of STEM subjects (Kassie, 2018; Melak & Singh, 2021), including "community expectations and domestic responsibilities" and "the complex relationship between marriage, schooling and career development" (Tukahabwa, 2018, p. 168). E-learning can potentially provide a culturally appropriate alternative to in-person education for female students (Sanga et al., 2013) but is hampered by low access to computing and internet resources. National or institutional admissions policies which give preference to female students positively impact enrolment (Appiah-Castel et al., 2020).

The achievement or success of female students within the higher education environment is affected by internal as well as external factors. Internal factors include agency, attitudes, persistence, coping strategies, learning habits and resilience (Hailu, 2018; Kebede, 2023; Melak & Singh, 2021). External factors which impact success are female role models, a supportive environment,

academic support for students who are struggling, national employment opportunities and gender-responsive practices (Baryeh et al., 2001; Hailu, 2018;
Melak & Singh, 2021).

Women's experiences in STEM higher education are negatively impacted by
gender inequalities and gender discrimination "manifested in comments, structures, and practices" (Boateng, 2016, p. 24), requiring that "female scientists
challenge the socio-economic and cultural constructions of society to pursue
careers in science" (Tukahabwa, 2018, p. 132). Kassie reports that "all participants have agreed on unwelcoming sphere of educational institutions" (2018,
p. 168), partly due to "[m]ale students' and teachers' perception and scorning
behaviour on girls" (2018, p. 168). Sadati records a variety of more serious
gender-based problems, including emotional violence and sexual harassment
(2018).

However, Boateng (2016) also reports that women's experiences of gender
discrimination vary depending on their personal support systems, which
may include support from their family, their faith, their community and
their employer. This points to the importance of intersectional approaches to
confronting the challenges experienced by female students (Sikhosana et al.,
2023).

Interventions affecting female success in STEM

Of the analysed studies, 11 studies reported on interventions aiming to improve
female student achievement or student performance in general.

Shishigu et al. (2017) used a five-step problem-solving strategy form of
problem-based learning (PBL) to improve female students' conceptual understanding in physics. The intervention had a substantial positive effect, and
students were motivated to continue using the strategy. Pair programming in
an introductory computer science course required students to work in pairs
to complete a six-week programming lab assignment. This was observed to
improve female students' performance as well as sense of self-efficacy (Mitchley
et al., 2014). Alternative assessment methods for mathematics, including group
discussions, reflective journals and portfolios were shown to improve female
pre-service mathematics teachers' attitudes towards mathematics as well as
their conceptual understanding (Eshun & Abledu, 2006). Mbano and Nolan
(2017) assessed two two-week bridging course camps run by the University of
Malawi for female students as preparation for entering university. The bridging course camps included sessions for study and research skills, personal
and self-development skills, tutorials for STEM subjects to enhance concept

understanding, guest speakers and field trips. Mbano and Nolan (2017) found that there was a positive impact on academic performance, and a more noticeable improvement in participants' motivation to study and in their study skills. Magunje and Brown (2013) investigated four female students' use of mobile phones as a primary computing device. One student felt increasingly disconnected and isolated, but the other students experienced this as an enabling pathway into using computers.

Several pedagogical interventions were not specifically linked to the success of female students or did not find any significant difference between male and female students. A constructionist approach to teaching programming was compared to a conventional teaching approach with lectures and unguided practical sessions by Campbell et al. (2023). The constructionist teaching approach emphasised student collaboration and exploration, with the students working in groups on different real-life projects. Students in the constructionist group showed greater improvement on a standardised programming test. However, there was no significant difference between male and female students (Campbell et al., 2023). An intervention to train spatial thinking as a core part of the first-year engineering graphics course has shown sustained benefits over 20 years (Potter et al., 2006). In this study, female students, as well as students with no prior exposure to technical drawing, entered university with lower spatial visualisation ability. The intervention demonstrated that spatial thinking is a teachable skill and it is predictive of success in engineering studies; thus, it is a valuable contributor to changing student outcomes (Potter et al., 2006). Peter et al. (2021) report on female engineering students' perceptions of entrepreneurship education as a curricular intervention to encourage startups. The curriculum was found to develop critical thinking and innovation, but not to offer enough practical exposure. The authors recommend that women collaborate with other women to learn most effectively (Peter et al., 2021).

Although the focus of our scoping review was on pedagogical interventions that are related to gender, other interventions emerged that, although non-pedagogical, had the potential to impact female students' academic performance and overall success. Wuhib (2017) found that creating residential communities of undergraduate women in STEM in Ethiopia played an important role in their social and academic integration, which in turn helped them in their academic programmes. Wignall et al. (2023) presented the Upskilling for Future Generations Project (Gen-Up), in partnership with the Salesian Don Bosco professional centres in Cameroon and Sierra Leone, which provide technical and vocational education and training (TVET). Gen-Up explores how TVET provides mentorship towards decent employability for vulnerable young women and can challenge systemic gender discrimination. The research has shown the great potential of TVET for transforming outcomes for women, albeit within communities which remain gendered.

Scholarships and admission strategies have also been effective in helping more women access STEM higher education. In Ghana, Kwame Nkrumah University of Science and Technology (KNUST) embarked on an initiative to deliberately increase the admission of females in STEM programmes by lowering the required aggregate score in 2009, and mentoring girls from secondary schools to choose STEM careers (Appiah-Castel et al., 2020). Additionally, KNUST has partnered with the MasterCard Foundation to provide scholarships for women.

Recommendations from studies for policy and practice

In this subsection, we summarise the policy and practice recommendations for government and HEIs made in the included studies. While some of the recommendations are specifically focused on gender, others aim to enhance success for all students.

To increase female enrolment in STEM, some studies recommend that governments and universities review and reframe access strategies for female students (Hailu, 2018; Mbano & Nolan, 2017). HEIs are recommended to provide pre-entry programmes or bridging courses for entering students (Mbano & Nolan, 2017; Sanga et al., 2013), and the government and the private sector are urged to offer scholarships, financial support and other incentives to women who enrol in STEM programmes (Baguant, 2021; Baryeh et al., 2001).

To promote women's success in STEM in HEIs, the included studies recommended that universities should use teaching and learning strategies that increase engagement, including more active and interactive forms of teaching and learning (Baguant, 2021), such as problem-based learning (Hailu, 2018; Shishigu et al., 2017) and peer learning (Melak & Singh, 2021). It is also recommended that marginalised students be provided additional academic support, including extra lessons in STEM subjects such as maths, physics and programming (Baryeh et al., 2001; Sikhosana et al., 2023). Sanga et al. (2013) propose e-learning as a complement to face-to-face teaching and learning, and recommend that HEIs teach computer courses to students, and that governments develop a plan to improve communications infrastructure and increase bandwidth and connectivity.

Melak and Singh (2021) recommend a holistic strategy to provide female students with psychological, economic and academic support, including creating supportive infrastructure and learning facilities, and protecting students from sexual harassment. In the same vein, Hailu (2018) recommends strengthening existing institutional support structures including increasing the scope of gender offices, reimagining first-year orientation and redesigning on-campus residence halls. Wuhib (2017) makes recommendations to improve the effectiveness of residential communities in supporting women in STEM, in particular, the design of residence halls as Living-Learning Programmes, with attention given to orientation and mentoring of female students. Wuhib (2017) also recommends, in the case of Ethiopia, that individual choice be considered when the government allocates students to study programmes.

Several studies emphasise the importance of interactions across institutional boundaries. Two studies recommend career counselling for girls in secondary schools and women in universities both before and after selecting STEM courses (Baryeh et al., 2001; Mbano & Nolan, 2017). Studies recommend role models and mentors for female STEM students in secondary and tertiary education. For example, Baryeh et al. (2001) believe that successful women engineers should be invited to secondary schools as role models. Baguant (2021) recommends connecting with female role models through collaborative linkages with industry. Sikhosana et al. (2023) advocate for progressive policies that ensure higher representation of Black women academics in positions of authority in STEM fields, to ensure the availability of women mentors.

The included studies recommend that HEIs employ gender-responsive curriculum practices, or gender-responsive pedagogy (GRP). This begins with awareness campaigns and workshops to develop STEM educators' awareness of gender (Kahamba et al., 2017) and of their role in perpetuating cultural norms (Chikunda, 2014). Professional development of lecturers is recommended for teaching staff to learn how to develop and implement gender-sensitive teaching and assessments (Chikunda, 2014; Kahamba et al., 2017).

The papers analysed and reported on in this chapter identify disjuncts between policy and practice regarding inclusive pedagogy in STEM higher education in SSA. For example, Kassie (2018) identifies a policy–practice gap in Ethiopia's implementation of affirmative action, allowing female students to be admitted to university STEM programmes with lower school marks than male students. The study found that women had higher rates of academic dismissals as compared to men, which was attributed in part to a lack of planned academic support for these less well-prepared female students (Kassie, 2018). The policy–practice gap is particularly clear in the two included studies where gender-responsive pedagogy was reviewed. According to Kahamba et al. (2017), lecturers' awareness of gender-responsive pedagogy at their Tanzanian university was high, but their understanding was limited, and they therefore did not fully or consistently implement gender-responsive pedagogy. This was explicitly studied, using activity theory, by Chikunda (2014), who identified that lecturers experience tensions between multiple value systems. Among the causes of these tensions are "gender blindness", "lack of conceptual tools for gender-responsive pedagogies" and "lack of learner-centred pedagogies". Chikunda argues that curriculum transformation requires more than policies but should leverage research in gender and science education to "reflexively engag[e] with intended policy implementers such as teacher educators to enable them to look at themselves; to examine their own practices and change them; and to reflect on and talk about the social world" (Chikunda, 2014, p. 274).

Conclusion

This scoping review summarises the extent of literature on external factors and interventions that influence the enrolment and retention of female higher-education students in STEM fields in sub-Saharan Africa. We found relatively few articles on this topic (25 articles), although we are aware of many more initiatives that have not been documented (Omari & Kouevi, 2023). From the data extracted, it is evident that most of the literature is from studies conducted in Ethiopia, South Africa, Ghana, Nigeria and Tanzania. The range of topics identified in the literature related to female students in STEM higher education includes student success, student resilience, academic achievement, academic performance and retention. Most of the studies (14 articles) are on factors affecting academic performance or student success in STEM in higher education. Fewer studies (11 articles) report on pedagogical interventions and policies that promote and encourage holistic success on the part of female students in STEM. Future research should focus on pedagogical interventions which create inclusive and affirming educational experiences.

Although some of the included literature describes the local contextual landscape, in most cases, the empirical work is not located in relation to the governing policy frameworks. We recommend that future research should be undertaken regarding the extent to which policy, pedagogical practice and research inform one another, and that contextual issues be reported in empirical studies.

Practice recommendations advocated in the surveyed literature include access strategies, career guidance, female role models and mentoring, scholarships, teacher development, interactive and collaborative learning activities, and gender-responsive pedagogies and support systems (see Chapter 1 for application of gender-responsive practices and pedagogy in Zimbabwe). The studies also highlight the policy–practice gap regarding gender in STEM in higher education, with policy interventions taking time and considerable effort to produce results in male-dominated and patriarchal institutional and cultural systems.

Practice can only become gender responsive as a result of sustained reflexive engagements with educators to allow them to examine and improve on their own teaching (Chikunda, 2014). A strong recommendation from this study is that there is a significant need for professional development of academic teaching staff. Such professional development should address two primary goals: (1) increasing awareness of and enabling implementation of active and inclusive pedagogical practices; and (2) facilitating lecturers' acknowledgement of their own biases regarding gender.

A possible framework for future research around women in STEM in higher education in SSA is one provided by Hailu and Parra Gaete (2024). They propose a research tool for comparative scholarship on women's involvement in engineering programmes in SSA that includes five components. These are: (1) understanding the socio-political and historical context surrounding women in engineering (which we have shown is seldom undertaken in our included STEM studies); (2) possible critical discourse analysis of gender-based policies (a significant avenue for future research); (3) more complete enrolment and graduation data for female students (where this data is not available); (4) investigation into the employability of women after graduation (which is beyond the scope of the current chapter, but worthy of investigation elsewhere); and (5) qualitative campus climate surveys of higher education institutions (another valuable avenue for future research). These five components address the policy and practice gaps in the reviewed studies and promise a strong analysis of the issues identified if applied.

This chapter recommends that researchers across the region work collaboratively to research and improve innovative teaching and learning, and to improve women's experiences and outcomes in STEM in higher education in SSA. Gender-responsive pedagogy requires dismantling of biases and stereotypes within the systems and the individuals that make up higher education. Ultimately, inclusive pedagogies have the potential to benefit *all* students in STEM, not just women.

Acknowledgements

The authors acknowledge the support of the International Development Research Centre (IDRC). We also gratefully acknowledge the insights of stakeholders from the Inter-University Council of East Africa (IUCEA), the Southern African Regional Universities Association (SARUA), the Association of African Universities (AAU), the Association for the Development of Education in Africa (ADEA) and the SoTL in the South 2023 conference, who participated in co-creation workshops.

About the Authors

Esther Matemba is an independent Engineering Education Consultant situated in Perth, Australia.

Baatseba Ramushu is a Doctoral Student at the University of Johannesburg, South Africa.

Zach Simpson is an Associate Professor at the University of Johannesburg, South Africa.

Helen M. Inglis is an Associate Professor at the University of Pretoria, South Africa.

Lucy A. Wakiaga is an Associate Research Scientist at the African Population and Health Research Center, Kenya.

References

Almukhambetova, A., Torrano, D. H., & Nam, A. (2023). Fixing the leaky pipeline for talented women in STEM. *International Journal of Science and Mathematics Education, 21*, 305–324. https://doi.org/10.1007/s10763-021-10239-1

Appiah-Castel, M. V. D., Lamptey, R. B., Titiloye, K., & Pels, W. A. (2020). Female enrolments in STEM in higher education: Trend analysis from 2003–2018: KNUST as a case study. *Library Philosophy and Practice (e-journal), 4327.*

Arksey, H., & O'Malley, L. (2005). Scoping studies: Towards a methodological framework. *International Journal of Social Research Methodology, 8*(1), 19–32. https://doi.org/10.1080/1364557032000119616

Association of African Universities. (2006). *A toolkit for mainstreaming gender in higher education in Africa.* AAU. https://www.aau.org/wp-content/uploads/sites/9/2019/07/Toolkit-module1.pdf

Baguant, N. D. (2021). Gender and civil engineering in higher education: The case of Mauritius. *International Journal of Higher Education, 10*(1), 157–165. https://doi.org/10.5430/ijhe.v10n1p157

Baryeh, E. A., Squire, P. J., & Mogotsi, M. (2001). Engineering education for women in Botswana. *International Journal of Electrical Engineering Education, 38*(2), 173–182. https://doi.org/10.7227/ IJEEE.38.2.8

Boateng, F. K. (2016, April 12). *In the birdcage of gender discrimination: A grounded theory study of STEM women's experiences in Ghana* [Paper presentation]. Paper presented at the 2016 annual meeting of the American Educational Research Association. Retrieved from the AERA Online Paper Repository.

Campbell, O. O., Adelakun-Adeyemo, O., Akinrinola, F. Y., Chewachong Akih, P., Tshukudu, E., & Becker, B. A. (2023). The impacts of a constructionist scratch programming pedagogy on student achievement with a focus on gender. *CompEd 2023: Proceedings of the ACM conference on global computing education* (Volume 1, pp. 29–35). Association of Computing Machinery. https://dl.acm.org/doi/10.1145/3576882.3617911

Chapin, J., Skovgaard, M., & Warne, V. (2020). *Integrating gender responsive pedagogy into higher education: Our approach*. International Network for Advancing Science and Policy (INASP). https://www.inasp.info/ sites/default/files/2021-01/Gender%20responsive%20pedagogy%20Approach%20paper.pdf

Chikunda, C. (2014). Identifying tensions around gender-responsive curriculum practices in science teacher education in Zimbabwe: An activity theory analysis. *African Journal of Research in Mathematics, Science and Technology Education, 18*(3), 264–275. https://doi.org/10.1080/10288457.2014.956409

Chikunda, C., & Chikunda, P. (2016). Patriarchy rules: Transforming resistance to gender inequalities in science teacher education in Zimbabwe. *Cultural and Pedagogical Inquiry, 8*(2), 11–22. https://doi. org/10.18733/C3JG64

Eshun, B., & Abledu, G. (2006). The effect of alternative assessment on the attitudes and achievement in mathematics of female pre-service teachers in Ghana. *African Journal of Educational Studies in Mathematics and Sciences, 1*(2001), 21–30. https://doi.org/10.4314/ajesms.v1i1.38574

European Commission: Directorate-General for Research and Innovation. (2019). *She figures 2018 – Gender in research and innovation: Statistics and indicators*. Publications Office of the European Union. https://data. europa.eu/doi/10.2777/124790

Fisher, M., Nyabaro, V., Mendum, R., & Moses Osiru, M. (2020). Making it to the PhD: Gender and student performance in sub-Saharan Africa. *PLoS ONE 15*(12): e0241915. https://doi.org/10.1371/journal. pone.0241915

Hailu, M. (2018). *Understanding why women stay: Examining persistence factors of women majoring in science and technology programmes in public Ethiopian universities using a mixed methods design* (Publication no. 1451). Doctoral dissertation, University of Denver. Digital Commons @ DU. https://digitalcommons.du.edu/ etd/1451/

Hailu, M. F., & Parra Gaete, I. (2024). Sub-Saharan women in engineering higher education: A literature-informed research tool. *Policy Futures in Education, 22*(7), 1278–1297. https://doi. org/10.1177/14782103241226527

Hill, C., Corbett, C., & St Rose, A. (2010). *Why so few? Women in science, technology, engineering, and mathematics*. American Association of University Women.

Kahamba, J. S., Massawe, F. A., & Kira, E. S. (2017). Awareness and practice of gender responsive pedagogy in higher learning institutions: The case of Sokoine University of Agriculture, Tanzania. *Journal of Education, Humanities and Sciences, 6*(2), 1–16.

Kassie, K. (2018). Gender difference in higher education in Ethiopia: A case of Addis Ababa University (AAU). *Africa Review, 10*(2), 157–172. https://doi.org/10.1080/09744053.2018.1485254

Kebede, W. (2023). Investigating female learners' attitude and challenges towards mathematics at the department of mathematics, Injibara College of Teachers' Education, Injibara, Ethiopia. *Cogent Education, 10*(2). https://doi.org/10.1080/2331186X.2023.2256202

Kouassi, A. (2016). Why Africa needs female scientists. *Mastercard Foundation*. https://mastercardfdn.org/ why-africa-needs-female-scientists/

Levac, D., Colquhoun, H., & O'Brien, K. K. (2010). Scoping studies: Advancing the methodology. *Implementation Science, 5*(69). https://doi.org/10.1186/1748-5908-5-69

Magunje, C., & Brown, C. (2013). From cellphone to computer: University students' use of technology in first year. In E. Ivala (Ed.), *Proceedings of the 8th international conference on e-learning* (pp. 496–502). Academic Conferences and Publishing International.

Mbano, N., & Nolan, K. (2017). Increasing access of female students in science technology, engineering and mathematics (STEM), in the University of Malawi (UNIMA). *Science Education International, 28*(1), 53–77.

Melak, A., & Singh, S. (2021). Women's participation and factors affecting their academic performance in engineering and technology education: A study of Ethiopia. *Sustainability, 13*(4), 2246. https://doi.org/10.3390/su13042246

Mitchley, M., Dominguez-Whitehead, Y., Liccardo, S. (2014). Pair programming, confidence and gender considerations at a South African university. In B. Thege, S. Popescu-Willigmann, R. Pioch & S. Badri-Höher (Eds.), *Paths to career and success for women in science* (pp. 133–148). Springer. https://doi.org/10.1007/978-3-658-04061-1_8

Namatende-Sakwa, L. (2018). The construction of gender in Ugandan English textbooks: A focus on gendered discourses. *Pedagogy, Culture & Society, 26*(4), 609–629. https://doi.org/10.1080/14681366.2018.1436583

Omari, R., & Kouevi, A. (2023). *Women in engineering education and careers in Benin and Ghana.* Final Technical Report submitted to International Development Research Centre (IDRC), Canada. IDRC Grant. https://idl-bnc-idrc.dspacedirect.org/handle/10625/61998

Onyeocha, E. I. E., Ukwuoma, U. F., & Onyeocha, O. M. (2023). Cultural barriers to females accessing technical and vocational education and training (TVET) in Nigeria: Remedial roles for National Board for Technical Education (NBTE). *African Journal of Educational Management, Teaching and Entrepreneurship Studies, 8*(1), 12–19. https://ajemates.org/index.php/ajemates/article/view/200

PASGAR (Partnership for African Social & Governance Research). (2023). *PedaL: A transformative learning experience.* https://pedal-africa.org/about-pedal/a-transformative-learning-experience/

Peter, F., Eze, S., Osigwe, K., Peter, A., Adeyemi, E., Okologbo, C., & Asiyanbola, T. (2021). Entrepreneurship education and venture intention of female engineering students in a Nigerian university. *International Journal of Higher Education, 10*(4), 9–20. https://doi.org/10.5430/ijhe.v10n4p9

Potter, C., Van Der Merwe, E., Kaufman, W., & Delacour, J. (2006). A longitudinal evaluative study of student difficulties with engineering graphics. *European Journal of Engineering Education, 31*(2), 201–214. https://doi.org/10.1080/03043790600567894

Sadati, S. M. H. (2018). Cellphilming in four ATVET colleges: A mirror, reflecting gender issues in Ethiopia. *Studies in Social Justice, 12*(2), 364–371. https://journals.library.brocku.ca/index.php/SSJ/article/view/1676

Sanga, C., Magesa, M. M., Chingonikaya, E., & Kayunze, K. A. (2013). Can e-learning promote participation of female students in STEM disciplines in higher learning institutions of Tanzania? *International Journal of Education and Development using ICT, 9*(3), 86–102.

Shishigu, A., Hailu, A., & Anibo, Z. (2017). Problem-based learning and conceptual understanding of college female students in physics. *Eurasia Journal of Mathematics, Science and Technology Education, 14*(1), 145–154. https://doi.org/10.12973/ejmste/78035

Sikhosana, H., Malatji, H., & Munyoro, A. (2023). Experiences and challenges of black women enrolled in a STEM field in a South African urban university: A qualitative study. *Cogent Education, 10*(2). https://doi.org/10.1080/2331186X.2023.2273646

Simpson, Z., & Bester, J. (2015). Cast in concrete? Constructions of gender in civil engineering laboratory practicals. In *Proceedings of the 3rd biennial conference of the South African Society for Engineering Education* (pp. 179–188). SASSEE.

Tandrayen-Ragoobur, V., & Gokulsing, D. (2022). Gender gap in STEM education and career choices: What matters? *Journal of Applied Research in Higher Education, 14*(3), 1021–1040. https://doi.org/10.1108/JARHE-09-2019-0235

Tukahabwa, D. (2018). Becoming women 'scientists': Negotiating gendered constructions of science at university in Rwanda. Unpublished doctoral dissertation, Canterbury Christ Church University, New Zealand.

UNESCO (United Nations Educational, Scientific and Cultural Organization). (2024a). *UNESCO call to action: Closing the gender gap in science* [Programme and meeting document]. https://unesdoc.unesco.org/ark:/48223/pf0000388641

UNESCO (2024b). *Advocacy brief: Support girls and women to pursue STEM subjects and careers* [Programme and meeting document]. https://unesdoc.unesco.org/ark:/48223/pf0000391937

Wignall, R., Piquard, B., Joel, E., Mengue, M.-T., Ibrahim, Y., Sam-Kpakra, R., Hyannick Obah, I., Ayissi, E. N., & Negou, N. (2023). Imagining the future through skills: TVET, gender and transitions towards decent employability for young women in Cameroon and Sierra Leone. *Journal of the British Academy, 11*(3), 121–151. https://doi.org/10.5871/jba/011s3.121

Wuhib, F. W. (2017). *The role of residential communities for the academic and social success of undergraduate women in STEM majors: The case of a public university in Ethiopia* (Order No. 10270982). Doctoral dissertation, Syracuse University, N.Y., U.S.A. ProQuest Dissertations & Theses Global. https://www.proquest.com/docview/1926757169

From Individuals to Institutions: Scaling Up Women Scientists' Impact in the Global South

Tonya Blowers, Sena Galazzi, Erin Johnson and Giulia Signori

Introduction

Efforts to close the gender gap in Science, Technology, Engineering and Mathematics (STEM) have increasingly emphasised the need for both individual empowerment and systemic reform. Global initiatives, such as UNESCO's 2024 call to action, have highlighted persistent disparities in women's participation in STEM, and have called for coordinated action to dismantle gender stereotypes, expand educational pathways and foster inclusive workplace environments. These goals reflect a dual challenge: ensuring that individual women are supported to pursue and thrive in STEM careers, while also transforming the institutional structures that continue to reproduce inequality.

In this chapter, we examine the activities and programmes of the Organization for Women in Science for the Developing World (OWSD) as a case study to explore how individual empowerment can drive systemic change in STEM across the Global South. Specifically, we ask:

1. How can investment in individual women scientists, through fellowships, awards and visibility, contribute to institutional transformation and the dismantling of gender stereotypes in science?

2. What mechanisms enable individual success stories to influence broader educational and policy environments, and how can these be scaled to promote gender equity in STEM?
3. What are the implications of OWSD's model for future funding strategies aimed at promoting women's leadership and participation in STEM fields?

Rather than providing definitive answers, this chapter offers insights drawn from OWSD's experience to illuminate these questions and inform future efforts to advance gender equity in science.

OWSD's mission, on the broadest scale, is to promote positive change in the opportunities available for women in STEM disciplines in higher education institutions throughout the developing world, based on evidence that the participation of more women in STEM improves both the quality and relevance of scientific research (Lleras, 2008). This research in turn can play a major role in mitigating the global challenges with which all citizens will be faced in the coming decades: climate change, disease and pandemics, food and water security, safe and affordable energy and housing. OWSD provides training and various activities, including access to scholarships and fellowships, to raise awareness and attract women to STEM fields. The organisation ensures that women have the resources and resilience needed to complete their education. OWSD provides networking support so that women scientists' experience and knowledge can be instrumental in both transmitting knowledge to their immediate and broader academic communities as well as implementing the results of their research within their wider communities.

> In a world characterised by a predominantly knowledge-based economy, well-trained and highly qualified human resources are key to sustainable development. It is now recognised that education, especially higher education, is critical for economic growth, job creation, competitiveness in the global market, socio-cultural revitalisation, and improvement in the standards of living of the populations. To succeed in these areas, countries must make substantial and intelligent investments in various fields of higher education and scientific research to train qualified higher-level professionals and a technical workforce capable of meeting development needs. (ADEA, 2022)[1]

---

1 The ADEA Triennale on Education is one of Africa's seminal high-level forums for political dialogue, knowledge sharing and fruitful experiences. It focuses on critical themes that transform Africa's education systems for sustainable social and economic development. Through the Triennale, ADEA fosters continental, regional and cross-country interactions in support of peer learning and knowledge exchange.

Background and context

The importance of women's participation in STEM

Why are we so keen for women to participate in STEM? Evidence suggests that if women are not involved directly in scientific research, we lose their specific experiences and local knowledge. In many countries across the developing world – as well as in parts of Europe and North America – women are at the forefront of major global challenges. For many, their daily routines are shaped by their roles as primary caregivers for children and the elderly. Women also make up the majority of agricultural workers, growing and harvesting food for their families and collecting fresh water for drinking. When women are included both as participants in scientific research and as its beneficiaries, the impact on children, the elderly and local communities is more likely to be meaningful, effective and successfully implemented.[2] In addition, there is a great deal of evidence to suggest that when women are not adequately represented in the design of research, the concerns and impact of the research on women are often left out of the methodology, creating inaccurate and often harmful, even lethal consequences (seatbelts not designed for pregnant women and diagnoses of heart attack symptoms based only on men, are only the best-known examples).[3]

Londa Schiebinger, founder of the Gendered Innovations project at Stanford University (USA), has argued that "sex and gender should be considered in each step of the research process from strategic considerations for establishing priorities and theory to more routine tasks of formulating questions, designing methodologies, and interpreting data" (Schiebinger, 2014, p. 3).

OWSD: Visible, active women in STEM

The Organization for Women in Science for the Developing World (OWSD) was founded in 1987 in Trieste, Italy, as a programme of The World Academy of Sciences (TWAS) and later established as a programme unit of UNESCO. From the beginning, the goal was to seek out existing and potential women scientists

---

2 "Why do we need women in STEM?", the National Commission for the Promotion of Equality's (NCPE) 7 February 2024 statement, as discussed by the 9th International Day of Women and Girls in Science Assembly (8–9 February 2024), under Women in science leadership: A new era for sustainability – Concept note and provisional agenda (https://www.un.org/sites/un2.un.org/files/2024/02/2024_idwgis_agenda_-_210124.pdf).

3 For more on which, see Tannenbaum et al. (2019). Londa Schiebinger's case study reports for Stanford University are well known, and examples are included in the European Commission's Directorate-General for Research and Innovation (2020) publication, *Gendered innovations 2*.

living and working in the Global South and encourage them to participate in a supportive network, *identifying the specific challenges they face and proposing means to* overcome these challenges. It was also important to ensure that women scientists were visible and represented in the notoriously male-dominated spheres of physics and maths. These goals of increased participation and visibility for women from the Global South in scientific research remain the bedrock of OWSD's mission. Importantly, through a global network of members and national chapters, OWSD has been able to ensure that women scientists are visible and included in research design and implementation at national, regional and international levels.

In 2025, OWSD counts nearly 11 000 members, and when membership in any one country reaches the threshold of at least 20, they can opt to establish an OWSD national chapter. At the time of writing (August 2025), OWSD counts 58 chapters throughout the Global South.[4] These chapters offer outreach and training activities and foster a much needed and appreciated sense of belonging and community. More and more, they are valued also as a source of information and feedback for national education systems regarding best practices for women in STEM (OWSD, 2024b).

In addition to supporting the work carried out by the chapters at a national and regional level, the OWSD Secretariat allocates funding for scholarships for individual women scientists from developing countries. For nearly 30 years, OWSD has been designing, developing and implementing master's, PhD and early-career fellowships in STEM subjects for individual women, as well as recognising outstanding women scientists each year through an awards scheme. More than 400 women scientists from least developed and under-resourced countries have completed their OWSD PhD fellowships in other Global South countries through a South-to-South mobility scheme and a further 100 are currently completing their fellowships. Further, 124 early-career women scientists have received up to USD50 000 each to set up centres of excellence in their home institutes in the South, and 69 women scientists have been recognised for their outstanding contributions to science.

OWSD's cornerstone activity has been the South-to-South PhD fellowships programme, established in 1997 when the first agreement was signed with the Swedish International Development Cooperation Agency (Sida). This fellowship model covers fellows' monthly stipends, return travel, visa and health insurance costs (and tuition and registration fees where necessary). In addition, OWSD also provides earmarked funding for alumnae-specific research and development activities, which enhances their work's impact. Alumnae benefit

---

4 https://owsd.net/national-chapters

from ongoing training, networking opportunities and collaborative support through national chapters and international conferences. This ecosystem fosters connections across OWSD programmes, ensuring that alumnae remain integrated into the broader community and can continue to support each other's work.

However, due to funding cuts, OWSD paused its annual call for PhD fellowship applications in 2023 for the first time in 25 years. This unexpected setback allowed OWSD time and space to re-evaluate the programme's sustainability, and to conduct a comprehensive survey of the successes and challenges of the longstanding programme. The results of that re-evaluation have played a substantial role in the development of the recommendations presented in this chapter and led to the reassignment of remaining funds to a new programme for displaced women scientists, which is discussed in further detail below.

It is clear that whereas fellowships confer visibility through specific opportunities over the long term, a popular and more immediate way to boost the visibility of individuals is by awarding prizes. Focusing on women from developing countries at the early-career stage, the OWSD Secretariat has co-designed a high-profile awards scheme with The Elsevier Foundation. Since 2013, the annual OWSD-EF awards recognise and celebrate the achievements of five early-career women scientists in the South who have worked hard against social, economic and cultural pressures to achieve internationally competitive results. Each year, awardees receive USD5 000 and an all-expenses-paid trip to a relevant international meeting, to present their research, network with others in their fields and receive recognition for their award. While the award itself is modest, the awardees are celebrated in international and national media and are highly visible. As a result, past awardees are often doubly recognised and awarded, some have even been received by their country's presidents, others go on to receive more awards and fellowships, including the L'Oreal-UNESCO Award for Women in Science Fellowships and the British Council Award.

Impact data collected from awardees revealed that nearly all recipients of the OWSD-EF Award report a positive influence of the award on their visibility (in the media and within their own institutes), increased collaborations, additional fellowships and research grants, and invitations as speakers or panellists, or on expert committees and funding boards, according to a survey conducted in 2020 (OWSD, 2024c). Award recipients also report that the award made them more confident and more motivated to continue in their scientific careers and to seek out more leadership opportunities (OSWD, 2024b).

The impact of visibility: In the words of OWSD-Elsevier Foundation awardees

> *"After getting the award, I was invited as editorial board member by three journals. Most of the university students wanted to do their research work under my guidance. I was invited for so many national and international conferences and seminars as a resource person and I am now a member of a high-level drinking water quality standard revision committee."*
> – Tista Prasai Joshi, 2019 award winner
>
> *"It's been a roller coaster ride ... one minute I was working quietly and following my dreams ... and then I am on the news, social media, etc. The impact on my career and professional development has been amazing. I've become more competitive at grants (I've won 3 out of 5 applied for so far), I have been invited to sit on a WHO expert committee and Research Funding Boards and review panels, I've had some high impact publications and I am now collaborating with many more people. I have also now mentored more people. On a personal level, it's been very humbling as I appreciate that the recognition from the Award is a privilege many black women do not have and so I use whatever platform and opportunity I have to be an ambassador for women scientists of colour."* – Uduak Okomo, 2019 award winner
>
> *"The award made me more prominent in my immediate community and I am taken more seriously in the international community. In my personal development, I have developed more confidence in interacting in many forums. For my collaborations, I got exposure to many international communities in my field of interest. For example, through the visibility I gained through the award, I networked with organisations in my country, became a climate change consultant and got nominated as a member of the Group on Earth Observation GEO working group on Climate Change and Data."* – Rabia Said, 2015 award winner

OWSD is enhancing and expanding programmes to further strengthen the impact and influence of women in STEM. This requires tracking and evaluating the impact of existing individual fellowship programmes, not only on the recipients themselves but also on the broader systems they interact with, including their institutions, research environments and local communities. By examining how these fellowships contribute to long-term systemic change, we can better understand and strengthen the pathways that enable more women to thrive in STEM leadership and drive transformative progress. This entails acknowledging that however successful any one individual may be, funds can only reach a limited number of individuals, and action needs to be taken at the structural level for changes in perception, access and promotion of women in STEM to occur. We suggest, however, that even at a structural level, the role of individuals can be decisive: by supporting and identifying outstanding women scientists, science granting councils and national educational programmes can have direct dialogue with women who have successfully navigated their own national systems and can recommend best practices as well as identify challenges and gaps. As 'insiders', fellowship alumnae are ideally placed to contact and liaise with other key players in the system. Moreover, as previously mentioned, they serve as influential role models for other women in their communities, creating a powerful multiplier effect that inspires and enables more women to pursue opportunities in STEM.

Methodology and framework for analysis

Methodology

This chapter draws on a mixed-methods approach, combining structured evaluations and qualitative testimonials to assess the impact of OWSD programmes on women's participation and leadership in STEM across the Global South. Structured data sources include:

- OWSD's 2023 comprehensive evaluation of its South-to-South PhD fellowship programme, which involved a survey of 176 alumnae and in-depth interviews with selected fellows.
- Impact surveys conducted by OWSD and the Elsevier Foundation on award recipients, measuring visibility, career progression and institutional influence.
- Quantitative data on fellowship distribution, graduation rates and chapter growth, extracted from OWSD's internal reports and publications.
- These structured evaluations are complemented by individual testimonials from OWSD fellows and awardees, which provide rich, narrative insights into personal experiences, challenges and achievements. While these stories are not generalisable, they illustrate the broader ripple effects of individual empowerment on institutional and community-level change.

The combination of structured data and personal narratives enables a nuanced understanding of how visibility, support and leadership development contribute to systemic transformation in STEM education and research environments.

Key stakeholders in STEM reform

STEM education reform is highly complex and must be adapted to diverse cultural, educational, geographical and political contexts. Its design and implementation require the engagement and coordination of a wide range of stakeholders. An inclusive and participatory approach is essential, ensuring that decision-making processes acknowledge and incorporate the expertise of those historically marginalised in shaping educational and scientific agendas – focusing, in this case, particularly on women. Equitable partnerships, both locally and globally, are critical to this process, requiring ethical collaboration that prioritises shared leadership, resource distribution and long-term systems change rather than extractive or one-sided engagement. Such stakeholders may include: institutional researchers (who act both as students and as teachers promoting and implementing change in the curriculum and pedagogy); academics and professors; institutional governors and policymakers (heads of departments, deans and vice-chancellors); as well as those involved in the nationwide creation and implementation of educational policies, including the various relevant national ministries (e.g. ministries of higher education; research and development; or science and technology). Additional critical actors are those who can provide specifically earmarked funds for the three interlinked areas of women, science and development, including cooperation agencies (e.g. GIZ, IDRC, Sida, UKRI[5]), foundations linked to corporations (MasterCard, IKEA, Ford, Elsevier Foundation, etc.) as well as private foundations and individuals (e.g. Bill & Melinda Gates; William and Flora Hewlett). Instrumental too are women in science organisations and associations who have on-the-ground experience of challenges and best practices. OWSD national chapters, for example, are key players here, not least because they are linked to a network across the Global South. Science granting councils also play a key role in determining how limited national research funds are distributed, and how success is evaluated, having a direct impact on which disciplines and research areas are promoted and supported. Critically, research councils can promote – during the design and implementation of programmes – greater inclusivity and diversity for the sake of excellent science.[6]

All these players and strategies can be brought together to determine an integrated nationwide strategy for implementing impactful higher education strategies. In order to effect institutional change to impact multiple parts of the STEM education system, teams of 'change agents' may select multiple strategies and tactics to enact at one time and over multiple years of a project.

---

5 GIZ – Deutsche Gesellschaft für Internationale Zusammenarbeit (German Agency for International Cooperation); IDRC – International Development Research Centre (Canada); Sida – Swedish International Development Cooperation Agency; UKRI – UK Research and Innovation.

6 The Athena SWAN Charter is an example of a successful mechanism for highly impactful change for diversity and inclusion in higher education, developed by a United Kingdom-based not-for-profit called AdvanceHE. See the Athena Swan Charter (https://www.advance-he.ac.uk/equality-charters/athena-swan-charter). See also, Wilkinson (2019) on the role Athena SWAN can play in gender equality and science communication.

Visibility and gender-transformative strategies

When women scientists from developing countries are increasingly visible on national and international stages as leaders and innovators in research, their presence becomes not only more accepted but also more valued, creating a ripple effect. This visibility fosters greater inclusion of women in research projects, breaking down barriers of bias and representation. Visibility also challenges entrenched gender norms and stereotypes, reshaping social perceptions of women's roles in science (Breda et al., 2023; González-Pérez et al., 2020). As women scientists gain recognition, the broader social, cultural and institutional structures around them become more supportive, leading to more equitable opportunities and fostering systemic change in research environments. The visibility of women scientists functions as both a symbolic and practical intervention: it challenges normative assumptions about who can be a scientist, while also altering the institutional and cultural landscapes that sustain gender inequities in science (Schiebinger & Schraudner, 2011).

Let us now consider how this applies to the key ideas introduced at the beginning of the chapter. The goal declared by UNESCO in 2024 was ensuring that "girls are never discouraged from pursuing their aspirations to become scientists" and to "dismantle the barriers that hinder women from realising their full potential in science" (UNESCO, 2024, p. 2).

On the one hand, a focus on visibility characterises the classic and effective role-model approach: highlighting successful women working in STEM, rewarding them for their achievements, publicising their success, asking them to manage outreach and passing on guidelines for how to reproduce these achievements, through word of mouth, thereby enabling others to achieve as they have done.

The second approach requires identifying and working with all the different actors in the systemic framework that 'prop up' scientific careers in any one country to provide awareness of challenges, suggested best practices and toolkits for action that can lead to policy change. Other chapters in this collection deal with the kinds of policies that might be introduced – but ultimately, policies are needed, for example, concerning the description and timing of courses, availability of places and grants, schedules, additional training and flexible career paths (see Chapter 3 for in-depth discussion on gender policies in African universities, or Chapter 9 for a scoping review of pedagogical efforts to address gender disparities in sub-Saharan Africa). Such policies can raise awareness of the barriers facing women in science among practitioners and decision-makers in higher education and ensure there are tools to overcome these barriers.

Benefits and challenges: The broader ripple effect of fellowships on research and communities

While individual awards offer significant opportunities for the women who receive them, upscaling such initiatives presents challenges. The number of fellowships awarded in any given programme is limited, meaning the overall impact on the number of women entering STEM fields is constrained by the number of available scholarships and awards. Additionally, PhD fellowships are long-term commitments (typically at least four years), and their results become visible only years after completion. This delay means that the impact on an individual's career can only be measured through surveys and longitudinal data gathered over time. Furthermore, funding priorities may shift over time, influencing the continuation of such programmes.

Despite these challenges, surveys conducted by OWSD reveal that our South-to-South PhD fellowships programme has been highly successful, with 576 fellowships awarded to women from Scientifically and Technologically Lagging Countries (STLCs) to study at host institutions in the South. By the end of 2024, 406 fellows had graduated, with 99 continuing their studies. Personal accounts from fellows illustrate how fellowships are both life-changing for recipients and can have measurable impacts on science policy and on communities. For example, Priscilla Nyadoi, an OWSD alumna (PhD 2011), used the knowledge she gained during her PhD to become a key advocate for wildlife conservation in Uganda. As Executive Director of the Uganda Wildlife Society, she influenced national legislation, including the Uganda Wildlife Act (2019) and the Community Conservation Policy (2020). Her work demonstrates how an individual fellow's expertise can shape national policies, ultimately benefiting both local ecosystems and global biodiversity conservation efforts. This case highlights how fellowships can have a ripple effect that extends well beyond the recipient.

Additionally, the influence of OWSD fellows can reverberate within their communities in unexpected ways. For instance, Myo Ma Ma Than, a 2004 alumna from Myanmar, has used her PhD research to drive women's empowerment within the agricultural sector. Through her 'female-led farming' projects, she challenges traditional male-dominated decision-making in rural communities and empowers women across the agricultural value chain. Despite significant infrastructure challenges in Myanmar, her work has demonstrated that empowering women in agriculture not only enhances livelihoods but also boosts food security in remote areas. Her contribution underscores how fellowship recipients can transform sectors traditionally dominated by men, improving both the local economy and women's social standing.

Furthermore, women who study abroad as part of these fellowships often bring back valuable knowledge and insights to their home countries, enhancing the relevance of local research to national and regional needs. Marycelin Baba, a 2005 alumna, exemplifies this broader impact. As a leading Nigerian virologist, she focused her research on underdiagnosed arboviruses such as West Nile, dengue and Zika. Her research has had profound implications for public health in Nigeria, where she has also played a crucial role in eradicating polio as head of Nigeria's WHO polio lab. Marycelin's work on neglected diseases highlights how a fellowship recipient's knowledge transfer can lead to significant improvements in healthcare outcomes, demonstrating the far-reaching effects of individual scientific contributions.

These case studies demonstrate that while fellowships promote individual careers, their broader impact is far-reaching, affecting not only the fellows themselves but also the scientific communities and policy landscapes of their home countries. Quantitative data further emphasise the benefits of fellowships (see Figure 1).

Figure 1: OWSD fellowship benefits in numbers

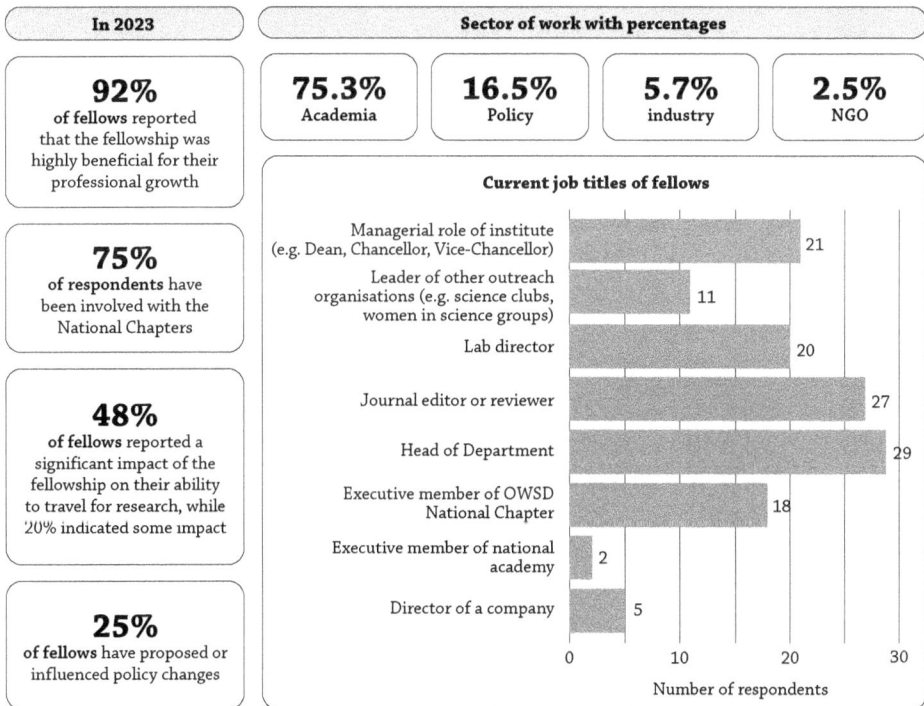

Note. Data and graphs are from an internal document (OWSD, 2024a).

An internal report (OWSD, 2024a) explored the findings of a comprehensive evaluation conducted in 2023, including a survey of 176 OWSD PhD alumnae and a series of in-depth interviews with select alumnae. The report highlights fellows' transformative achievements and significant contributions to science and society over 25 years. Through both numbers and narratives, OWSD demonstrates the profound and lasting impact of sustained investment in women scientists.

These case studies also illustrate the incidental and non-systematic nature of the impacts that investment in an individual can bring, reliant on selection processes that ensure women are selected for awards because of their all-around contribution to the scientific endeavour. In order to scale up the impact such fellowships can have on the entire scientific ecosystem, we need reliable, repeatable methods at the structural level. Can resources focused on individual women in STEM effectively 'change the system', or are they rather more limited to promoting individual women's careers?

OWSD's comprehensive review of the PhD programme's impact, conducted in 2023, shifted from primarily reporting quantitative results (such as the number of fellows and countries represented) to capturing long-term outcomes. This includes the personal growth of fellows – such as promotions, increased research recognition and leadership roles – and the systemic changes at their institutions, such as gender policy reforms. The focus on these long-term effects not only reinforces the programme's value but also strengthens the case for continued funding and partnerships.

Accelerating institutional change through individual fellowships

In 2024, in recognition that conflict and climate change in many countries were causing additional and complex challenges for women to participate and remain active in scientific research, OWSD partnered with host institutes in Jordan and Türkiye to launch an innovative science, gender and displacement programme. Twenty-four women from conflict-affected countries have already begun this two-year programme in 2024 and OWSD works alongside the host institutes (Hashemite University in Jordan and Aydin Istanbul University in Türkiye) to ensure that the institutions themselves identify the specific challenges faced and resources needed, equipping academic supervisors and university administrators with the skills, frameworks and systems necessary to integrate refugee women scientists into their student populations. This approach aligns with the United Nations Refugee Agency (UNHCR) 15by30 Roadmap, which sets out strategic actions to achieve 15% refugee enrolment in higher education by 2030.[7]

This model of institutional support alongside individual fellowships is highly effective. For women refugee scientists, accessing a master's programme is not merely a step in their educational journey but a vital bridge between learning and earning, between dependence and self-reliance. It determines whether their talents are lost to brain drain or channelled into meaningful contributions to their host countries, diaspora communities, the global scientific community (through the right to science), and eventually, their home countries when conditions allow their return. Investing in institutions that can systematically support the inclusion of refugee students ensures that education is not an isolated opportunity but a sustainable, long-term mechanism for integration, capacity-building and resilience.

By supporting institutions that are committed to these goals, OWSD is helping to create a more inclusive academic and research environment where displaced women scientists are not just accommodated but actively empowered to contribute to science and society.

Interventions to promote systemic change

Creating centres of excellence through OWSD fellowships

OWSD early-career fellowships (funded by IDRC since 2017) are intended to create research centres of excellence in the Global South, focused on one outstanding individual. The fellowship is a highly flexible grant (up to USD50 000) to be spent on a broad range of training, teaching and technical assistance, communication skills, equipment, laboratory set-up and management, and linking with industry, that will allow the individual scientist to continue her research at an advanced level. To be eligible, she must have been residing in one of the eligible STLCs for at least five years and be already employed at an institute there as the grant does not cover the researcher's stipend. Although the programme has only been in place for a short period, its impact is already visible, with 124 fellowships awarded to date, and ongoing fellows contributing to long-term change.

A striking example of the programme's success is Elizabeth Bandason, an OWSD Early-Career Fellow from Malawi. She was able to overcome a significant barrier in her research – access to equipment – by using the fellowship

---

7 https://www.unhcr.org/uk/media/15by30-roadmap-expanding-higher-education-skills-and-self-reliance-refugees

to acquire the tools she needed to continue her groundbreaking work in insect control in Malawi. Elizabeth was determined not to leave Malawi for a post-doctoral opportunity, as she saw her potential to create change in her home country. This commitment to staying and building a research team highlights how the fellowship has helped to support individual women scientists in their pursuit of excellence while contributing to the scientific capacity in developing countries. Beyond her research, Elizabeth's leadership in the OWSD Malawi Chapter and mentoring of young women scientists in Malawi exemplify the ripple effect of empowering individual women in STEM. Her contributions are not only transforming agriculture but are also fostering a new generation of female scientists in her country.

> When I got awarded the PhD, my next question was, what next? I desper-ately wanted to continue what I was doing in Michigan back home in Malawi, but I couldn't because there was no way I could access the equip-ment I needed. Either I let my dreams go down the drain and do what I could in Malawi, or I went back to the United States to continue working with my supervisor (she had offered me a postdoc). But I knew that if I went back there, I would be denying myself an opportunity to grow as an African woman scientist – and I would delay the changes in insect control I wanted to see in Malawian farming. I had to find a way to stay in Malawi and build a team. OWSD gave me that once-in-a lifetime opportunity! (Elizabeth Bandason, OWSD Early-Career Fellow)

The fellowships are not only about supporting individual careers; they are also about creating centres of research excellence that can address regional challenges. Early-career fellows are selected using the scientific communi-ty's standard parameters to determine how competitive their research is (e.g. international publications, peer-reviewed journals, collaborations) but also additional 'soft skills' such as leadership qualities, evidence of mentoring and training, ability to communicate her science to diverse and non-specialist audi-ences, and to go beyond academia to link with industry, the private sector and policymakers. Only with these skills can her work have the broadest impact and ultimately become sustainable.

Pendo Bigambo, a lecturer at the University of Dar es Salaam, is addressing the environmental impact of cotton farming through her innovative research in textile technology, materials science and mechanical engineering. As co-founder and vice-chair of the OWSD Tanzania National Chapter, she actively advocates for women in STEM, organising conferences and workshops to inspire and empower future generations. Her groundbreaking work focuses on developing sustainable cotton recycling processes to reduce the environmental footprint of cotton farming. By offering alternatives to traditional cotton farming, which competes with food crops for limited land and resources, Pendo is driving sustainable textile solutions that benefit both the environment and local communities. Her work is an example of how science can provide innovative, locally relevant solutions to global challenges.

Visibility again plays a crucial role here. OWSD fellows, having seized opportunities to enhance their science communication and leadership skills, are well-versed in advocating for STEM education for women and presenting their own cutting-edge research. They are increasingly sought after as articulate, confident panellists whose dynamic presence directly challenges the dominant international academic practice of favouring male, Western scientists. This practice often relies on the unfounded rationale that exceptional women scientists from developing countries are difficult to find.

Figure 2: OWSD early-career fellows' achievements in numbers

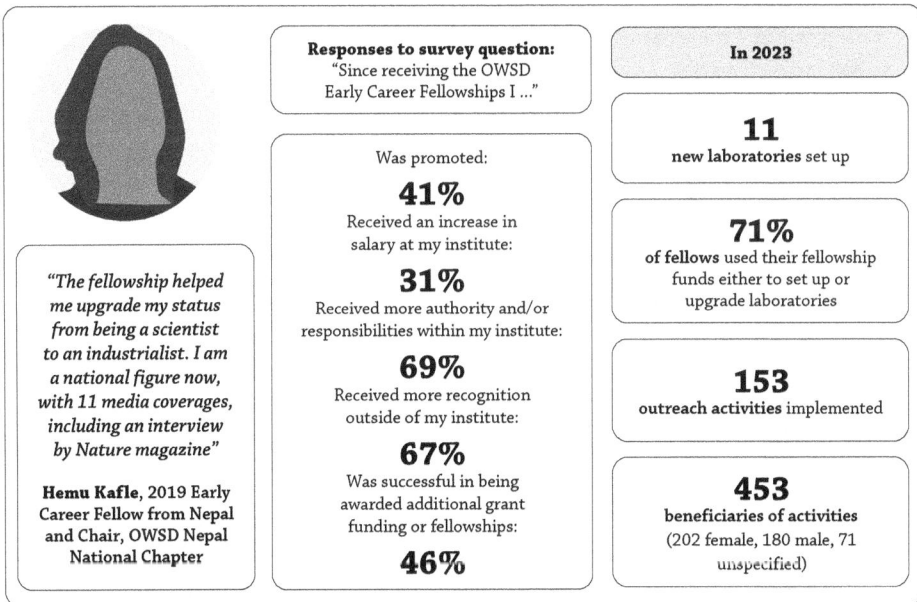

Responses to survey question:
"Since receiving the OWSD Early Career Fellowships I ..."

Was promoted:
41%

Received an increase in salary at my institute:
31%

Received more authority and/or responsibilities within my institute:
69%

Received more recognition outside of my institute:
67%

Was successful in being awarded additional grant funding or fellowships:
46%

"The fellowship helped me upgrade my status from being a scientist to an industrialist. I am a national figure now, with 11 media coverages, including an interview by Nature magazine"

Hemu Kafle, 2019 Early Career Fellow from Nepal and Chair, OWSD Nepal National Chapter

In 2023

11
new laboratories set up

71%
of fellows used their fellowship funds either to set up or upgrade laboratories

153
outreach activities implemented

453
beneficiaries of activities
(202 female, 180 male, 71 unspecified)

In this regard, the value of visibility for individuals participating in and presenting at key scientific events cannot be overstated. These events are where reputations are built, collaborations are initiated and groundbreaking publications emerge. For women scientists from developing countries, their visibility at these stages not only shifts perceptions but actively disrupts entrenched biases, fostering a more inclusive and diverse scientific landscape. The ultimate aim, indeed, of these fellowships is not only to support individual careers but to create lasting, self-sustaining research centres that contribute to regional development and generate innovative solutions relevant to the needs of their countries.

The visibility and recognition of outstanding women scientists are crucial in igniting this transformation, serving as the catalyst for the establishment of research centres of excellence, attracting talent, resources and institutional support to sustain their impact.

Training workshops for systemic change

OWSD's Early-Career Fellowships are enhanced by training workshops that aim to foster systemic change in STEM, focusing on empowering women scientists and advancing gender equity. These workshops have produced significant outputs and introduced innovative practices that support OWSD's broader mission of creating more inclusive and equitable research environments.

The annual Orientation Workshop, for example, run by OWSD for incoming early-career fellows, serves as a critical starting point, providing training in essential areas such as grant management, leadership, communication and intellectual property. This workshop ensures that fellows possess the skills necessary to manage their research projects, navigate academic systems and engage with the broader professional landscape effectively.

An additional core component of OWSD's training efforts offered to early-career fellows is the Gamechangers Workshop, an innovative platform designed to equip women scientists with the tools needed to engage with policymakers and advocate for institutional change. The workshop emphasises advocacy, leadership and policy engagement, empowering fellows to initiate and influence gender-responsive policies in STEM. A notable innovation within this workshop is the use of gamification, where fellows participate in a specially developed board game, Best in Her Field, created in collaboration with the Humanitarian Engineering Department of the Royal Melbourne Institute of Technology (RMIT). The game simulates the challenges faced by women scientists in developing countries, offering an interactive experience that helps participants brainstorm policy solutions and best practices. This gamified approach fosters deeper engagement with real-world issues, allowing for a more creative and collaborative exploration of potential policy solutions. The workshops have also demonstrated a significant impact on the fellows' professional visibility and policy influence. For example, after participating in the Gamechangers Workshop, one fellow was invited to contribute to her country's national climate adaptation policy, illustrating how visibility and expertise gained through these workshops can translate into tangible changes in policy at both the national and global levels.

Through these workshops, OWSD not only strengthens the technical and research skills of women scientists but also builds their leadership capacity, ensuring they are well-equipped to drive systemic change. By combining technical training with leadership development, these workshops provide a comprehensive approach to fostering both personal and professional growth. Moreover, they create a platform for women scientists to connect with policymakers and international funding agencies, amplifying their voices in global discussions on STEM and gender equity.

The role of OWSD national chapters

While OWSD has been offering fellowships since 1998, the organisation was established in 1987 as first and foremost a membership organisation, with (by the end of September 2024), close to 11 000 members – all women with postgraduate degrees in (natural and social) science subjects living and working in developing countries. The spread of countries where members can be found is impressive (115 out of a possible 152 developing countries). But even more impressive is that this membership is consolidated and activated through the establishment of national chapters.

Currently, OWSD has 58 national chapters and aims to reach 60 by 2026 (see Figure 3 below). These chapters are grassroots organisations that empower local women scientists by providing a platform for advocacy, networking and leadership development. To establish a chapter, a country must have at least 20 OWSD members. Once formed, chapters elect an executive committee and conduct surveys to understand the unique challenges women face in STEM, providing tailored solutions.

National chapters have demonstrated significant success in organising STEM outreach events and public lectures, which enhance the visibility of women scientists. For example, the OWSD Ghana National Chapter hosts an annual Women in Science Forum that attracts policymakers, educators and journalists, resulting in increased media coverage of women-led research. Similarly, the OWSD Nigeria National Chapter has successfully advocated for female scientists' inclusion in national science advisory boards, reinforcing their role in decision-making spaces.

Figure 3: OWSD national chapters around the world

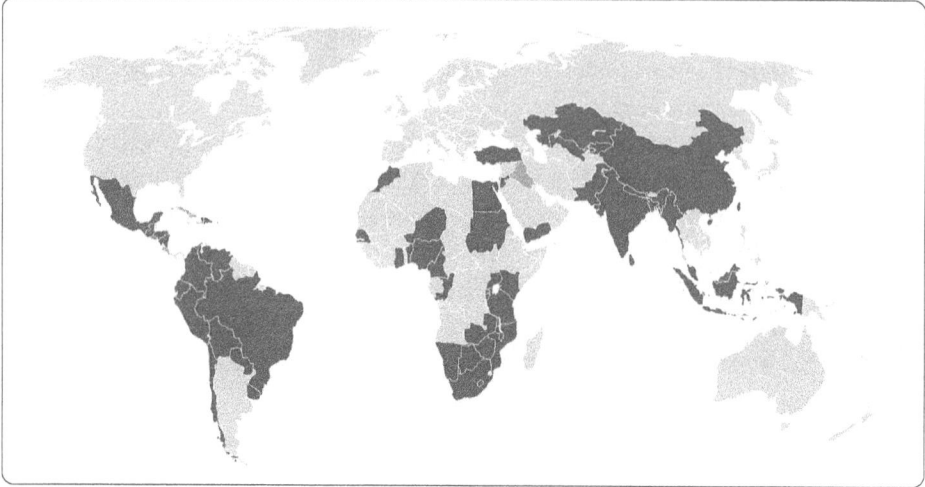

These efforts contribute to shifting societal perceptions of women in STEM, making it more likely for young girls to see female scientists as role models and pursue STEM careers themselves. In fact, many chapters have also launched initiatives that connect women scientists with young students to encourage participation in STEM fields. For instance, the OWSD Rwanda National Chapter organises outreach activities where female mathematicians visit schools to inspire girls by sharing their personal stories.

One of the key strengths of OWSD's national chapters is their ability to collect data and advocate for policy change. Through initiatives such as the National Assessments and pilot studies in Zimbabwe, Rwanda and Bolivia, chapters are collecting and analysing sex-disaggregated data on women in STEM, which is crucial for identifying gaps and shaping policies that support female scientists.

OWSD chapters have been organising local and national events since the first chapter was established in 1994 but since 2022, chapters have been encouraged to apply for small awards of USD1–3 000 to support activities of their choice, including synchronised events throughout the Global South on the International Day of Women and Girls in Science (11 February). Beyond this small 'startup' contribution, chapters are expected to do their own fundraising or attract/ provide in-kind support. These small but impactful initiatives are not only instrumental in increasing the number of women applying for fellowships but also in creating a network of support that extends beyond individual achievements.

Notably, 15% of the executive members of national chapters are recipients of OWSD fellowships or awards, illustrating the strong 'give-back' culture within the community. These alumnae are not only shaping the future of OWSD but are also mentoring the next generation of women scientists, reinforcing the organisation's mission to promote systemic change.

The national chapters represent a dynamic force for change, empowering local women scientists, driving policy reforms and fostering a community of collaboration and mentorship that influences the broader STEM ecosystem.

There has always been a strong correlation between the number of applications for fellowships received and the presence of national chapters. These numbers increase significantly around the establishment (both pre- and post-) of new chapters, when visibility and promotion of the chapter are at their peak.

Conclusion

The OWSD community of scientists, by being highly visible role models, can make substantial inroads into traditional and cultural expectations of appropriate career paths for women. Their visibility not only challenges stereotypes but also encourages other women to consider STEM careers, seeing first-hand what is possible. Additionally, the support and mentorship provided through national chapters further motivates applications. Mentoring helps women navigate professional challenges and boosts their confidence, while the community's encouragement fosters a sense of belonging and purpose. Together, these factors create a strong, reinforcing cycle where role models and support systems drive more women to pursue and succeed in STEM fields.

> EC fellowships emphasise mentoring researchers and students so that their scientific capability is grown. After taking part in this project, two of my researchers have received full scholarships to pursue PhDs in immunology and virology in reputed universities in the US, and this is a huge asset for the country as well, because these researchers plan to come back to Nepal after their training. For me science is not just about what it can do today, but how it will shape the type of just and prosperous world that I would like our future generations to thrive in. (Prativa Pandey, OWSD Early-Career Fellow, Nepal)

OWSD's impact studies are evidence that prioritising individual women scientists can have profound, far-reaching effects. The work of research fellows not only pushes the boundaries of scientific knowledge but also shapes policy, fosters community development and enhances educational systems. By high-lighting the intersection of individual achievements and broader societal impact, it becomes clear that empowering women in STEM catalyses trans-formative change at multiple levels. Ultimately, upscaling the impact of women in STEM requires a dual approach: supporting individual careers while simulta-neously dismantling the systemic barriers embedded in educational and policy frameworks. The work of OWSD over the past four decades underscores this approach, showing that, when provided with the right opportunities, women scientists are not just contributors to scientific advancement but leaders capable of driving sustainable, lasting change within their communities and on a global scale.

While fellowships focused on individual women scientists are essential, systemic change necessitates addressing the broader context in which these individuals operate. This chapter highlights that investing in women scientists leads to systemic change in STEM. While individual fellowships are crucial, long-term transformation requires working with all stakeholders at a national level to identify challenges and collaborate on tailored solutions for attracting and retaining women in STEM fields.

The connection between individual and systemic change is vital in creating a sustainable and inclusive STEM environment. As women scientists succeed, they not only transform their own careers but also serve as catalysts for broader shifts in institutional and societal structures. Their leadership and contribu-tions challenge entrenched norms, influence policy reforms and inspire future generations of women. At the same time, by addressing systemic barriers, such as unequal access to resources, mentorship and leadership opportunities, we ensure that the successes of individual women scientists can be replicated on a larger scale, fostering a more equitable and inclusive scientific community. This integrated approach is essential for lasting change that benefits both individu-als and the larger ecosystem they are part of.

We conclude this chapter by outlining recommendations that are relevant both to our organisation, which is constantly evolving, and to others who are considering or have already implemented similar initiatives. These recommen-dations, drawn from the data presented above as well as our experience and reflections over nearly 30 years of activity at OWSD, aim to summarise some of the key ideas discussed in this chapter.

Recommendations for future initiatives

- **Promote long-term partnerships between funders, institutions and networks** to ensure sustainability and scale. Encourage science granting councils and development agencies to integrate gender-transformative criteria into funding mechanisms.
- **Support award and mentorship programmes** that connect fellows with early-career women scientists, fostering long-term professional development and creating strong networks of support within the scientific community.
- **Enhance collaboration with policymakers** to ensure that women's contributions in STEM are recognised, valued and integrated into national development strategies and research agendas.
- **Engage women scientists** by implementing additional community-building programmes (e.g. OWSD's national chapters).
- **Begin collaboration with science granting councils** to ensure their priorities align with efforts to increase the participation and recognition of women in STEM.
- **Develop robust frameworks to track both individual and institutional outcomes of fellowships and awards**, while using both quantitative and qualitative data to inform adaptive programme design and policy advocacy.

Beyond supporting individual scientists, key national actors in higher education such as academic institutions, science granting councils and programmes like OWSD's national chapters can play a critical role in shaping environments that enable women in STEM to thrive. Institutions and organisations that are aware of their own research priorities and national development agendas can align their policies, funding mechanisms and institutional cultures to better support women scientists. By embedding gender equity considerations into hiring practices, research funding and leadership pathways, these institutions and organisations can create a more level playing field and reinforce systemic progress. Ultimately, when visibility is matched with structural commitment, women's presence in STEM ceases to be the exception and becomes an expected, integral part of the scientific landscape – strengthening not only those who lead, but the science they help to advance.

Acknowledgements

Our sincere thanks to OWSD's two major donors, the Swedish International Development Cooperation Agency (Sida) since 1997, and the International Development Research Centre (IDRC) since 2017. The Elsevier Foundation has co-designed and funded awards since 2012. Many thanks to the following members of the OWSD Secretariat: Tanja Bole, Fiona Dakin, Lucia Fanicchi, Erika Hrvatic, Marina Juricev and Zabeeh Ullah Sahil for their invaluable contributions collecting and compiling the data we have used for this chapter.

About the Authors

Tonya Blowers is the UNESCO OWSD Coordinator, Italy.

Sena Galazzi is a Technical Adviser at UNESCO OWSD, Italy.

Erin Johnson is an Administrative Assistant at UNESCO OWSD, Italy.

Giulia Signori is an Administrative Assistant at UNESCO OWSD, Italy.

References

ADEA (2022). *3rd ADEA high-level policy dialogue forum: Higher education and scientific research in the light of digitalisation and the fourth industrial revolution (4IR) – Concept note*. Association for the Development of Education in Africa. https://worlddidac.org/wp-content/uploads/2022/03/Concept-Note_HLPDF-Higher-Education-and-Scientific-Research.pdf

AdvanceHE. (n.d.). *Athena swan charter*. https://www.advance-he.ac.uk/equality-charters/athena-swan-charter

Breda, T., Grenet, J., Monnet, M., & Van Effenterre, C. (2023). How effective are female role models in steering girls towards STEM? Evidence from French high schools. *The Economic Journal, 133*(653), 1773–1809. https://doi.org/10.1093/ej/uead019

European Commission: Directorate-General for Research and Innovation. (2020). *Gendered innovations 2 – How inclusive analysis contributes to research and innovation: Policy review*. Publications Office of the European Union. https://data.europa.eu/doi/10.2777/316197

González-Pérez, S., Mateos de Cabo, R., & Sáinz, M. (2020). Girls in STEM: Is it a female role-model thing? *Frontiers in Psychology, 11*, 2204. https://doi.org/10.3389/fpsyg.2020.02204

Lleras, C. (2008). Race, ethnicity, and inequality in educational achievement. In *Handbook of research on education and inequality* (pp. 67–84). Springer.

OWSD (Organization for Women in Science for the Developing World). (2024a). A quarter-century of scientific leadership: The OWSD PhD Fellowships Programme. Internal document.

OWSD. (2024b). *OWSD annual report 2024*. OWSD. https://owsd25.interfase.tv/sites/default/files/attachments/reports/OWSD_Annual%20Report_2024.pdf

OWSD. (2024c). OWSD-Elsevier Foundation Award Impact Survey. Internal document.

Schiebinger, L. (2014). Gendered innovations: Harnessing the creative power of sex and gender analysis to discover new ideas and develop new technologies. *Triple Helix, 1*, 9. https://doi.org/10.1186/s40604-014-0009-7

Schiebinger, L., & Schraudner, M. (2011). Interdisciplinary approaches to achieving gendered innovations in science, medicine, and engineering. *Interdisciplinary Science Reviews, 36*(2),154–167. https://doi.org/10.1179/030801811X13013181961518

Tannenbaum, C., Ellis, R. P., Eyssel, F., Zou, J., & Schiebinger, L. (2019). Sex and gender analysis improves science and engineering. *Nature, 575*, 137–146. https://doi.org/10.1038/s41586-019-1657-6

UNESCO (United Nations Educational, Scientific and Cultural Organization). (2024). *Call to action: Closing the gender gap in science* [Programme and meeting document]. UNESCO. https://unesdoc.unesco.org/ark:/48223/pf0000388641

Wilkinson, C. (2019). What role can Athena SWAN play in gender equality and science communication? *JCOM, 18*(04), C06. https://doi.org/10.22323/2.18040306

Voices of Change: Gender and Knowledge Journeys in the Construction of Public Policies for Women in STEM in Bolivia

Mariana Santa Cruz Terrazas and Mary Cruz De Urioste Vidaurre

Introduction

Women's access to Bolivian universities began in the 1950s and gained visibility in the 1970s, with women's significant participation in Science, Technology, Engineering and Mathematics (STEM) fields emerging in the 1990s. Despite increased enrolment, women's representation in engineering and technology in Bolivia remains low; in 2015, women comprised 40% in natural sciences and only 29% in engineering (UNESCO, 2017).

Barriers to women's participation in STEM begin early in life, with girls losing interest in science as early as primary school. Although young girls perform well in math competitions – holding 70% of top positions in primary school – representation drops to approximately 25% in secondary school (Guevara, 2021). In secondary school, problem-solving skills and teachers play vital roles in encouraging science careers. However, gender stereotypes and discriminatory behaviours by teachers often deter students (Cerinsek et al., 2013; Radovic et al., 2021). Gender barriers persist in undergraduate programmes, further limiting women's opportunities (De Urioste, 2016).

Gender stereotypes and hierarchical discrimination exacerbate women's drop-out rates at all levels, reinforcing inequality in STEM (Radovic et al., 2021). Addressing these challenges requires multisectoral and sustainable measures that consider the complex barriers women face in these fields.

Understanding the low participation of Bolivian women in STEM fields requires a multidimensional approach. However, understanding data alone will not bring about significant change. It is necessary to create spaces for reflection and to work with stakeholders to co-construct solutions to gender inequality in STEM. This chapter narrates the journey through this process of understanding the experiences of women in STEM in Bolivia and using this information to design effective solutions. Our work is guided by the voices of successful women in STEM fields in Bolivia, as well as their parents, teachers and principals from secondary schools and universities.

This chapter details two key phases of the project. The first phase focused on data collection and analysis through three distinct approaches: (1) life stories of successful women in STEM; (2) social representations[1] within the community; and (3) statistical analysis of female participation (Avolio & Chávez, 2023). These methods provided a comprehensive understanding of the barriers and opportunities present in STEM. The second phase focused on the co-construction of participatory workshops with key stakeholders, culminating in the development of concrete proposals for extracurricular programmes to promote inclusion and gender equity in STEM (Arredondo Trapero et al., 2019; Mariaca, 1999). In these co-construction spaces, key stakeholders collaborate to provide solutions to this issue.

Developing the study: Reflection on women's participation in STEM in Bolivia

The motivation to study the gender gap in STEM in Bolivia emerged from the Research Committee of the Interuniversity Observatory for Gender Equality, composed of 14 universities in the city of Santa Cruz de la Sierra. This committee highlighted the urgent need to address the issue, as women's participation in STEM areas was significantly lower than men's. This gender disparity not only limits the personal and professional development of women but also hinders the country's innovative and economic potential (Paredes-Walker, 2020).

One of the main challenges identified by the research committee was the lack of detailed information on the factors that influence women's participation in STEM. A lack of data makes it difficult to have a comprehensive understanding of the phenomenon and, consequently, to implement effective

---

1 Social representations refer to the shared beliefs, values, ideas and understandings that people in a society or group hold about a particular topic or social phenomenon. These representations are constructed through communication, culture and social interaction, and they shape how individuals perceive and relate to the world around them.

strategies (Abdulkadri et al., 2022). To overcome this limitation, a mixed-methods research approach was adopted, integrating both qualitative (e.g. life stories and social representations) and quantitative methods (statistical data analyses) to provide a more complete view. Quantitative methods provide statistical data that reveal patterns of women's participation in STEM, while qualitative methods, through interviews and focus groups, explore the experiences and obstacles women face (Carrasco Mercado, 2018).

Life stories offer a qualitative perspective on personal challenges and achievements, revealing patterns of resilience (Denzin & Lincoln, 2018). These narratives, along with social representations of what it means to be a female engineer in Bolivia, uncover stereotypes and cultural barriers that influence women's aspirations (Connell, 2009). Additionally, statistical analyses provide a quantitative understanding of women's participation in STEM, identifying trends and critical areas. This comprehensive approach not only sheds light on the complexity of the gender gap but also facilitates the design of more effective policies and programmes to promote gender equality in STEM in Bolivia (UNESCO, 2017).

The project focused on addressing the gender gap in STEM through an inclusive, collaborative and comprehensive approach. Led by the Interuniversity Observatory for Gender Equality,[2] this initiative emphasised the importance of plural participation from key stakeholders, including universities, the private sector, local governments and civil society organisations, to ensure sustainable and effective solutions.

Our mixed methods approach identified structural and cultural barriers that limit women's participation in STEM (Connell, 2009; Denzin & Lincoln, 2018; López, 2021). The intersectoral (i.e. involving key stakeholders from multiple sectors) reflection spaces facilitated the co-construction of public policies aligned with national and local priorities. Plural participation enriched the process, ensuring that the proposals reflected the actual needs of communities.

Additionally, pilot programmes, including mentorships and educational workshops, were developed, tested and adjusted to maximise their impact. This inclusive approach seeks to close the gender gap in STEM and create meaningful change within Bolivian communities.

Phase 1: Voices and data of women in STEM in Bolivia

The participation of women in STEM should be understood through their own experiences, which highlight both the barriers and empowering factors

---

2 www.ouig.org

they face in their careers. Participatory action research (PAR) was used in this project to explore and promote female participation in STEM, offering a collaborative and inclusive approach that involves both researchers and the affected community (Kemmis et al., 2014). PAR is effective in addressing challenges faced by marginalised groups in STEM and provides a deeper understanding of power dynamics and inequalities (Somekh, 2006). Additionally, it empowers women by fostering the ability to transform their educational and professional environments (Bergman & Danermark, 2015).

PAR not only facilitates the co-construction of knowledge but also promotes transformative actions that go beyond the generation of academic data. These actions drive concrete changes in policies and institutional practices, strengthening gender equity and inclusion in scientific and technological fields.

The following section explains how we designed the project to understand women's participation in STEM. We began by investigating the characteristics, limitations and opportunities that affect women's STEM participation. We implemented three research strategies to understand how personal perceptions, social factors and institutional practices influence women's access to and development in STEM.

The first method (life stories) focused on how successful Bolivian female engineers overcame barriers, using the life stories of 40 accomplished Bolivian women in STEM. These women were selected based on specific criteria, including their professional trajectories, academic degrees obtained, publications and visibility in their respective fields. Another key criterion was that professionals in the field identified them as role models or exemplars of success. Additionally, their participation in leadership roles or mentorship initiatives within STEM was considered an indicator of their impact and influence. These life stories are complemented by interviews with 60 outstanding students, revealing that family support, motivation and resilience are key to overcoming gender barriers.

The second method (social representations) focused on how society perceives women engineers and how these perceptions affect their participation (family, school, universities and the labour market). The recruitment process for participants in the research was carried out at three educational levels, following the criteria of accessibility, convenience and gender equity. At the school level, participants were selected from public and private educational institutions, with preference given to those involved in STEM areas. The selection process focused on students, teachers and parents, prioritising individuals from the three study communities: (1) school directors; (2) teachers with experience in STEM areas; and (3) parents with children in secondary education. At the university level, professors and students enrolled in STEM programmes were recruited, along with administrators with relevant experience. For interviews with employers in the public and private sectors, participants were selected from nationally recognised companies in the fields of technology, mathematics and sciences, with preference given to those with experience in human resources management in STEM areas and those holding senior positions.

The study, conducted in five Bolivian cities, reveals through focus groups and interviews with 408 participants that women in STEM face unequal treatment in education, employment and professional development. This perpetuates stereotypes and cultural barriers that discourage their participation.

The third method (statistical analysis) focuses on women's participation in STEM and the factors that influence participation rates. The quantitative data show that although female participation in primary and secondary education is almost equal, it significantly decreases at university and in the labour market, particularly in engineering and technology. Qualitative analyses also reveal what factors are related to women's interest in STEM participation.

The combination of these approaches offers a multidimensional understanding of the gender gap in STEM in Bolivia. Social representations expose cultural barriers, life stories reveal individual experiences and statistical analysis quantifies these trends. Together, they highlight the need for comprehensive public policies to promote gender equality in STEM, which is crucial for the country's development.

Roots of success: Factors driving Bolivian women in STEM

In Bolivia, a total of 40 professional women in STEM fields were interviewed, representing five cities: three in the central axis – La Paz, Cochabamba and Santa Cruz – and two intermediate cities, Sucre and Tarija. In addition, eight Bolivian women living abroad participated in the study, each from a different region.

The research, which followed a qualitative approach, utilised grounded theory to analyse life stories, identifying eight categories of analysis: (1) family context; (2) self-perception; (3) education; (4) teacher influence; (5) career choice; (6) university life; (7) labour market integration; and (8) gender treatment. The information was coded and analysed using Atlas.ti. The results reveal how women from various regions and ethnic groups are forming a new generation of middle-class professionals with a more homogeneous culture, highlighting their experiences and challenges in science and technology.

One of the key findings from our analysis was around the intersection between gender and generation (see similar results from Mexico in Chapter 5).

While the grandmothers, coming from rural farming areas, faced the transition to urban life through precarious jobs, the mothers reached technical and, to a lesser extent, university levels. Finally, the daughters achieved university degrees in fields that are not traditionally pursued by women, breaking barriers that their predecessors never imagined possible.

> We don't come from a financially well-off family; my grandmother was a farmer, my mother moved to a small city, but for my parents, education was important ... They always say that: 'Your inheritance is your education'. (Engineer, 43 years old, La Paz)

We also find that Bolivian women in STEM mostly come from upwardly mobile middle-class households, where gender equity was promoted, and self-esteem and discipline were encouraged. Despite challenges, such as discouragement from some teachers, these women managed to excel in STEM.

In general, the school context in Bolivia tends to discourage girls' interest in STEM, with factors like the curriculum and teacher interactions playing a role. Teachers were of particular importance; some inspired girls to challenge norms, while others demotivated and rendered them invisible, limiting their progress. "*They respond rudely ... They leave you with unresolved doubts, they don't acknowledge you when you raise your hand to answer*" (Systems Engineer, 40 years old, Tarija).

Parental support contributed to women choosing STEM careers, and mothers seemingly contributed the most in supporting their daughters. By the time these women reached university, they had a clear understanding of their academic choices, showing that gender biases have significantly diminished compared to previous generations. The gender perspective of the younger generations is more focused on freedom of choice and the right to exercise their individuality, marking a departure from past generations where marriage was seen as the main path. As a 43-year-old systems engineer from Santa Cruz notes, "*The path before was marriage, now it's the profession.*"

This younger generation of women engineers arrives at university with a clear vision of their academic choices, indicating that gender biases are no longer as relevant. However, these women face discrimination and sexism at university, reporting derogatory and sexist comments from both peers and professors. The women interviewed reported feeling forced to normalise such language to fit into a male-dominated environment. This sexist environment has had severe consequences, such as some women abandoning their careers after feeling harassed and devalued.

There were sexist professors who made very inappropriate comments. For example, in engineering, we measure the volume of things, so the professor would say, 'Let's say I want to measure the volume of Miss X,' referring to a female student present in the course, 'then I would have to completely undress her and put her in a bathtub full of water.' I mean, how did we, as young people, tolerate those kinds of comments? What mindset did we have, what immaturity, what kind of upbringing, that we couldn't stand up to those comments and instead laughed – it all seemed natural. (Chemical Engineer, 48 years old, Santa Cruz)

In the workplace, these women struggle with the difficulty of balancing family and professional life, especially in male-dominated environments where gender discrimination limits their opportunities. A key finding was their tendency to postpone marriage and question the possibility of having children due to a work culture that demands total dedication, making it difficult to reconcile work and family life. Male-dominated work environments often show a lack of empathy toward their family needs and impose barriers to career advancement due to gender discrimination: *"Getting married is not in my plans, and if I ever do, I don't plan on having children"* (Industrial Engineer, 35 years old, Cochabamba).

While the first generations of women in STEM were better able to balance professional life and childcare thanks to family support, the new generations lack this level of support, as their mothers are typically also active professionals. Despite this, STEM professionals have achieved good job placement, especially in the public sector, where it is easier to balance work and caregiving responsibilities. The private sector, although generally more hesitant to hire women, is showing greater openness in regions like Santa Cruz and in sectors such as banking.

Women in STEM are committed to continuous training and international networking, which has allowed them to access global networks and receive recognition. Despite facing sexism and harassment in male-dominated environments, many have overcome these adversities by consistently demonstrating their skills, creating support networks among women engineers and strengthening their positions. Perseverance and personal effectiveness are key to their success in male-dominated fields. Some of these sexist experiences are reflected in the following quote:

They talk to you as if you were a little girl. Consistent with the anonymity they try to impose on women, they limit our right to speak. I told them I wanted to invite them to the business roundtable, and I clearly remember one of them, an older man, said to me: 'Little girl, look, those women over there might be talking about soap operas, maybe they're talking about something else, but we're talking business here. Go chat with them for a bit and then come back.' (Systems Engineer, 40 years old, Cochabamba)

Social barriers faced by Bolivian women in STEM

We analysed the social representations of women in STEM in five Bolivian cities with 412 participants. The recruitment process for the research ensured diverse and equitable participation, with 58% women across all study groups. The selection criteria were both rigorous and tailored to each educational level and type of informant. At the school level, priority was given to students, teachers and parents of 5th- and 6th-grade secondary school students, preferably from STEM fields, ensuring representation from both major and intermediate cities. At the university level, faculty members, administrative authorities and students from STEM disciplines were selected, with a strong emphasis on gender equity. For the in-depth interviews with employers, human resources managers or executives from leading national companies in technology and engineering were chosen, for their expertise in human resources management and their holistic understanding of the sector. In all cases, gender equity was prioritised, and participants were selected based on their willingness to share their experiences.

We conducted qualitative analyses with focus groups and interviews in three key communities: (1) schools; (2) universities; and (3) employers. These communities were selected to shed light on the social representations derived from cultural practices. The results reveal a gender gap where women face detrimental treatment compared to men, affecting their educational experience, access to jobs, and professional progression in STEM. The low female participation reflects complex and subtle mechanisms of segregation that perpetuate this inequality.

Women facing significant barriers to accessing and thriving in STEM fields reflects a deeply rooted gender gap in Bolivia's cultural, social and structural dynamics. Through 50 focus groups and eight interviews with key informants, we investigated the complexities of this inequality. Women, from their school years to their entry into the workforce, faced unfavourable treatment compared to men, affecting their educational experiences, access to job opportunities and professional growth.

The school environment is where these barriers first become evident. Although progress in female participation in STEM has been recognised, particularly in private schools, family and cultural prejudices persist as signif-icant obstacles. Teachers and parents, consciously or not, tend to reinforce gender stereotypes that limit girls' aspirations. A secondary school teacher observed:

> Society conditions men and women to differentiate which careers they can study. There are few people who say you can study whatever career you want. From my point of view, a more male-oriented career would be engineering or automotive mechanics, while careers more encouraged for women are teaching subjects like literature, biology and social sciences.

These practices are more pronounced in rural cities like Sucre and Tarija, where traditional careers are still preferred, compared to urban places like La Paz or Santa Cruz, where women in STEM are more recognised. Many students face pressure to conform to societal expectations that confine them to traditional roles, while others challenge these norms, often at a significant personal cost.

As they transition to university, women begin to encounter new forms of social pressure. Some students, initially interested in fields like civil engi-neering, describe how the predominantly male environment and discouraging comments from peers and family led them to change majors. A private-school student shared:

> My cousin started studying civil engineering, but she felt a bit intimidated by the men there, so she didn't feel very comfortable in that environment and ended up switching to financial engineering. Even her family would ask, 'Why are you studying a man's career?' So, with all that social pressure, including from people at the university, she decided to change her major.

This shift reflects not only an internal struggle but also a battle against soci-etal norms that continue to assign genders to academic disciplines. However, higher education also presents opportunities to overcome these barriers. With adequate support, students can develop competencies that empower them to face a demanding job market.

The labour market, however, presents even greater challenges. Women in STEM face subtle and sometimes explicit discrimination, particularly regarding motherhood. A human resources manager explained:

> In practice, when there is an obvious case among executives or staff, there are committees that try to avoid hiring women who are at a stage where

they might start a family, as they would need to be given leave, subsidies, etc. In this sense, some women manage to get hired without problems and perform well during the first few years, but then their performance and participation in the company decline due to pregnancy and the 'young child' stage, where they request transfers to more family-friendly environments.

These dynamics perpetuate a cycle of inequality in which women face a "career tax" associated with motherhood.

Motherhood is seen as a public good from an economic standpoint, but this responsibility disproportionately falls on women. As a technology area manager noted:

Motherhood, from an economic standpoint, is seen as a public good – everyone wants it, but the career tax is always applied to women. Often, domestic activities fall on the woman, creating a slight disadvantage in the labour market because men do not always take responsibility for these tasks. Some women even choose to delay motherhood because otherwise, they risk their careers. Cases like this are caused by inflexible labour policies. This is the big dilemma where motherhood is always the turning point that decides the future of Bolivian women's careers. I believe this needs to evolve because we need women to continue wanting to have children, as it is a societal need, and policy should align with society's needs.

Statistical analysis of women's participation in STEM in Bolivia

This exploratory research utilised document analysis to systematise data on enrolment, academic performance and employment outcomes in Bolivian public and private schools and universities. We use historical and statistical data from both secondary and primary sources, covering education from primary school to the labour market.

The study followed a non-experimental, cross-sectional design with a descriptive and correlational approach. Data analysis involved the application of univariate and bivariate statistical methods, such as correlation and regression, using R (R Core Team, 2020), SPSS (IBM Corp., 2021) and EViews (IHS Markit, 2020). The integration of these three software platforms enabled a comprehensive and rigorous analytical approach, accommodating diverse data types and research needs.

The findings offer valuable insights into women's participation in STEM fields, providing a foundation for developing interventions aimed at promoting gender equity in these disciplines.

Table 1: Statistically representative samples

	Universities												
Group	Women and men		Women		Women STEM		Women STEM Private		Women STEM Public		Women STEM Rural		Women STEM Language	
	n	%	n	%	n	%	n	%	n	%	n	%	n	%
Sample	3.643	100	2.427	66.6	1.863	51.1	1.293	35.5	570	15.6	1.085	29.8	1.236	33.9
	Educational units												
Group	Women and men		Women		Women STEM		Women STEM Private		Women STEM Public		Women STEM Rural		Women STEM Language	
	n	%	n	%	n	%	n	%	n	%	n	%	n	%
Sample	1.389	100	948	68.3	365	26.3	92	6.6	273	19.7	246	17.7	295	21.2

The results are presented in two groups: (1) educational units, focusing on the entry of girls into STEM; and (2) universities, addressing both entry and retention of women in STEM. Educational units provide information on education at the primary and secondary levels. They are regulated by ministries of education at the national or regional level and aim to offer basic and secondary education. In contrast, universities are higher education institutions that grant professional and academic degrees such as bachelor's, master's and doctoral degrees. They focus on specialised training, research and innovation.

Significant correlations were found among different groups of women in educational settings who are interested in STEM. We investigated how specific questionnaire items were correlated with demographic (e.g. gender, rural background and use of another language) and contextual (e.g. area of study – STEM or otherwise, and school – educational unit or university) factors (see Table 2). For ease of interpretation of the table, non-significant correlations are not included.

In addition to the correlations presented above, a multivariate analysis was conducted with interest in STEM subjects as the dependent variable and 44 potential explanatory variables. Using the Stepwise Regression technique in R software, the final model was reduced to 15 statistically significant variables ($\alpha=0.05$) that best explain interest in STEM in educational units. To determine the significance of the variables, confidence levels of 95% ($\alpha=0.05$) were established, prioritising those with greater statistical robustness. The final model

Table 2: Correlations between the items of the questionnaire and gender, area of study, school, rural area and other language

Dimensions		Variables	Bivariate Pearson Correlations (r)				
			Gender	Study area	School	Rural area	Another language
Individual dimension	Self-perception	My favourite subjects are mathematics, chemistry and physics.					
		I feel that I have an ease in learning mathematics, physics and chemistry.		.635**			
		6. I think it's easier for men to learn mathematics, chemistry and physics than women.	.166**	.086**			-.129*
		7. I think the engineering profession is more suitable for men than for women.	.220**				
		8. I think that service careers such as psychology, social work, medicine and other assistance to people are best suited for women.	.132**	.086**			
	Personal effectiveness	9. I am confident that I will be successful in any career I study.	.058*	.150**			
		10. I would like to study a career related to mathematics, physics or chemistry, but think I do not have the capacity to succeed in it.		.098**			.104*
Familiar and peer dimension	Socio-cultural characteristics of parents	11. My parents or guardians spent their childhood:			.312**		-.179**
		12. One of my grandparents was born and lives in a rural area or province.		-.094**	.214**		
		13. In addition to Spanish, my parents, guardians or grandparents speak any of these languages:					
		14. My parents are of religion:		.087**			
		15. The highest level of education of your mother or guardian is:			.309**		
		16. The highest level of education of your parent or guardian is:	-.074**		.297**		
		17. My parents would like me to study a career related to mathematics, chemistry or physics.		.350**			
		18. My parents would like me to study a service career such as psychology, social work, nursing, law or other similar.	.196**	.094**	-.109*		
	Socio-economic level	19. My parents have an economic level that would allow me to support myself financially until the end of a university degree.	.067*	.092**			
		20. I don't think my parents support me in the career I chose.		.087**			

Dimensions		Variables	Bivariate Pearson Correlations (r)				
			Gender	Study area	School	Rural area	Another language
Familiar and peer dimension (con.)	Other family characteristics	21. In my family there are several professional engineers that motivate me to study a similar career.			-.126*		
		22. My relatives (grandparents, uncles, cousins, others) consider that I should choose a career appropriate to my gender.					
	Peers or friends	23. My friends would support me if I told them I wanted to study a career related to mathematics, physics or chemistry.	.182**	.262**			
		24. My friends would support me if I told them I wanted to study a service career such as psychology, social work, nursing, law or others similar.	.225**	.119**			
Academic dimension	School experience	25. My educational unit is:				.214**	
		26. The educational unit where I did primary school is:	.054*	.069*	.202**		-.126*
		27. My mathematics, physics and chemistry teachers have a way of teaching that makes me interested in those subjects.	.055*	.354**	.144**		
		28. My mathematics, physics and chemistry teachers demonstrate mastery of the subjects they teach.		.195**	.125*		
		29. Having teachers of my sex teaching mathematics, physics or chemistry at my school motivates me to study a career related to those areas.	.210**	.207**			
		30. To choose which career to study in the future, in my school:		.081*	.196**	.152**	
		31. While I was studying at school, I participated in the scientific olympiads in the area of:	.096**	.356**	.178**		-.145**
		32. At my school, the physics and chemistry laboratory is used:		.090**			
		33. At my school, the library, videos and other teaching materials for mathematics, physics and chemistry were used:		.137**	.285**		
		34. At my school, the teachers think materials related to mathematics, physics and chemistry are more suited to boys than girls.	.108**			.226**	
		35. My classmates see the female students as less intelligent for mathematics, physics and chemistry due to their being female.		.127**		.122*	
		36. I think my class teachers see female students as less intelligent for mathematics, physics chemistry because they are female.		.124**		.119*	-.106*

Dimensions		Variables	Bivariate Pearson Correlations (r)				
			Gender	Study area	School	Rural area	Another language
Academic dimension (con.)	School experience (con.)	37. My teachers prefer to select boys for scientific olympiads.	.116**	.141**	.142**		
		38. At my school, the teachers valued the work of students of the opposite sex to mine.	.173**			.133*	
		39. At my school, I have been harassed in exchange for receiving support with homework and exams.		.112**			
		40. I feel that my teachers evaluate me more strictly because of my gender.	.104**	.115**		.139**	-.106*
Social dimension	Social perception	41. Who do the media promote most as typical of an engineering professional?	-.097**	-.140**	-.213**		
		42. For whom is university education more important?	.145**			-.111*	
		43. In general, in terms of gender, who are better leaders?	.182**				
		44. Who is the best boss?	.252**		.184**		
		45. When jobs are scarce, who should have more right to a job?	.118**				
	Job prospects	46. I thought it would be easy to find a job in the career I want to study.		.082*			
		47. I think it could take time to find a job once I graduate as a professional due to my gender.					
		48. Career area you want to study:	-.191**	.118**			

Notes

**. Correlation is significant at 0.01 level. (two-sided).

*. Correlation is significant at 0.05 level. (two-sided).

was optimised using the Akaike Information Criterion (AIC) to ensure model parsimony and minimise overfitting.

Significant variables explaining women's preference for STEM subjects include: the perceived ease of mathematics, physics and chemistry; perception that service-based careers such as psychology, social work, medicine and other careers that help people are the most appropriate for women; place where the parents spent their childhood; grandparents' rural origins; parents' religion; fathers' education levels; parental influence on STEM career choices; parental interest in a service-based career such as psychology, social work, nursing, law or similar; perception of lack of parental support in the chosen career; support from friends; teaching methods used by STEM teachers that generate interest in these subjects; the quality of STEM teaching; participation in science olympiads; teachers' preference for selecting boys for the science olympiads and whether men, women or both make better bosses.

The analysis of dimensions reveals several key insights. At the individual level, only two survey questions were significantly related to interest in STEM subjects. In the family and peer dimension, eight out of 14 survey questions were significantly related to interest in STEM subjects. In the academic dimension, four out of 16 survey questions were statistically significant. At the social level, only one out of eight survey questions were significantly related to interest in STEM subjects. While it is important to note that the number of questions in each dimension differed, it seems clear that family-level factors are of particular importance to Bolivian women based on the statistical analyses above.

In the family and peer dimension, eight out of 14 survey questions were significantly related to interest in STEM subjects. In the academic dimension, four out of 16 survey questions are statistically significant. At the social level, only one out of eight survey questions were significantly related to interest in STEM subjects. While it is important to note that the number of questions in each dimension differed, it seems clear that family-level factors are of particular importance to Bolivian women based on the statistical analyses above.

Taken together, these three methods illustrate key factors related to women's participation in STEM in Bolivia. Our work highlights that women's preferences for STEM careers in universities are influenced by factors such as an interest in theoretical and numerical subjects, the perception of good career opportunities despite challenges, and concerns about balancing family and work life. Support from teachers and effective teaching methods are critical, as is parental approval, particularly in private universities. Academically, no significant discrimination is reported, and satisfaction with STEM teaching remains high. However, social and cultural barriers, such as gender stereotypes and harassment, continue to affect women's access to and retention in STEM fields. Despite these challenges, family support and perceptions of gender equality in private universities act as facilitating factors.

Overall, this research provides an in-depth understanding of the factors influencing female participation in STEM in Bolivia. Through the analysis of life stories, it becomes evident that female engineers overcome gender barriers with the support of their families, motivation and resilience. Social representations highlight the persistence of stereotypes that limit opportunities, while statistical analysis confirms significant disparities despite advances in equity. These findings underscore the need for educational policies and strategies that promote gender equality – essential for personal development and the country's social progress.

Collaboration among educational institutions, government, the private sector and civil society is crucial for achieving gender equality in STEM. Proposals such as teacher training programmes and curriculum redesign illustrate the potential for progress through joint efforts.

Phase 2: Co-construction of the pilot project

Despite these challenges, women in STEM in Bolivia demonstrate resilience and determination in overcoming the barriers they face. However, to truly transform these dynamics, structural change is necessary. Public policies must address not only the visible barriers but also the subtle mechanisms that perpetuate inequality. This includes improving vocational guidance in schools, creating support programmes in universities and developing labour policies that allow for a balance between personal and professional life.

Gender equity in STEM is not only a matter of social justice but also an opportunity to harness human potential and foster the country's economic and technological development. Ultimately, closing this gap will benefit Bolivian society by building a more inclusive, equitable and innovative environment for future generations.

The challenges women face in STEM in Bolivia are compounded by intersectional factors such as gender, ethnicity and region (see Chapter 5 for further discussion on how intersectional factors may be considered and addressed). Women from rural or Indigenous backgrounds encounter layered barriers, including limited access to quality education, fewer role models and entrenched cultural norms that reinforce traditional gender roles. Further, while younger generations, especially in urban areas, show greater support for gender equity, traditional norms continue to constrain progress in rural regions. As Crenshaw

(1989) highlights, addressing these disparities requires an intersectional approach that considers the interplay of social categories. Public policies and programmes must go beyond gender equality to include tailored strategies for women from diverse ethnic and regional backgrounds, fostering a more inclusive and equitable STEM environment.

With this understanding, we piloted a project that brought together key stakeholders in STEM field education to propose policy-level changes designed to improve women's participation in STEM in Bolivia. Stakeholders represented the following three groups:

- University directors and professors: Comprising directors and professors from public and private universities, this group analysed the institutional and professional challenges faced by women in STEM fields.
- School system faculty and staff: Composed of teachers and educational coordinators, especially in psychology, pedagogy and STEM, this group proposed solutions to increase female participation in STEM starting from basic education.
- Women engineers, professors and entrepreneurs in STEM: Prominent women in engineering, academia and business contributed an analytical perspective on the problems and offered proposals to overcome structural and cultural barriers in the workplace and education.

Methodology

The workshop methodology was based on a participatory approach inspired by Orlando Fals Borda's concept of popular education and grounded in participatory action research (PAR). This approach empowers communities through the collective construction of knowledge, fostering reflective and educational processes rooted in participants' realities. The workshops were designed as spaces for horizontal dialogue, integrating local knowledge and individual perspectives to identify problems and generate meaningful learning. In response to the pandemic, some workshops were adapted to a virtual format, reorganising dynamics and schedules while maintaining the participatory spirit, the centrality of lived experiences and the transformative practice of PAR (Fals Borda, 1987, 2001).

The facilitation was led by experts in gender and education, professionals with experience in educational projects with a gender perspective in universities, secondary education institutions and programmes in collaboration with local governments. The workshops were structured into the following phases:

programme presentation, problem identification and proposed solution development. Open and constructive dialogue was promoted throughout all phases.

Participatory techniques such as brief presentations, plenary discussions and the use of cards were employed to capture diverse perspectives and co-create proposals. The contributions were systematically organised in Microsoft Excel matrices, categorising the information according to the programme's objectives. This methodology allowed for in-depth analysis and the formulation of effective proposals to reduce the gender gap in STEM, ensuring that all voices were heard and valued.

Workshops were initially held separately for the three stakeholder groups (university, school and workplace groups). However, towards the end of this phase, the groups of stakeholders were brought together.

Presentation

The workshops began with a presentation of findings from previous research, providing a scientific framework to contextualise the causes and factors affecting women's participation in STEM. This enabled participants to reflect and debate in an informed manner during the participatory phase, enriching proposals with data and evidence.

Problem identification

The inputs collected during the participatory workshops focused on identifying problems and formulating proposals based on the presented findings. Based on the presented research, workshop participants identified five barriers that limit women's participation in STEM:

- **Gender stereotypes:** Perceptions of women's abilities in STEM are shaped by stereotypes that discourage them from pursuing these fields from basic education through to university.
- **Lack of institutional and family support:** The lack of motivation from teachers, the absence of family support and the scarcity of role models prevent many women from choosing STEM.
- **Workplace challenges:** Women face wage discrimination, inadequate infrastructure and biases in hiring practices that favour men for certain roles.

- **Cultural barriers**: Cultural norms and caregiving responsibilities limit women's professional development, and policies like maternity leave can act as additional obstacles.
- **Educational inequality**: STEM education is not sufficiently integrated, resulting in inadequate preparation in key areas and a lack of proper vocational guidance for female students. This stems from the insufficient integration of STEM subjects into the curriculum, reliance on traditional teaching methodologies and inadequate training in critical subjects such as mathematics and technology. Furthermore, vocational guidance is often limited, and when combined with persistent gender stereotypes, it further discourages female students from pursuing STEM careers.

Proposed solutions

The participants formulated various proposals to address these barriers:

- **Training and awareness**: Develop training programmes for teachers, counsellors and families to raise awareness about the importance of female participation in STEM and to include gender topics in the educational curriculum.
- **Promotion and visibility**: Create communication campaigns that highlight women's achievements in STEM and establish scholarships and specific competitions for women.
- **Educational strengthening**: Review curricula to include incorporating playful activities and workshops to foster interest in STEM from an early age, as well as specific programmes to strengthen soft skills, mathematical competencies and entrepreneurship among final-year high school and first-year university students.
- **Institutional alignment**: Create partnerships between universities, businesses and governments to promote gender equity and encourage the hiring of women in male-dominated fields.
- **Support for work–life balance**: Establish policies that allow women to balance their work and family responsibilities, thereby facilitating their professional development in STEM.

The co-construction of the pilot project in the workshops was a collaborative process focused on addressing the barriers that perpetuate the gender gap in STEM. Participants identified problems and formulated proposals to develop programmes that strengthen basic mathematics skills, soft skills and entrepreneurship, particularly for students transitioning from high school to university. These contributions are key to empowering young women and promoting a more equitable and inclusive environment in STEM, driving lasting transformation in Bolivian society.

To evaluate the effectiveness of these proposals in reducing the gender gap, the pilot project will include a comprehensive evaluation framework. This framework will establish clear indicators to assess teacher training, visibility campaigns, curriculum improvements, institutional partnerships and work–life balance policies. The evaluation process will involve data collection through surveys, interviews and focus groups, complemented by longitudinal studies, to provide insights into both short- and long-term outcomes. Guided by the principles of PAR, this inclusive approach will empower stakeholders to refine and scale the most successful initiatives, promoting sustainable gender equity in STEM across Bolivia.

Conclusion

This chapter reflects on the barriers that limit the access and development of women in STEM in Bolivia. The participatory action research (PAR) approach employed here gathers data while actively involving teachers, students, professionals and decision-makers as co-creators of solutions. The participatory workshops became spaces of empowerment, generating concrete proposals to overcome these barriers.

The study's findings challenge us to question the structures that perpetuate gender inequality in STEM. The life stories reveal that family support and resilience are crucial for women to overcome stereotypes and advance in their careers. The social representations analysed show how negative expectations continue to limit career options for women. These findings are not merely observations but a call to action for those who seek social justice.

Collaboration across sectors – educational, governmental, private and civil society – is essential to achieving gender equality in STEM. The proposals, ranging from teacher training to curricular redesign, demonstrate what can be achieved through joint effort. Our multi-pronged approach to understanding and promoting women's participation in STEM is yet to be evaluated in terms of efficacy. That said, we hope our approach can serve as a blueprint for others looking to engage in similar efforts across other contexts.

Acknowledgements

We would like to express our sincere gratitude to all the participants in this project, including students, parents, teachers, faculty and researchers, whose valuable collaboration and willingness to share their experiences made the data collection and success of this study possible. We are especially grateful to the women engineers, whose commitment and knowledge were crucial to the realisation of this project. We also extend our deep thanks to the International Development Research Centre (IDRC), whose financial support was essential for carrying out this research and whose collaboration was key throughout the entire process. Without their contribution, this project would not have been possible.

About the Authors

Mariana Santa Cruz Terrazas is affiliated with the Universidad Católica Boliviana San Pablo, Bolivia.

Mary Cruz De Urioste Vidaurre is affiliated with the Universidad Privada de Santa Cruz de la Sierra (UPSA), Bolivia.

References

Abdulkadri, A., John-Aloye, S., Mkrtchyan, I., Gonzales, C., Johnson, S., & Floyd, S. (2022). Addressing gender disparities in education and employment: a necessary step for achieving sustainable development in the Caribbean. *Studies and Perspectives series-ECLAC Subregional Headquarters for the Caribbean, No. 109*. https://repositorio.cepal.org/server/api/core/bitstreams/617fc7ac-82b0-4b2f-be83-5a14d825caf4/content

Arredondo Trapero, F. G., Vázquez Parra, J. C., & Velázquez Sánchez, L. M. (2019). STEM y brecha de género en Latinoamérica. *Revista de El Colegio de San Luis, 9*(18), 137–158. https://revista.colsan.edu.mx/index.php/COLSAN/article/view/947/

ATLAS.ti Scientific Software Development GmbH. (2023). *ATLAS.ti Mac* (Versión No. 23.2.1) [Software de análisis de datos cualitativos]. Lumivero, LLC. https://atlasti.com

Avolio, B., & Chávez, J. (2023). Professional development of women in STEM careers: Evidence from a Latin American country. *Global Business Review, 0*(0). https://doi.org/10.1177/09721509221141197

Bergman, M. M., & Danermark, B. (2015). *Participatory action research: A new approach to research on gender and STEM. International Journal of Gender and STEM, 3*(1), 42–57.

Carrasco Mercado, G. J. (2018). Situación de la mujer en la ciencia y tecnología: relaciones de poder al interior de una entidad académica pública con autonomía universitaria. *Trilogía Ciencia Tecnología Sociedad, 10*(19), 45–58. https://doi.org/10.22430/21457778.1015

Cerinsek, G., Hribar, T., Glodez, N., & Dolinsek, S. (2013). Which are my future career priorities and what influenced my choice of studying science, technology, engineering or mathematics? Some insights on educational choice – Case of Slovenia. *International Journal of Science Education, 35*(17), 2999–3025. https://doi.org/10.1080/09500693.2012.681813

Connell, R. W. (2009). Gender and education: A perspective on the power of knowledge. In D. Epstein, R. Deem, F. Rizvi & S. Wright (Eds.), *World yearbook of education 2009: Childhood studies and the impact of globalization* (pp. 59–75). Routledge.

Crenshaw, K. (1989). Demarginalizing the intersection of race and sex: A Black feminist critique of antidiscrimination doctrine, feminist theory, and antiracist politics. *University of Chicago Legal Forum, 1989*(1), 139–167. https://chicagounbound.uchicago.edu/uclf/vol1989/iss1/8/

De Urioste, M. C. (2016). Estadísticas de género de las Universidades de la Ciudad de Santa Cruz. *Aportes de la Comunicación y la Cultura, 1*(20), 40–46. https://doi.org/10.56992/a.v1i20.98

Denzin, N. K., & Lincoln, Y. S. (Eds.). (2018). *The SAGE handbook of qualitative research* (5th ed.). Sage.

Fals Borda, O. (1987). The application of participatory action-research in Latin America. *International Sociology, 2*(4), 329–347. https://doi.org/10.1177/026858098700200401

Fals Borda, O. (2001). Participatory (action) research in social theory: Origins and challenges. In P. Reason & H. Bradbury (Eds.), *Handbook of action research: Participative inquiry and practice* (pp. 27–37). Sage.

Guevara, M. E. (2021). Factores que influyen en la participación de la mujer en carreras de ciencia, tecnología, ingeniería y matemática. *Ciencia Cultura y Sociedad, 6*(2), 66–82.

IBM Corp. (2021). *IBM SPSS statistics for Windows* (Version 28.0) [Computer software]. IBM Corp. https://www.ibm.com/analytics/spss-statistics-software

IHS Markit. (2020). *EViews 11* [Computer software]. IHS Markit Ltd. https://www.eviews.com/

Kemmis, S., McTaggart, R., & Nixon, R. (2014). *The action research planner: Doing critical participatory action research*. Springer. https://doi.org/10.1007/978-981-4560-67-2

López, S. (2021). Mujeres en STEM: Factores que inciden en la elección de carreras científicas y tecnológicas. *Revista Iberoamericana de Educación Superior, 12*(33), 83–102.

Mariaca, G. (1999). *La democratización de las elites: Apuntes sobre género y educación superior*. Ministerio de Desarrollo Sostenible y Planificación, Viceministerio de Asuntos de Género, Generacionales y Familia.

Paredes-Walker, V. (2020). Mujeres que marcan precedentes en Ingeniería. Su experiencia en la carrera académica en una universidad de investigación en Chile. *Revista Iberoamericana de Educación Superior, 30*(11), 137–159. https://doi.org/10.22201/iisue.20072872e.2020.30.592

R Core Team. (2020). *R: A language and environment for statistical computing* (Version 4.0.3) [Computer software]. R Foundation for Statistical Computing. https://www.r-project.org/

Radovic, D., Veloso, R., Sánchez, J., Gerdtzen, Z., & Martínez, S. (2021). Entrar no es suficiente: Discursos de académicos y estudiantes sobre inclusión de mujeres en ingeniería en Chile. *Revista Mexicana de Investigación Educativa, 26*(90), 841–865. https://ddg.ingenieria.uchile.cl/wp-content/uploads/2020/09/Radovic_RMIE_Aceptado.pdf

Somekh, B. (2006). *Action research: A methodology for change and development*. Open University Press.

UNESCO (United Nations Educational, Scientific and Cultural Organization). (2017). *Cracking the code: Girls' and women's education in science, technology, engineering and mathematics (STEM)*. UNESCO. https://unesdoc.unesco.org/ark:/48223/pf0000253479

Universidad Privada de Santa Cruz de la Sierra (UPSA). (2018). Informe de participación femenina en olimpiadas científicas. UPSA.

Verdugo, C., Martínez, P., & Soto, A. (2019). Género y permanencia en carreras STEM en universidades públicas chilenas. *Revista de Educación Superior, 48*(192), 45–62.

CHAPTER 12

The Underrepresentation of Women in STEM Research in Afrika* – Can Nego-Feminism Offer a Solution?

Ulrike Rivett and Joshua Ishaku Azaki

Introduction

The Nigerian novelist Chinua Achebe once said, "There is that great proverb – that until the lions have their own historians, the history of the hunt will always glorify the hunter" (Achebe, 1958). In other words, the perspective of the storyteller affects the story being told. Reflecting on this idea, we consider how most research and narratives around gender inequalities in STEM come from the Global North.

Specifically, we seek to address the underrepresentation of women in Science, Technology, Engineering and Mathematics (STEM) in the Afrikan context, which begins with our intentional spelling of 'Afrika' (Madhubuti, 1979). Throughout the continent, 'Afrika' is spelt with a 'k'; the introduction of the letter 'c' represents the global dispersion of Afrikans, which is frequently linked to a loss of Afrikan identity. Colonialist and patriarchal systems have contributed to this loss of identity, and we highlight the importance of considering these influences when considering gender equity in STEM. Using the 'k' spelling is a deliberate choice to reclaim agency and acknowledge the significant contributions Afrikan women make in the 21st century.

Why focus on STEM? STEM fields have become integral to global and economic prosperity (Olaitan & Mavuso, 2022). STEM fields attract researchers, problem solvers and professionals who advance critical aspects of life, such as education, health, security and others. However, as highlighted by this collection, gender parity in STEM fields remains skewed (Blackburn, 2017; Bloodhart et al., 2020; Kahn & Ginther, 2017). Studies investigating this phenomenon show that stereotyping, as well as institutional and systemic biases, are among the factors contributing substantively to women's underrepresentation (Bloodhart et al., 2020; Nakayiwa et al., 2020; Odaga, 2020; Siwale et al., 2023). However, research investigating women in STEM originates in the Global North and limited input can be found from the Global South (Prozesky & Mouton, 2019; Siwale et al., 2023).

We reiterate ideas shared throughout this collection, highlighting how the body of research from Afrika suggests that gender stereotyping from an early age has meant that girls and young women have not been encouraged to pursue careers in STEM (CHE, 2016; Mbirianjau et al., 2019; Odaga, 2020). For example, in Kenya's public universities, women's enrolment is approximately 30% (Mbirianjau et al., 2019). The 2020 study by The Afrikan Academy of Sciences, comprising Afrikan countries sub-Sahara, showed the percentage of women graduates in STEM stood at 12% (The AAS, 2020).

Even more concerningly, in a World Economic Forum blog, the projected year for closing the gender gap (STEM inclusive) was moved from 2095 to 2133 (Harry, 2018); suggesting that efforts towards gender equality are moving more slowly than expected. The delay in achieving gender equality has far-reaching impacts, from economic growth to social implications, but also a mental and emotional impact on women themselves. This 38-year delay should act as a call to re-examine efforts and investigate potentially ineffective policies.

The previous chapters of this collection, through the diverse perspectives shared and contexts explored, seek to address the lack of Global South voices contributing to conversations around gender equality in STEM. Conversely, the current chapter looks to highlight alternative pathways through which we might interrogate the issue. More specifically, we consider how Afrikan perspectives can address the underrepresentation of women in STEM on the Afrikan continent. There is, to date, a lack of literature originating in Afrika, that discusses and conceptualises gender inclusion with an awareness of cultural nuances. This is despite the continent's diverse cultural heritage, which encompasses relevant principles such as ubuntu and Afrikan feminism (Cruz, 2016; Menon, 2022).

Ubuntu is an Afrikan philosophy rooted in communal interdependency. It engages with social justice, interdependence, empathy as well as collaboration and compassion (Ewuoso & Hall, 2019). By reflecting on togetherness, ubuntu provides an opportunity to reflect on Afrikan culture (Ewuoso & Hall, 2019;

Menon, 2022). Afrikan feminism aligns with the philosophy of ubuntu (Cruz, 2016) and provides a nuanced approach to addressing gender disparities in STEM using Southern theory. Understanding the Afrikan approach and its nuances (Prozesky & Mouton, 2019; Siwale & Mwalemba, 2023) can help chart a course towards specific targeted actions that could be effective in an Afrikan context.

Existing Afrikan literature highlights the experiences of women in STEM fields (see Chapter 9 for a scoping review of literature on gender disparities in undergraduate learning in sub-Saharan Africa). Gender biases within structural inequalities significantly contribute to the challenge of the leaky pipeline in STEM (Siwale & Mwalemba, 2023; The AAS, 2020). The absence of role models and limited funding opportunities hinder women's advancement (Nakayiwa et al., 2020; Olaitan & Mavuso, 2022). Insufficient digital access is compounded by low infrastructure availability, including mobile broadband, internet connectivity and power supply limitations, impacting women's educational opportunities and skill development in STEM fields, including information and communication technology (ITU, 2019; The AAS, 2020). Education disparities are evident in inadequate learning infrastructure, lack of teaching materials and shortages of skilled teachers, affecting enrolment and retention rates in STEM fields (UNESCO, 2020). Research output in STEM is influenced by the scarcity of women academics and researchers, emphasising gender imbalances in scholarly contributions. Women's family responsibilities impede their career progress, while insufficient social capital limits women's leadership roles, resulting in underrepresentation and an underrepresentation of women in influential positions (Mbirianjau et al., 2019; Nakayiwa et al., 2020; Siwale & Mwalemba, 2023).

Understanding gender stereotypes and biases in science through an Afrikan feminist framework

To contextualise Afrikan women's experiences, it is worth considering the framing typically used when discussing gender inequalities, including by UNESCO (2024) and IDRC: *dismantling gender stereotypes and biases in science*. The term 'dismantling' reflects a call to conflict, which is challenging in a context where community is understood as supportive. When terms such as 'dismantling' are used, the understanding and discourse about gender representation in STEM in Afrika can feel threatening or intimidating, contradicting the sense of togetherness that underlies much of the Afrikan philosophy of ubuntu and Afrikan feminism. Challenging gender bias or stereotypes often has a negative, even combative connotation. Nnaemeka (2004) aptly captures it this way: "you cannot mobilise a movement that is only and always against; you must have a positive alternative".

To unpack the concept of stereotype and what it means for Afrikan women, it is pertinent to factor in and value contexts and experiences that are rooted in a sense of community, togetherness and complementary shared roles, which may be at odds with the Global North's feminism of competitiveness and individualism (Biwa, 2021; Cruz, 2016; Nnaemeka, 2004). The sense of complementarity is typified in the writings of Afrikan feminists who highlight that Western and Afrikan feminism are not contradictory theories; such contributions often identify the nuances of both theories and then suggest ways to go forward, respectfully engaging in scholarship (Akin-Aina, 2011; Cruz, 2016). Similarly, Afrikan feminism acknowledges the roles of all people and organisations as allies in coming up with solutions to problems that Afrikan women face.

> Afrikan women are not problems to be solved. Like women everywhere, Afrikan women have problems. More important, they have provided solutions to these problems. We are the only ones who can set our priorities and agenda. Anyone who wishes to participate in our struggle must do so in the context of our agenda. In the same way, Afrikan women who wish to contribute to global struggles (and many do) should do so with a deep respect for the paradigms and strategies that people of those areas have established. In our enthusiasm to liberate others, we must not be blind to our own enslavement. Activities of women globally should be mutually liberating. (Nnaemeka, 2005, p. 57)

Nnaemeka (2005) highlights that Afrikan women have the solutions to their problems and those who would like to partner in resolving those problems must align with their agenda. In her seminal article "Nego-feminism: Theorising, practicing and pruning Afrika's way", she advocates the feminism of negotiation (nego-feminism) as an agency to go around the patriarchal landmines such as negative stereotypes as well as detonate them respectfully with little to no casualties in an Afrikan-centric way.

> First, nego-feminism is the feminism of negotiation; second, nego-feminism stands for 'no ego' feminism. In the foundation of shared values in many Afrikan cultures are the principles of negotiation, give and take, compromise and balance. Afrikan feminism[s]

(or feminism as I have seen it practiced in Afrika) challenges through negotiations and compromise. It knows when, where, and how to detonate patriarchal land mines; it also knows when, where, and how to go around patriarchal land mines". (Nnaemeka, 2004, p. 376–378)

When using *role models* to *dismantle* gender stereotypes, the danger is one of aesthetics. Aesthetics relegate social action and promote egocentrism and individualism above collective action (Nnaemeka, 2004). In the Afrikan context, the function of role models is to benefit the collective and not to promote some hidden agenda. What are the driving forces of role modelling as a form of agency for *dismantling* gender stereotypes? According to an Afrikan feminism of negotiation, the term *role model* requires a collective engagement to define role models in the Afrikan context to promote a communal discourse about the role of such *role models* in *dismantling gender stereotyping,* particularly women in STEM fields. The superficial studies of Afrikan women need to go deeper as Nnaemeka (2004, p. 364) states: "Afrikan studies' focus on the idea of Afrika rather than the reality of Afrika mimics women's studies' foregrounding of the notion of the Afrikan woman rather than the humanity of Afrikan women." The challenge put to us is to reflect on how we identify role models and to challenge ourselves in seeking role models. In other words, we must ensure we are not defining role models based on male or Global North norms. Instead, our role models should represent success as defined by Afrikan women. Some questions to wrestle with while seeking to use the agency of role models are:

- Is it possible to have/raise role models at diverse stages of life – from childhood to adulthood, covering different educational and career stages?
- How can structures be put in place that promote raising role models?
- What would be the best or appropriate ways/approaches/strategies to develop these structures?
- How can these structures be sustained?
- What tools would be needed in building such systems that should produce role models?
- What technologies can be leveraged in (the system of) raising role models?
- How will these technologies be developed to ensure that Afrikan women benefit optimally?

These are pertinent questions to consider to effectively *dismantle gender stereotypes* using role models. These questions go beyond the aesthetics of showcasing a role model and reflect the true nature of Afrikan engagement. By asking these questions through the lens of gender-awareness combined with Afrikan engagement (i.e. considering barriers faced by and perspectives of Afrikan women specifically), we can emphasise the value of creating community and intentionality when confronting the underrepresentation of women in STEM. Indeed, role models are not the only way to dismantle gender stereotypes. An initiative that may serve as an example of intentionality and creating a community is the Forum for Afrikan Women Vice Chancellors (FAWoVC); among its responsibilities is included mainstreaming gender within higher education institutions through "spearhead[ing] gender responsive training in higher education institutions and ... increase[ing] the enrolment of female students in ... STEM" (Nakayiwa et al., 2020, p. 66).

To engage more appropriately in questions of gender, stereotypes and biases, we must enhance our own gender-awareness and in doing so, our ability to go beyond a superficial analysis of the commonly accepted gender studies terminologies and their conclusions. By being mindful of the different perspectives and working towards a more equitable approach, a holistic comprehension of the structural and societal implications of using those terminologies will encourage sensitivity in interactions and decision-making.

Ensuring support across education and career pathways – Understanding women's needs

Supporting women in STEM requires educational and workplace environments that actively recognise and respond to their specific needs, ensuring retention, advancement and equity across career pathways. Research has mainly reviewed unconducive work environments causing many women to exit STEM fields at various stages in their education or careers – often referred to as the leaky STEM pipeline (Mbirianjau et al., 2019; Nakayiwa et al., 2020; Siwale & Mwalemba, 2023; The AAS, 2020). The leaky pipeline, marked by systemic barriers such as discrimination, harassment and inadequate policies, continues to push women out of STEM fields at various stages (see Chapter 11 for an approach to understanding and addressing such barriers in Bolivia). Addressing these issues requires both structural reform and culturally grounded feminist approaches.

To address these persistent barriers, nego-feminism offers a culturally grounded approach to reimagining support systems for women in STEM to challenge these areas of tension through the art of negotiation and compromise. Scholars of Afrikan feminism agree on the power of negotiation in creating awareness about different parties' needs leading to "detonating" or "charting a course around patriarchal landmines" manifested through the various hostilities faced by women (Akin-Aina, 2011; Cruz, 2016; Nnaemeka, 2004). Nego-feminism's "third space of engagement" provides a platform for women in STEM to develop a common charter that can be used to engage with workplace leadership. As Nnaemeka (2004, p. 360) puts it, "The third space allow[s] the mediation of policy. The third space, which allows for the coexistence, interconnection and interaction of thought, dialogue, planning and action, constitutes the arena where I have witnessed the unfolding of feminisms in Afrika." In other words, the third space of engagement refers to a theoretical space that lives between the worlds of theory, policy and practice, wherein ideas can be openly shared and continuously evolving.

Within this framework, the concept of a 'third space of engagement' emerges as a powerful tool for collective action, enabling women in STEM to articulate shared needs and influence institutional policies. If educational institutions and workplaces are to become spaces where women feel welcomed and accommodated, such a space needs to be created. Otherwise, the undesired consequences become inevitable, and we continue to perpetuate the existence of unconducive educational and workplace environments. The manifestation of systemic barriers reported in the literature has made more women become victims of the leaky pipeline. The relevance of these ideas becomes clear when examining real-world policies that disproportionately affect women, such as the study by Mbirianjau et al. (2019) examining restrictions on campus housing for pregnant students. This type of policy applies exclusively to women and leads to women dropping out of university programmes when they start families. Societal and cultural norms downplay the need for providing women with opportunities as women are perceived to be family and home caretakers (The AAS, 2020). With this notion, women's participation in STEM is threatened and undermined.

Motherhood, while culturally valued in many Afrikan contexts, often intersects with institutional policies in ways that disadvantage women in STEM. This duality, where motherhood confers social respect but also institutional penalties, highlights the need for policy reform that aligns with cultural realities. Cruz (2016) highlighted the agency of socialisation through motherhood as a way for women to gain visibility. In the Afrikan sense, motherhood comes with a substantial benefit which includes status, respect and a sense of being valued (Cruz, 2016). Research suggests women are challenged with weighing the costs and benefits of motherhood when making decisions about their educational or career trajectories. Many women ascend to the peak of their careers during childbearing ages, which leaves women to choose between their career and family; most forfeit their career to raise a family (Nakayiwa et al., 2020; Odaga, 2020; Siwale et al., 2023; The AAS, 2020; Thornton, 2019). There is an additional punitive aspect of motherhood in certain, often male-dominated, spaces, including STEM fields. For example, in Kenyan public universities, pregnant women are given penalties like losing on-campus boarding privilege (Mbirianjau et al., 2019). The cited study noted that no policy existed to support nursing mothers in university residences, leading to delayed graduation or drop-out. Contrarily, in Uganda, the affirmative action introduced in 1990 has increased the intake of female students into the university, though the corresponding outcome is yet to significantly increase the number of women taking up STEM courses (Nakayiwa et al., 2020).

In light of these disparities, scholars advocate for a gender-awareness lens to be applied to research infrastructure, curriculum and human resources to foster more inclusive environments (see a detailed discussion in Chapter 1). There is a need to urgently put policies in place that will address "the perceptions and stereotypes about the performance and participation of females in the ST&I [Science, Technology and Innovation] realm and workplace", and "policy engagement and advocacy should target the socio-cultural, technological and financial aspects that will narrow the gender [gaps] in education, ST&I as well as technical and leadership positions" (Nakayiwa et al., 2020, p. 85).

Beyond policy reform, it is essential to interrogate the theoretical foundations guiding gender research in STEM, particularly when Global North perspectives dominate the discourse. Dimensions of positionality and intersectionality are crucial considerations for research on women in Afrika (Cruz, 2016; Nnaemeka, 2004). Nnaemeka (2004) remarks that positionality will bring about a reconsideration of different aspects of life such as the social, personal, political and others. Intersectionality, she argues, will bring together the ontology and evolution of being and becoming. Akin-Aina (2011) adds that continuous engagement is required to promote scholarship and praxis of Afrikan feminism and allow room for constant negotiation with evolving 'elements of custom and tradition' whose end goal is emancipation.

Theorising women's underrepresentation in STEM on the Afrikan continent as a subset of gender equality using Global North methods of analysis raises important questions such as: who benefits from the theories developed? Who does the theory serve? Whose agenda is pursued? Nnaemeka (2004, p. 362) cites Lugones and Spelman (1983) to capture a crucial aspect of theory building:

> Theory makers and their methods and concepts constitute a community of people and shared meanings. ... Why do we engage in this activity and what effect do we think it ought to have? As Helen Longino has asked: 'Is "doing theory" just a bonding ritual for

academic or educationally privileged feminist women?' Again, whom does our theory making serve?

We argue theories should be developed and used contextually and intersectionally to contribute to positive and meaningful change (Nnaemeka, 2004, p. 367). Ultimately, theories addressing gender in STEM must be rooted in Afrikan contexts, informed by intersectional realities and aimed at transformative change, not merely academic discourse. Only then can they serve the women they intend to support.

Conclusion

The pervasive influences of patriarchy and colonialism significantly shape the cultural norms prevalent across the Afrikan continent, permeating societal structures and influencing the trajectory of development, particularly within technological advancement. Within patriarchal systems, the reinforcement of binary gender constructs tends to privilege men while constraining women and non-binary individuals' opportunities for participation and contribution in processes crucial to societal progress. The ramifications of this systemic bias have historically been overlooked and downplayed, perpetuating an ongoing cycle of inequality.

We aimed to introduce a new perspective on the narrative of women in STEM across the Afrikan continent. Exploring local perspectives on gender and social dynamics within Afrikan contexts holds critical significance for driving positive change. With this, the imperative arises to delineate what constitutes the dismantling, stereotyping, creating role models and conducive workplace environments from an Afrikan perspective. Western feminist approaches continue to navigate the historical legacies of colonialism and systemic suppression that have shaped perceptions of gender and representation in STEM. We argue that by using an Afrikan feminism of negotiation to unpack perceptions and experiences, the possibility of redefining gender norms and reimagining Afrikan STEM spaces can evolve into equitable and inclusive domains.

In conclusion, we emphasise the crucial need for a broader consideration of Afrikan perspectives in addressing the underrepresentation of women in STEM fields across the continent. Recognising that the challenges faced by Afrikan women are deeply embedded in unique socio-cultural, historical and economic contexts is vital. The application of solutions derived from the Global North often fails to resonate with the realities on the ground, leading to ineffective approaches that overlook the invaluable insights and agency of Afrikan women themselves.

The integration of frameworks such as Afrikan feminism and the philosophy of ubuntu is essential in redefining gender norms and creating inclusive STEM environments in Afrika. These frameworks not only acknowledge the communal and relational aspects of Afrikan cultures but also promote the active participation of women in dialogues about their representation and advancement. By centring local narratives and contexts, stakeholders can better understand what it truly means to dismantle gender stereotypes and biases and how to create role models and supportive workplace environments that genuinely reflect Afrikan realities.

Moreover, the importance of engaging in gender-aware research that transcends superficial analyses cannot be overstated. This research must consider the complexities of intersectionality and positionality, allowing for a nuanced understanding of the barriers women face in STEM and the potential pathways for overcoming them. The limited visibility of role models and systemic inequalities perpetuated by cultural perceptions must be addressed through collective action, driven by the voices and experiences of women in science and technology across Afrika.

Ultimately, this chapter advocates for a shift in the global discourse surrounding gender in STEM, urging for partnerships that are respectful of Afrikan agency and aligned with local aspirations. Such an approach requires both an acknowledgement of historical injustices and a commitment to fostering environments where Afrikan women can thrive as innovators and leaders in STEM fields. It is through this paradigm shift that we can hope to achieve meaningful progress, ensuring that gender parity in STEM is not just an ideal but a reality in Afrika.

Acknowledgements

We acknowledge the International Development Research Centre (IDRC), Ottawa, Canada for funding the GeJuSTA[1] project, which gave us the insights for the reflection in this chapter.

---

1 https://sit.uct.ac.za/gejusta

About the Authors

Ulrike Rivett is a Professor in the Department of Information Systems at the University of Cape Town, South Africa. She was the PI on GeJuSTA, a research project that provides the background to this chapter.

Joshua Ishaku Azaki is currently a Doctoral Student at the University of Cape Town, South Africa, and was the GeJuSTA Project Manager.

References

Achebe, C. (1958). *Things fall apart*. William Heineman Ltd.

Akin-Aina, S. (2011). Beyond an epistemology of bread, butter, culture and power: Mapping the African feminist movement. *Nokoko, 2*, 66–89.

Biwa, V. (2021). African feminisms and co-constructing a collaborative future with men: Namibian women in mining's discourses. *Management Communication Quarterly, 35*(1), 43–68. https://doi.org/10.1177/0893318920973988

Blackburn, H. (2017). The status of women in STEM in higher education: A review of the literature 2007–2017. *Science & Technology Libraries, 36*(3), 235–273. https://doi.org/10.1080/0194262X.2017.1371658

Bloodhart, B., Balgopal, M. M., Marie, A., Casper, A., Sample Mcmeeking, L. B., & Fischer, E. V. (2020). Outperforming yet undervalued: Undergraduate women in STEM. *PLoS ONE, 15*(6), e0234685. https://doi.org/10.1371/journal.pone.0234685

CHE (Council on Higher Education). (2016). *VitalStats: Public higher education 2014*. Council on Higher Education. https://www.che.ac.za/sites/default/files/publications/CHE_VitalStats_2016%20webversion_0.pdf

Cruz, J. M. (2016). Reimagining feminist organizing in global times. *Women & Language, 38*(1), 23–41.

Ewuoso, C., & Hall, S. (2019). Core aspects of *ubuntu*: A systematic review. *South African Journal of Bioethics and Law, 12*(2), 93–103. https://journals.co.za/doi/pdf/10.7196/SAJBL.2019.v12i2.679

Hammond, A., Matulevich, E. R., Beegle, K., & Kumaraswamy, S. K. (2020). *The equality equation: Advancing the participation of women and girls in STEM*. World Bank Group.

Harry, N. (2018, January 19). Will the fourth industrial revolution be a revolution for women? [Blog post]. *World Economic Forum*. https://www.weforum.org/stories/2018/01/gender-inequality-and-the-fourth-industrial-revolution/

ITU (International Telecommunications Union). (2019). *Measuring digital development: Facts and figures*. ITU Publications. https://www.itu.int/en/ITU-D/Statistics/pages/facts/default.aspx

Kahn, S., & Ginther, D. (2017). *Women and STEM*. NBER Working Paper 23525. National Bureau of Economic Research. https://www.nber.org/papers/w23525

Lugones, M. C., & Spelman, E. V. (1983). Have we got a theory for you! Feminist theory, cultural imperialism and the demand for 'the woman's voice'. *Women's Studies International Forum, 6*(6), 573–581.

Madhubuti, H. R. (1979). Four reasons for using 'K' in Afrika. In *From plan to planet – Life studies: The need for Afrikan minds and institutions*. Third World Press.

Mbirianjau, L. W., Chege, F., & Oanda, I. (2019). Exploring enabling interventions for increasing female students' access and participation in science, technology, engineering and mathematics (STEM) disciplines in Kenyan public universities. *Msingi Journal, 1*(2), 1–6. https://journals.ku.ac.ke/index.php/msingi/article/view/107

Menon, D. M. (Ed.). (2022). *Changing theory: Concepts from the Global South*. Routledge India. https://www.taylorfrancis.com/books/9781003273530

Nakayiwa, F., Elhag, M. M., Santos, L., Kifle, D., & Tizikara, C. (2020). Strengthening higher education capacity to promote gender inclusive participation in science, technology and innovation. *African Journal of Rural Development, 5*(3), 65–86. https://afjrdev.org/index.php/jos/article/view/606

Nnaemeka, O. (2004). Nego-feminism: Theorizing, practicing, and pruning Africa's way. *Signs: Journal of Women in Culture and Society, 29*(2), 357–385. https://doi.org/10.1086/378553

Nnaemeka, O. (2005). Bringing African women into the classroom: Rethinking pedagogy and epistemology. In O. Oyěwùmí (Ed.), *African gender studies: A reader* (pp. 51–65). Palgrave Macmillan, https://doi.org/10.1007/978-1-137-09009-6_3

Odaga, G. (2020). Gender in Uganda's tertiary educational distribution. *Social Sciences and Humanities Open, 2*(1), 100023. https://doi.org/10.1016/j.ssaho.2020.100023

Olaitan, O., & Mavuso, N. (2022). Investigating the challenges faced by female students in STEM courses: Case study of a traditional South African university. *Perspectives in Education, 40*(4), 19–37. https://doi.org/10.38140/pie.v40i4.6638

Prozesky, H., & Mouton, J. (2019). A gender perspective on career challenges experienced by African scientists. *South African Journal of Science, 115*(3/4), 2–6. https://doi.org/10.17159/sajs.2019/5515

Siwale, K., & Mwalemba, G. (2023). Societal influences on career decision making: Perspectives of African women pursuing technology-related professions. *Electronic Journal of Information Systems in Developing Countries, 89*(4), 1–17. https://doi.org/10.1002/isd2.12259

Siwale, K., Mwalemba, G., & Rivett, U. (2023, September 14). *Experiences of African women in STEM careers: A systematic literature review* [Paper presentation]. 9th annual African conference on information systems and technology, Harare, Zimbabwe. https://digitalcommons.kennesaw.edu/acist/2023/presentations/9

The AAS (The African Academy of Sciences). (2020). Mukhwana, A. M., Abuya, T., Matanda, D., Omumbi, J., & Mabuka, J. *Factors which contribute to or inhibit women in science, technology, engineering, and mathematics in Africa*. The AAS. https://portal.aasciences.app/storage/publications/01112022071736Women%20in%20STEM%20Report_Final.pdf

Thornton, A. (2019, March 5). Gender equality in STEM is possible. These countries prove it. *World Economic Forum*. https://www.weforum.org/agenda/2019/03/gender-equality-in-stem-is-possible/

UNESCO (United Nations Educational, Scientific and Cultural Organization). (2020). *A new generation: 25 years of efforts for gender equality in education*. UNESCO. https://www.unesco.org/gem-report/en/publication/new-generation-25-years-efforts-gender-equality-education

UNESCO. (2024). *Call to action: Closing the gender gap in science* [Programme and meeting document]. UNESCO. https://unesdoc.unesco.org/ark:/48223/pf0000388641

Conclusion

Matilda Dipieri and Hannah Whitehead

This collection outlines researchers' efforts to advance gender equity in Science, Technology, Engineering and Mathematics (STEM) within their institutions, national governments and interregional networks. Organised around four critical themes – (1) Building gender-responsive and equitable STEM institutions; (2) Leveraging data to address gender disparities; (3) Fostering leadership and mentorship for women; and (4) Ensuring support across education and career pathways – each chapter offers unique perspectives and insights. While these themes provide a structured lens through which to view the contributions, the impact of the research extends far beyond these categories.

Though these contributions emerge from the Global South, gender inequities in STEM are resonant at a universal scale, as gender disparities in STEM remain a global problem. This collection not only sheds light on these pervasive challenges but can serve as a beacon, guiding and informing efforts to create an inclusive and equitable STEM landscape worldwide.

What the case studies reveal

Building gender-responsive and equitable STEM institutions

Chapter 1 highlighted the importance of institutional intentionality when evaluating and promoting gender in STEM. Despite gender equality being integral to the institution's inception, evaluations of the Women's University of Africa revealed that barriers to women's participation in STEM remained. The authors highlight the value of intentionality – including consistent evaluation and adaptation – from the institution and all parties within it to create a more equitable environment for women.

Similarly, Chapter 2 illustrates the importance of an institutional approach to developing a lasting, equitable learning environment. This project included a commitment from multiple stakeholders (apprentices, instructors, coordinators and community members) to improving gender equality within Colombian apprenticeship institutions.

Chapter 3 furthered this narrative by highlighting the value of addressing gender equity above the level of institutions. The authors highlight the limitations of policies adopted by individual institutions in siloes and call for an overarching framework for the African Research Universities Alliance. Taken together, these contributions emphasise the key role of institutions in ensuring gender equity and the value of intentionality in efforts towards gender equality in STEM.

Leveraging data to address gender disparities

Chapter 4 illustrates the importance of a multi-pronged approach to data collection and analysis. The multi-country team collected qualitative and quantitative data in Benin, Côte d'Ivoire and Niger. Their analyses reveal numerous barriers to gender equality in agricultural work and research, emphasising the importance of understanding and adhering to the norms of the population being studied. Their findings illustrate similarities and differences across the three countries, highlighting the value of collaboration as well as the importance of considering specific contexts.

Chapter 5 leverages the evaluation of a scholarship programme for Indigenous women in STEM in Mexico to develop critical insights into the trajectories and experiences of a previously understudied population.

Chapter 6 highlights the complex process involved in making data highly accessible and user-friendly. The interdisciplinary team outlines the design of the database as well as potential use cases while emphasising the importance of ease of access for diverse stakeholders. Taken together, these chapters highlight the value of large collaborations, be it between researchers in multiple disciplines and/or multiple countries, to ensure the collection of and access to relevant gender-disaggregated data.

Fostering leadership and mentorship for women in STEM

Chapter 7 underscores the importance of supervision and mentorship in supporting women's STEM postgraduate training. The researchers' framework, which has been adopted within East Africa, emphasises comprehensive planning, stakeholder engagement, capacity-strengthening initiatives and policy evaluation as essential to the success of supervision and mentorship in the region.

Chapter 8 evaluates how policies relate to women's participation in STEM leadership roles. The authors showcase that while there are policies in place to support women's leadership, a lack of understanding of policy and a lack of clarity within policies are barriers to women's success. The chapter highlights mentorship and capacity initiatives, as well as greater policy clarity, as critical to attracting and retaining women in leadership roles. Taken together, these contributions highlight the limited number of women in leadership roles in STEM, but the crucial importance of these role models and their role in changing the paths that other women may take.

Ensuring support across education and career pathways

Chapter 9's scoping review demonstrates that, to date, only a small body of literature has considered how pedagogical practices and interventions can support women students in STEM. Among existing publications, research suggests that gender-responsive pedagogies, teacher development, female role models and mentorships are among the strategies that can support women's progress in STEM in higher education.

Chapter 10 highlights that although investments in individual women scientists are not on their own sufficient to achieve gender equity in STEM, they can dismantle stereotypes and biases within institutions. Through fellowships and awards, OWSD supports women scientists in master's, PhD and early-career stages. The authors outline how investments in women scientists and the institutions in which they work can lead to better working conditions for women and greater visibility, both of which contribute to dismantling barriers and keeping women in science.

Chapter 11 provides insights into women in STEM in Bolivia from those in the university and the workforce. The authors identify stereotypes, workplace barriers, lack of support, cultural barriers and educational inequalities as the driving forces behind women's low rates of STEM participation in the country. They highlight improvements to educational curricula and workplace commitment to change among potential solutions. Taken together, these chapters suggest that despite barriers at all levels of education and in the workplace, gender-responsive pedagogies, role models and institutional commitments to gender equality can serve to make necessary changes.

Following the four main themes of the collection, Chapter 12 offers critical insights into the value of understanding contextual (e.g. national, regional) factors in efforts to advance gender equity in STEM. Using Africa as a model, the authors explore how relevant theory can guide research questions, intervention efforts and even the language we use to discuss gender inequality in STEM. The authors suggest that African feminist perspectives may be more suited to addressing the underrepresentation of women in STEM in the African context than theoretical frameworks and perspectives from the Global North.

Navigating context in STEM equity

It is clear throughout this edited collection that context matters – there is no one-size-fits-all approach to understanding or addressing gender disparities in STEM. Chapters 5 and 11 highlight the intersectional nature of challenges faced by Indigenous women and women in rural communities. As illustrated by Chapter 8, policies in place to combat gender-based disparities vary by country, even within the same sector (i.e. WASH). These factors affect the barriers faced by women in STEM fields as well as the rates of women in STEM fields. Only through the investigation and understanding of unique contexts can we find solutions to make STEM more equitable within those contexts.

That said, there is also value in understanding commonalities across contexts. This edited collection presents promising solutions to address these gender disparities in STEM across contexts. For example, a prevalent theme across multiple chapters is institutional commitment and multi-stakeholder engagement. Efforts that directly involve stakeholders in research (Chapter 11), practice (Chapter 2) and policy (Chapters 1 and 7) provide more robust solutions with a greater likelihood of lasting change.

Another common theme is the value of investigating and addressing gender disparities from multiple perspectives. Successful projects attribute some of their successes to interdisciplinary research teams (Chapter 6) and/or multi-country collaborations (Chapter 4). While contextual factors do play a role, broader and more globally applicable insights can be gained when experts from multiple research fields or different countries come together.

In addition to overall themes and implications, these research projects have led to concrete progress towards gender equity in STEM. Multiple projects have focused on increasing women's participation in STEM via changes to specific programmes (Chapter 2), institutions (Chapter 1) or through funding access (Chapters 5 and 10). This cohort of researchers has also improved the visibility of women scientists – an effort designed to combat stereotypes (Chapters 2, 5, 6 and 10). Increased access to data (Chapters 4, 5, 6) serves not only our understanding of gender inequalities but having concrete metrics against which we can measure positive progress. Further, multiple contributions include investigations of and policy recommendations (Chapters 3 and 8). Chapters 1, 7 and 11 move a step beyond this, to actively work with stakeholders, including policymakers, to develop and implement changes to policy. These concrete actions or deliverables move the needle towards progress on a global issue.

Advancing a Southern-led research agenda

The inequities we observe in science are reflections of our national, regional and global institutions. To challenge these inequities requires a strong belief in science's capacity to drive development and respond to the communal challenges we face as a society. The research and reflections that make up this edited collection speak to the role of women in driving development in agriculture, green industries, engineering and mathematics, as well as change in the research and education institutions they are a part of. This collection's focus on the Global South takes this belief in science's potential a step further, asserting that just as we cannot afford to act on assumptions about the obstacles women face and their needs, we cannot afford to act on assumptions about the change that needs to happen in the Global South.

The Breaking Barriers Network comes together to show that every voice in science matters and that every challenge is unique in its complexity and requires unique solutions. While no roadmap can lead us to gender equity in science, a research agenda that reflects the learning, experiences and evidence from researchers across Latin America and Africa presents a promising start. The priority areas and suggested steps forward are important pieces of the puzzle and help move us towards promoting changes to our institutions.

First, there is a need to evaluate existing gender-responsive policies at national and institutional levels to identify gaps and areas for improvement, ensuring alignment with national science priorities. We should explore the impact of advocacy efforts on women's representation in leadership and decision-making roles within STEM to generate evidence that supports policy refinement.

Our researchers have also shown just how essential it is to prioritise the collection and analysis of comprehensive data on the factors contributing to attrition and low participation rates among marginalised groups in STEM. This includes examining existing mechanisms and platforms for data collection at both institutional and national levels. Demand for data and clear use cases for the data across institutions helps drive this forward. Future efforts should focus on identifying high-risk moments for drop-out throughout the educational spectrum and during transitions into the workforce. It is with these data that we can continue to test and develop targeted interventions based on empirical findings to address these critical gaps.

We should also explore the effectiveness of mentorship frameworks in supporting women, particularly those from underrepresented groups, in STEM fields. Future initiatives should assess the impact of partnerships with advocacy organisations and digital platforms in enhancing mentorship connections. Additionally, it's important to investigate leadership training programmes that equip women with the necessary skills and confidence to take on decision-making roles – a key step in moving from equal participation to representative leadership.

Furthermore, we need to investigate strategies to create a seamless support system that bridges education and workforce transitions for women in STEM. Collaborative approaches among educational institutions, government agencies and industry partners should be explored to implement gender-sensitive curricula, capacity-building initiatives and reintegration programmes. Future research must also address the prevalence and impact of gender-based violence and discrimination in academic and professional settings, providing recommendations for fostering safe and supportive environments.

Beyond the collection: Building the future of inclusive STEM

To sustain this momentum and address the critical next steps outlined above, it is crucial to continue to build sustainable knowledge networks, linking perspectives and shared learning from across the globe. The network of researchers that have come together in this collection are a part of this movement, each employing diverse approaches to tackle gender biases and systemic barriers, such as conducting gender audits at universities, supporting fellowship programmes for Indigenous women scientists, digitising and sharing important data from physical archives and building confidence among young women to engage in male-dominated fields like agricultural training and research. These networks are crucial for the continuous sharing of evidence-informed strategies and interventions, which are essential for making substantial and lasting changes.

The sustained action required to break persistent barriers to women's participation and leadership in science involves a shared commitment from all stakeholders. The initiatives listed throughout this collection and their subsequent phases are designed to mould and adapt to changing research needs and circumstances, ensuring that the efforts remain relevant and effective. By committing to this movement, we are helping to create a more inclusive and equitable environment in STEM fields, paving the way for more women to participate and lead in science.

www.ingramcontent.com/pod-product-compliance
Lightning Source LLC
Chambersburg PA
CBHW050836300326
41935CB00043B/1768